Canto is an imprint offering a range of titles, classic and more recent, across a broad spectrum of subject areas and interests. History, literature, biography, archaeology, politics, religion, psychology, philosophy and science are all represented in Canto's specially selected list of titles, which now offers some of the best and most accessible of Cambridge publishing to a wider readership.

Disraeli

This new and revisionary 'brief life' of Benjamin Disraeli (1804–81) focuses on the substantial reassessment of Disraeli's life and personality which is currently taking place. Particular reference is made to the role played in Disraeli's conception of life and politics by his Jewishness and his romanticism. The book also tries to understand Disraeli in a European as well as a British frame of thought.

These new elements are set alongside all the principal biographical elements of Disraeli's life and career. The book can therefore be read both as a standard, up-to-date biography of one of the greatest statesmen of the later Victorian age and as a reinterpretation of key aspects of Disraeli's life and times.

Disraeli

A BRIEF LIFE

PAUL SMITH

CAMBRIDGE
UNIVERSITY PRESS

Published by the Press Syndicate of the University of Cambridge
The Pitt Building, Trumpington Street, Cambridge CB2 1RP
40 West 20th Street, New York NY 10011-4211, USA
10 Stamford Road, Oakleigh, Melbourne 3166, Australia
© Cambridge University Press 1996

First published 1996
Canto edition 1999

Printed in Great Britain at the University Press, Cambridge

A catalogue record for this book is available from the British Library

Library of Congress cataloguing in publication data

Smith, Paul, 1937–
Disraeli: a brief life / Paul Smith.
p.   cm.
Includes bibliographical references.
ISBN 0 521 38150 9
1. Disraeli, Benjamin, Earl of Beaconsfield, 1804–1881.
2. Conservative Party (Great Britain) – Biography.   3. Great Britain –
History – Victoria. 1837–1901.   4. Prime ministers – Great Britain –
Biography.   5. Jews – Great Britain – Biography.   6. Romanticism –
Great Britain.   I. Title.
DA564.B3S65   1996
941.081'092-dc20   [B] 95-51407   CIP

ISBN 0 521 38150 9 hardback
ISBN 0 521 66990 1 paperback

CONTENTS

PREFACE

This book is designed to provide in a single volume a new interpretation of Disraeli which takes fully into account recent thinking about his personality and ideas.

Among those who have helped to guide my thoughts on various aspects of Disraeli's life, by allowing me to see unpublished material and in other ways, I must particularly mention Benjamin Braude, Bryan Cheyette, P. J. Chilcott, Todd Endelman, David Feldman and Charles Richmond. They bear, of course, no responsibility for what I have made of their promptings. I am most grateful to those individuals and bodies who have allowed me to consult and quote from material of which they hold the copyright.

No attempt has been made to supply a comprehensive bibliography. For Disraeli bibliography up to about 1970, the reader is referred to R. W. Stewart, *Benjamin Disraeli, a List of Writings by Him and Writings About Him with Notes* (Metuchen, N.J., 1972), and *Disraeli's Novels Reviewed, 1826–1968* (Metuchen, N.J., 1975).

For Disraeli's letters, and such other documents as it includes, the edition in course of publication by the Disraeli Project at Queen's University, Kingston, is cited as the standard text, up to 1856, the date which it had reached at the time of preparing this edition. For the letters to Lady Bradford and Lady Chesterfield, Monypenny and Buckle's text is preferred to that of the Marquis of Zetland's edition, where the letters appear in both. Disraeli's novels and his biography of *Lord George Bentinck* are cited by chapter, so that any edition of them may be used (but a few quotations from the first editions of *Vivian Grey* and *The Young Duke* will not be found in the later editions which Disraeli expurgated).

The opportunity of this edition has been taken to correct a few errors in the original publication and to provide references to the latest volume (vi) of *Benjamin Disraeli Letters*.

ABBREVIATIONS

DISRAELI'S WRITINGS

CF	*Contarini Fleming*
HT	*Henrietta Temple*
Letters	*Benjamin Disraeli Letters*
	vols. I–II (1815–1834; 1835–1837), ed. J. A. W. Gunn, J. Matthews, D. M. Schurman and M. G. Wiebe (Toronto, 1982)
	vols. III–V (1838–1841; 1842–1847; 1848–1851), ed. M. G. Wiebe, J. B. Conacher, J. Matthews and M. S. Millar (Toronto, 1987; 1989; 1993)
	vol. VI (1852–1856), ed. M. G. Wiebe, M. S. Millar and A. P. Robson (Toronto, 1997)
	(Letters are cited by their serial number in the edition; other documents included in the edition by page number.)
VG	*Vivian Grey*
Vindication	*Vindication of the English Constitution in a Letter to a Noble and Learned Lord*
YD	*The Young Duke*

OTHER WORKS

Blake	R. Blake, *Disraeli* (London, 1966)
M & B	W. F. Monypenny and G. E. Buckle, *The Life of Benjamin Disraeli, Earl of Beaconsfield*, 6 vols. (London, 1910–20)
Reminiscences	H. M. and M. Swartz (eds.), *Disraeli's Reminiscences* (London, 1975)
Stanley	J. Vincent (ed.), *Disraeli, Derby and the Conservative Party. Journals and Memoirs of Edward Henry, Lord Stanley 1849–1869* (Hassocks, 1978)

INTRODUCTION

I N APRIL 1907, twenty-six years after his death, in Bloomsbury
Square where he had lived as a boy, Disraeli was the subject of a
paper delivered to the progressive discussion group, the Rainbow
Circle, by the Liberal MP J. M. Robertson.

Disraeli [the Circle heard], the most notable egoist of his generation, entered
public life to push his own fortunes. His talk, like his dress, was an act of self-
obtrusion, a flaunting of his cleverness. He had no political ideals or convic-
tions, and never cared for any cause as such ... The secret of his ultimate
popular success was his appeal to the passions of racial enmity & belligerence –
as witnessed for example in his antagonism to Russia. All that he did was to
create jingoism. Tried by the standards of moral character and moral aim,
Disraeli has no aspect of greatness. He was a man of abnormal pertinacity &
determination, a strong-willed & self assertive eccentric, but as a statesman &
as a politician, he was outclassed by his opponents in his own country & in his
own day.

Not surprisingly, among these heirs to the philosophic radicalism
Disraeli had lampooned, the minutes record 'general agreement' with
Robertson's views, but, less predictably, they also record some elements
of a warmer appreciation and a subtler analysis. It was suggested in the
discussion

that Disraeli was great in that he captured the great tory party, that his Irish
policy was sincere, that the democratic idea that permeates the tory party at the
present day was due in some measure to him, & that there was a certain amount
of elevating ideas beneath all his eccentricity & egoism. Some stress was laid
upon his essentially Asiatic temperament, character & outlook.

('Asiatic' was a nice progressive synonym for 'Jewish'.)[1]

1

It was not a bad miniature of the debate that began in Disraeli's lifetime and has continued to this day, as to whether he was a mere cynical careerist and charlatan or a statesman of constructive achievement and genuine vision, and as to how far his British life had to be understood in terms of adaptation to local prejudices and manipulation of native materials by one who, in his inmost nature and feeling, was not what Britons meant by British. The images of actor, artist and alien have vied with those of statesman, sage and patriot, to the immense confusion of those who have innocently supposed that they could not all be true – an error Disraeli would never have made.

As the Rainbow Circle's minutes suggest, evaluation of Disraeli's career has had much to do with political partisanship, moral fastidiousness and prejudice against the outsider. His role in giving the Conservatives a plausible title to be a 'popular' and 'national' party, by the passing of the Second Reform bill in 1867 and a clutch of social measures between 1874 and 1880, and by his seizure in the 1870s of the national and imperial platform which was to sustain them so effectively for some eighty years, made him an inevitable totem of the party and even a guru of its progressive wing. It simultaneously caused opponents whose political patents it infringed or whose political opportunities it undermined to regard him as a political necromancer, who by black arts had corrupted the soul of the Tory party and the British nation, exploiting the greed for office of the one, the pride of power of the other, in order to take the first place in a country to which by blood and sentiment he did not truly belong. The two views have intermingled as much as clashed. Conservatives have sometimes disliked Disraeli's methods and suspected his motives, at the same time as admiring his achievement and profiting by his legacy. Those to the left have enjoyed the wit and bravado of an outsider's capture of the Tory party and the prime ministership, even while deploring the uses to which his victories were put and the cynical egoism which they subserved; or, by emphasising Disraeli's youthful radicalism and later appropriation of much that passed for liberalism, have managed to regard him almost as one of their own, marooned in the wrong party but beguiling it into broader views and better courses.

The ambiguities of these interweaving attitudes reflect the ambiguity of their subject. Through them runs the difficulty even close and sympathetic contemporaries experienced in gauging whether Disraeli was 'genuine' or 'serious', whether any backbone of principle or belief underlay his brilliant instinct of performance and his ceaseless manoeuvring for position. 'How', wrote his friend and political pupil, Lord Stanley, in 1861, 'can I reconcile his open ridicule, in private, of all religions, with his preaching up of a new church-and-state agitation? or how can I help seeing that glory and power, rather than the public good, have been his objects? He has at least the merit, in this last respect, of being no hypocrite.' Allies and opponents, admirers and critics, alike, often combined a lively appreciation of Disraeli's talents with the sensation, resentful or amused, that they were being had. Disraeli, wrote Wilfrid Scawen Blunt in 1903, was

a very complete *farceur* ... you cannot persuade me that he ever for an instant took himself seriously, or expected any but the stolid among his contemporaries to accept him so. His *Semitic* politics of course were genuine enough ... Our dull English nation deserved what it got, and there is nothing funnier in history than the way in which he cajoled our square-toed aristocratic Party to put off its respectable broad-cloth, and robe itself in his suit of Imperial spangles, and our fine ladies after his death to worship their old world-weary Hebrew beguiler under the innocent form of a primrose.

Shorn of the distancing references to Disraeli's Jewishness, this has much in common with the verdict of a historian who has practised as a politician, Lord Jenkins, that Disraeli is, among British political figures, 'captain of the impudents'.[2]

Recent interpretation of Disraeli has rested less on new research than on shifts in the angle of vision. Much of the evidence on which we depend for our knowledge of him he broadcast himself, in his novels and other writings and in his speeches. They and his letters and papers are so extensively quoted in the six-volume biography published between 1910 and 1920 by W. F. Monypenny and G. E. Buckle, Conservative imperialists both, but not altogether uncritical admirers, that their work constitutes a compendium of source materials broad and honest enough to permit evaluations differing widely from their own. Writing in the 1960s the standard modern account of Disraeli, Lord Blake was able to be franker about such things as his sexual and financial entanglements, and to take advantage of B. R. Jerman's important exploration of his early years,[3] but for the main lines of Disraeli's career the corpus of knowledge he had to work with was not very much larger than that available to Monypenny and Buckle. So it has remained, despite a steady flow of monographs touching on aspects of Disraeli's political and literary career, and the publication in the diaries of the fifteenth earl of Derby of an important set of glimpses by a close friend and colleague. Even the majestic Kingston edition of Disraeli's letters (often mangled in previous publication), which began to appear in 1982, has reached the 1850s without so far bringing to light anything which compels major revision of existing views, though its uncovering of a hitherto unrecognised novel of 1834 by Disraeli and his sister, *A Year at Hartlebury or The Election*, has enlarged our insight into the former's first venture in politics. It seems improbable that new caches of evidence of first-rate significance will appear, and likely that, while research will continue to extend our grasp of the detail and context of Disraeli's career, advance in understanding will come primarily by more sensitive reflection on what has, for the most part, been long familiar.

The ease and lucidity of its style, the urbanity and shrewdness of its judgements, and the apparent comprehensiveness of its treatment readily explain why, since its publication in 1966, Robert Blake's *Disraeli* has sometimes seemed to render further reflection unnecessary. As a narrative of Disraeli's career, it is hard to think that it will be surpassed. As an analysis of what drove and shaped that career, however, some recent writing has found it less commanding and complete. The crux lies in Disraeli's intellectual and emotional, rather than political, biography, or in the problem of how to integrate the one with the other, and the questions at issue were already largely familiar to the Rainbow Circle. They centre around the problem of Disraeli's intellectual integrity. Are the social, political, religious and racial ideas which he propounded so vividly in the 1830s and 1840s, and repeated or re-endorsed at intervals later on, to be taken seriously, even regarded as 'principles' supplying unity and coherence to his public career, or must they be seen as a glittering farrago of youthful exuberances, largely or wholly set aside in the shifts and exigencies of climbing to political eminence? Or again, should they be understood, as I suggested in a 1987 article,[4] not as a blueprint for political action or as a mere scattering of intellectual wild oats, but as an attempt to create and impose a definition of the identity, needs and destiny of the Tory party and the English nation which would offer a home and a leading role in both to an outsider who might seem to belong naturally to neither?

The tendency of Lord Blake's essentially political biography is to push Disraeli's ideas to the periphery. Blake defends his subject against the charge of insincerity and lack of principle, but only by treating the 'Tory idea' he elaborated in his youth as a flourish unconnected with his subsequent career as a front-bench politician, which was directed, not by the notions of Young England, but by a sincere, if commonplace, Tory belief in the supreme value of the landed interest as the guarantee of the stability and greatness of England and the liberties of her people. A somewhat similar disjunction is operated by Peter Ghosh's view that, even if Disraeli had 'principles sufficient to justify his personal integrity', they did not direct his actions: he was guided as a Tory leader from the late 1840s by a set of working principles resting on such prosaic foundations as 'Francophilism and his estimate of the political value of low taxation', the tactical advantage of which was to enable him to spend most of his mature career competing with Gladstone for that supreme electoral talisman, the Peelite mantle of economical finance and moderate progress.[5] This chopping of Disraeli into two intellectually unconnected or inconsistent halves, the young swashbuckler and the mature, pragmatic leader, presents some problems. It tends to deny that the child is father of the man, and to deprive Disraeli of a consistency of outlook and wholeness of political conception which it was, throughout his life, one of his central aims to assert. It turns into the epiphenomena of the career much that was central in the living of the life.

In a dashing survey of Disraeli's ideas in 1990, John Vincent restored them to prominence partly by inverting the normal order of importance between Disraeli's intellectual achievement and his political. Losing most of the general elections he fought, inept at handling public opinion and his own party, largely ineffectual in government, Disraeli is downgraded as a politician, at the same time as he is seen as an acute exponent of political sociology, ahead of his age in analysing the problems of emergent urban and industrial society, even if his recipe for tackling them hardly went beyond 'the achievement of an era of good feeling' through charismatic leadership, well chosen 'social platitudes', and the restoration of the sense of social responsibility among the upper classes.[6] Others, myself included, have focused on the origin and function of Disraeli's ideas in terms of their instrumentality in the task of integrating what he described as his 'continental' and 'revolutionary' mind into his English environment in a way which would enable him to achieve not a mere passive assimilation but the pinnacle of power. How far these ideas corresponded to 'reality', embodied 'truth', or constituted 'principles' intended to materialise in policies, has been seen as a less illuminating question than that of what they were meant to do, and did, in relation to the intellectual and emotional needs, as well as the tactical necessities, of their author. The English compulsion to give Disraeli marks on some notional scale of seriousness of purpose and consistency of belief and practice has been modified by a concern to elucidate the way in which he struggled for success, not simply in advancing his fortunes but in reconciling the diverse aspects of his personality and inheritance with each other and with the society in which he had to operate, in an emotionally harmonious, intellectually satisfying, and aesthetically pleasing synthesis. Disraeli was, or aspired to be, an artist: the problem is to discern the sources and mechanism of his art and the kind of wholeness it aimed to achieve.

In this, Disraeli's Jewishness and his romanticism have been highlighted, the one as presenting an acute problem of identity for a convert to Christianity seeking to rise in a formally Christian polity and to claim the leadership of the English nation, the other as a mode of thought and feeling, largely continental in inspiration, which combined with Jewishness both to accentuate Disraeli's quality of strangeness in English life and in so doing to supply the peculiar, detached and transformational vision which enabled him to conjure up a 'pure' Tory tradition and a 'true' English nation within which he could live and lead. Lord Blake's study has little truck with either. Romanticism, as a *modus operandi* helping Disraeli to establish the terms of composition between his 'genius' and the external world, does not figure. Jewishness is largely

6

dismissed as a matter of practical import with the argument that it was rather the Italian than the Jewish temperament that predominated in Disraeli (though his need to come to terms with his Jewish identity does receive recognition in the discussion of *Tancred* and in Blake's subsequent sketch of his journey to the Near East).[7]

Following the lead of such perceptive commentators as Israel Zangwill and Philip Rieff (who do not appear in Blake's bibliography) and Isaiah Berlin (whose important lecture on Disraeli and Marx came later), more recent writers such as Todd Endelman and Stanley Weintraub have sought to bring out the character of Disraeli's Jewishness and the problems which it posed for him.[8] Preceded by the impressive but little known work of Raymond Maitre, literary scholars such as Daniel Schwarz and students of Disraeli's intellectual formation like Charles Richmond have looked at the role of the romantic vision in the frantic process of self-fashioning which occupied the early years.[9] Both streams have contributed to a growing sense of the intricacy of Disraeli's performance and of the need to relate it to European currents of thought and feeling, against which the 'continental' and 'revolutionary' mind appears, not strange and anomalous, as when set in a narrowly conceived English frame and prodded by the blunt instruments of Anglo-Saxon empiricism, but familiar and even fashionable.

Sometimes, too, it appears derivative and commonplace. Disraeli was not an original or a profound thinker. As Richard Faber has said, he was 'not so much deep as complex', and it is the complexities that fascinate. His thought presents not a compelling system but an intriguing reticulation. Some of it, like some of his self-presentation in speech, manner and dress, was extravagant to excess, fantastical to the point of absurdity, ambiguous and ironical in the highest degree. Alarmed, as Lord Blake notes, by the irony and the fancy, sober Britons have tended to approach Disraeli with their guard up, determined not to be cozened.[10] But the guard is better dropped, for only by taking Disraeli on his own terms can we discover what those terms were. If that risks taking him at face value, it avoids the grosser error of ignoring the value which attaches in human transactions – and which he certainly attached – to face. In standing none of his nonsense, you catch very little of his drift.

The task of Disraeli's biographers has always been daunting, to the degree that some of his contemporaries wondered whether it was even possible. Carnarvon, who had sat in two cabinets with him, noted at his death: 'I doubt much if there is anyone living who combines all the conditions for a faithful description & analysis of so singular a life & character.' 'There was', Gladstone declared in 1895, 'no life which required so much to be written as that of Disraeli and which it was so difficult, if not impossible, to write with any approach to faithfulness.' The need to integrate recent study of Disraeli's mentality into the familiar story of the political career makes matters no easier. None the less, it is time to march to the sound of the guns. 'Every book', Disraeli once told Metternich, 'is a battle lost or won.'[11]

I

THE THEATRE OF LIFE

To ENGLAND in 1748, in search of opportunity in the straw bonnet trade, came an eighteen-year-old Italian Jew, Benjamin D'Israeli, from the small town of Cento in the Papal States, some seventy miles south-west of Venice. Prospering eventually as a merchant and stock-broker in London, he was able on his death in 1816 to leave the sub-stantial fortune of £35,000 to the only child of his second marriage, Isaac, born in 1766. Isaac had married in 1802 Maria Basevi, daughter of another well-to-do Italian Jewish family settled in London for forty years, whose father was a president of the Jewish Board of Deputies. With her, he had five children, of whom the second and the eldest son, Benjamin, was born in what is now Theobald's Road, on 21 December 1804.

By the time of his first son's arrival, Isaac D'Israeli had long since broken out of the narrow world of immigrant London Jewry into which he had been born. Reacting against the commercial atmosphere surrounding his youth, he had turned out to be an impulsive, high-strung, romantically-minded intellectual, whose temperament in his early years displayed a number of features that were to be still more strongly marked in his eldest son. Fascinated by literary genius, but unable to whip his own very modest creative talent into a convincing semblance of it, he ended by becoming its chronicler and analyst, achieving celebrity at the age of twenty-five with the first volume of a work which he was to go on revising and expanding for many years, the *Curiosities of Literature*, a collection of anecdotes, character sketches and observations on books and authors, which, highly popular in his own day, retained sufficient vitality to achieve a paperback edition in the twentieth century. To this he added, after the fashion of the time for exploring the psychology of genius, a study of *The Literary Character*, and a number of other works, including poetry, novels and history. In 1809, he helped his publisher, John Murray, launch what was to be one of the most distinguished and influential organs of a great age of periodical journalism, the *Quarterly Review*. Mainly through Murray, he had access to a literary circle comprising leading figures like Scott, Southey and Moore, and touching the world of politics through men such as J. W. Croker. In that fellowship, in the reading room of the British Museum, in the Athenaeum of which he was one of the earliest members, and in his own extensive library, he passed the agreeable and undemanding existence of a bookish man with private means.

Benjamin Disraeli's origins were thus less obscure than later myth, anxious to dramatise his ascent, sometimes painted them. He grew up as the son of a mildly celebrated, comfortably-off author, with wide contacts in a certain society. But he did not grow up with the sense of security that so solid a middle-class background might seem to imply. First of all, the admittedly scanty evidence suggests that he did not receive the affection he craved from his mother, and that this led to the aggressive need to compel attention and admiration from other sources which was apparent from his childhood. Then, the transition from home to his first schools, Miss Roper's at Islington and the Rev. Potticary's in Blackheath, inevitably brought the consciousness of his difference from most of his schoolfellows, a difference of intelligence and, more profoundly, of 'race' and religion. The personal difficulty involved in his separateness, the shock of emergence into a society in which he was to a degree alien, were enhanced by the failure of his family to help him see his Jewishness as a source of pride. Yet if he was ever tempted to the self-disgust which was a not uncommon form of response to such a situation, he was preserved by that extraordinarily proud and mettlesome temperament which informed his life from first to last. The theme of desire to master a hostile and excluding environment is a prominent one in his early writing. Disraeli was an outsider, but in him this produced no grovelling for acceptance but a fierce determination to achieve dominance on his own terms. It also conferred on him a certain detachment and sharpness of vision, which could shade easily into calculating cynicism. The hero of his novel *Contarini Fleming* sees in his schoolfellows 'only beings whom I was determined to control'.[1]

The need to command attention and admiration, the need of an outsider to impose himself on his environment, the need of an intelligent, sensitive and spirited being to express his strong sense of his own powers, these were basic elements of Disraeli's personality, the working of which can be seen throughout his life, but which manifested themselves with a specially raw intensity in his youth. They were fused in youth with another which Disraeli's circumstances rendered unusually acute, the need of the growing boy to discover and assert his individual identity. The problem of adolescent identity, commonplace enough in itself, was complicated for Disraeli by a fundamental turn which was arbitrarily imposed on the course of his life in his thirteenth year. Isaac's young romanticism had early been replaced by a rational and sceptical outlook which left him indifferent to the forms and dogmas of religion. His children were initially brought up in the Jewish faith, and Benjamin seems even to have received some elementary instruction in Hebrew. But his links with Judaism and the Jewish community became very tenuous, and a dispute with his synagogue over his refusal to compound for non-acceptance of office with a fine led to his resigning from it in 1817. In the same year, he allowed his children to be baptised into the Church of England, Benjamin on 31 July. This step was vital to Disraeli's future career – without it he could not have sat in the House of Commons until his mid-fifties – but it left him still more ambiguously situated than before between his Jewish inheritance and his Christian environment. The recognition and resolution of that ambiguity was not something that a boy could achieve, and the problem lay for the time being dormant. Its operation in the long run was to contribute profoundly to determining the peculiar cast of Disraeli's life.

The young Benjamin's integration into English society might have been facilitated had he undergone the communal rites of passage supplied by its public schools. He seems to have thought so himself in later years, to judge by the wistful envy apparent in the references to public-school life in his novels, and it is a question why his father did not send him to Winchester, as he did the younger boys. In fact, in 1817, he went to a school at Higham Hill, Walthamstow, kept by a self-taught Unitarian minister, the Rev. Eli Cogan, whom Isaac had met in a bookshop. It was not a random or a bad choice: Cogan was a scholar, whose school enjoyed a well-to-do clientele and a high reputation, and provided a relatively progressive education for the day, paying attention to English literature as well as to the customary classical studies. Disraeli may have benefited by being saved from the often stultifying classical grind of the public schools, and the comparatively broad nature of his education was further enhanced when he left Cogan's to pursue the expansion of his mind in his father's well-stocked library, where history and modern European literature bulked large. He was one of those in whom the faculty of rapid apprehension never allows time for deep study, and his knowledge was often superficial, but it was also more wide-ranging than that of many of the men, crammed in youth with Latin and Greek, whom he was later to encounter in public life. Still, the difference between their education and his, between their classical formation and his more expanded, more cosmopolitan, more modern outlook, formed an additional barrier to sympathy.

In November 1821, just before his seventeenth birthday, Disraeli was articled at his father's bidding to a substantial firm of City solicitors. This remarkably misconceived attempt to set him on a legal career no doubt helps to explain his telling Montagu Corry more than fifty years later that 'his father never understood him',[2] and the persistence in his early novels of the theme that a child's parents are often poor judges of its true character. It may be that Isaac was not so much ignorant of his son's natural bent as anxious to correct it. If Disraeli's novels can be taken as in some measure autobiographical, it is tempting to relate to this period the account of the hero's adolescence in *Contarini Fleming*. Contarini is maddened by the burgeoning consciousness of powers and aspirations for which he cannot as yet find adequate expression. 'A deed was to be done, but what? I entertained at this time a deep conviction that life must be intolerable unless I were the greatest of men.' He looks to achieve fame in literature, and is appalled by the inability of his stripling talent to answer his purposes. His father, who has known the misery of frustrated intellectual ambition in his own youth, brings him down to earth by pointing out the dismal prospects for postulant poets and suggesting that his poetic yearning does not represent a genuine high talent: 'in you, as in the great majority, it is not a creative faculty originating in a peculiar organization, but simply the consequence of a nervous susceptibility, that is common to all'.[3] Contarini becomes a politician's secretary. Disraeli became a lawyer's.

Poetry, however, was stronger than probate, and the ardour of youth was not to be confined by contract. In after life, Disraeli remembered how he had grown 'pensive and restless ... nothing would satisfy me but travel. My father then made a feeble effort for Oxford, but the hour of adventure had arrived. I was unmanageable.' The effort for Oxford was perhaps not very serious, and perhaps Disraeli felt, like his character Vivian Grey, that London life had already developed his mind and experience too much for the society of newly emancipated schoolboys in a provincial town ('The idea of Oxford to such an individual was an insult!').[4] He went not to university but, in the summer of 1824, to Belgium and the Rhineland, on a tour with his father and a young friend, Meredith, which seems to have reinforced his desire to part company with the law. His articles were given up in the following year, though he retained at least the possibility of a legal career by inscribing himself as a student of Lincoln's Inn. The hour of adventure had indeed arrived. It was a peculiarly tempting moment for a young man stirring with the sense of nascent powers and limitless ambitions, for a vacancy had just occurred in the leadership of romantic youth: 1824 was the year of Byron's death.

But which direction was adventure to take? The next ten years of Disraeli's life saw a frenetic search for the true path of self-definition and self-realisation in thought and action. It is too simple to characterise this decade as one of mere vulgar efforts to climb. Disraeli did strenuously and shamelessly pursue success by whatever means came to hand, but it was success the point of which lay as much in the acquisition of self-knowledge, in the location and development of his powers and the materialisation of his real nature, as in the capture of fame and the carving out of a worldly position. He sought it in his twenties through most of the channels that could attract a young man: in financial speculation, literature, dandyism, politics and love. The quest had in it less of the lofty and tragic heroism of the artist's struggle for creation and survival than he sometimes liked to imagine. The bohemianism of his early life can be exaggerated: it is doubtful that he ever set foot inside a garret, certain that he never starved. The comfortable family home and the comfortable family income were always there to fall back on, and Disraeli could indulge the impulses of a teeming brain and impetuous spirit with the full support of the creature comforts to which he was noticeably addicted. But it was a period of struggle and inner tumult all the same, the most exciting of his life. Nearly all his novels are about youth, that stage of life when Vivian Grey's principle 'that every thing was possible' seems self-evident. The half-erotic sensation of undisciplined and unfocused force, of strong and all-enveloping desire, of boundless aspiration and limitless potentiality, was an intoxicant the power of which he never forgot; and when his capacity to experience it waned (though it never entirely died), he clung to it through his fiction and through his association with the young. His ability, indeed his need, constantly to catch the hopes and fears, splendours and miseries of youth, and above all the sense of the sun newly rising on a world waiting to be stormed gave his life and writings much of their freshness and appeal.

'To enter into high society', we are told in *Vivian Grey*, 'a man must either have blood, a million, or a genius.'[5] Disraeli had not yet devised the litmus test of romanticised origins that would show his blood to be blue; there remained as tickets of admission the million and the genius. He was always attracted by quick results, and the acquisition of the first seemed likely to be a speedier business than the cultivation of the second. With a couple of partners, he speculated in Latin American shares. By the middle of 1825, the syndicate had lost £7,000, and he had saddled himself with the debts which, even if underwritten in the last resort by Isaac, would dog him for many years. He had also produced his first public writings, three anonymous pamphlets designed to bolster confidence in the Latin American mining companies. His next venture again linked the commercial and the literary. It speaks for the impression he had made on his father's friend, Murray, that the publisher should have employed him as confidential agent in the organisation in late 1825 of a new daily newspaper, for which he was to put up – though it is hard to see how – a quarter of the capital. The role gave ample scope for callow intrigue, complete with coded letters, and boyish delusions of power and influence, and Disraeli's blunders did not improve the prospects of the *Representative*, which after the lapse of his connection with it, appeared for six months of feeble life. From the first, he had the knack of turning even his failures to practical account, and the experience gained in the affair was at once put to use in a fresh assault on success. If the million would not materialise, the genius might. In April 1826 appeared the first part of *Vivian Grey*, and Disraeli's career as a novelist was launched.

It was natural for a young man of Disraeli's background and facility with the pen to turn to writing in the hope of speedy recognition and ready cash. But it is a serious mistake to see even in his early work nothing more than the search for rapid returns. From *Vivian Grey* until the publication of *Contarini Fleming* in 1832 – perhaps until the fiasco of the *Revolutionary Epick* in 1834 – literature was the principal medium of his pursuit not only of fame but of himself. It was the arena in which he struggled, before a paying public, to explore his consciousness and to discern the shape and gauge the force of the genius which he felt himself to possess. The nature of the struggle, the temperament of its protagonist and the epoch in which it took place alike dictated the idiom in which it was conducted. Disraeli, at once by irresistible predisposition and by conscious predilection, was a romantic; and it is essential to perceive the function which romanticism performed for him and the way in which it helped to mould not only his literary expression but his whole manner of treating with reality, if his life is to be understood as a spiritually coherent whole. Much incomprehension arises from the tendency to see the young Disraeli in an exclusively English frame and to regard him as though he were simply an aberrant Victorian, a deviant from a norm in fact established, if at all, only in his middle age. Observed in the wider setting of European romanticism, what in the English context appears outlandish and bizarre becomes normal, and even, in some aspects, banal: the aberrant becomes conventional. 'My mind is a continental mind', Disraeli wrote in the so-called 'Mutilated Diary' in 1833. 'It is a revolutionary mind.'[6] In the right understanding of what he meant lies a vital key to his vision.

Romanticism was a fashionable intellectual mode when he began to write, and it was virtually inevitable that he should experiment with its forms, not least because his creative talent, though lively, was always more derivative than original, and at that age, in any case, everyone needs models to imitate. But it offered him something much more fundamental than a handy set of conventions: it presented a natural affinity with his deepest needs and purposes. It gave him not only an artistic stance but a transforming view of life. It was not a pose, though it involved posing, but an energising principle of existence. To Disraeli, on the border of two cultures, the frontier position of the romantics, between imagination and mundane reality, was immediately sympathetic: they, too, with their ambiguous relation to society and the special perception derived from it, were outsiders. Yet in identifying with them, he became, paradoxically, an insider, a member of a European fraternity and, in narrower English terms, an acolyte in a sphere where intellectual sympathy was his only claim even to marginal status; it was the world of bucks, beaux, wits and poets, with its aristocratic tone, which he did not possess, its athleticism, which he could not emulate, its freemasonry of school and college, to which he did not belong, symbolised in his adolescence by Byron, whom he idolised, and on a lower plane by Scrope Davies, to whom he made his bow with the character of Sir Berdmore Scrope in *Vivian Grey*. To be a romantic was to be at the same time a freebooter of the spirit and at least a candidate member of a high-toned and exclusive club.

The preoccupations of romanticism, its cult of the individual self and its fascination with genius, were his own. It furnished him with a technique of self-examination, indeed self-obsession, and a justification for it in moral and aesthetic terms; with a satisfying emotional experience and mode of catharsis; and above all with a redeeming vision, which permitted him to transcend reality (that is, the limitations and frustrations of his situation) through the power of the imagination to transform the external world. The modalities of self-realisation and self-creation which it offered would absorb the literary energies of his twenties; their transference to the sphere of collective identification and destiny would set the tone of his conceptualisation of the Tory party and the English nation in his thirties and forties. Always their artifices and artificialities would baffle and annoy a part of the public on which he practised them, and always their cosmopolitan character would emphasise the extent to which he stood outside a purely English frame of reference. Because he seldom made explicit reference to them, it is not easy to trace the sources of Disraeli's ideas, but it seems clear that, however much he shared his generation's fascination with Byron, an important part of the romantic outlook which he imbibed came from Germany. It was probably in 1824, the year of his visit to the Rhineland, that he made copious notes on Madame de Staël's *Germany*, the prime conduit of German thinking for those who could not approach it in the original; another key work, Goethe's *Wilhelm Meister*, became available in English in Carlyle's translation in the same year. Later he would read, at least, Wieland and Heine, again in translation, for, as he admitted to Lady Blessington, he had no talent for languages. His knowledge of German literature and thought was certainly glancing, but his typical quick grasp of current ideas was enough for him to converse on German literature, in 1837, with a leading British student, Crabb Robinson, without the latter's finding anything amiss.[7] He was sufficiently taken with Germany to set there the third and fourth volumes of *Vivian Grey*. Much of that work evoked in its undisciplined exuberance and wild melodrama the turbulence of the 'Storm and Stress' school rather than romanticism proper, and the higher flights of German idealism came in for some shrewd and sceptical mockery, yet already Disraeli was sampling the possibilities of the novel of self-development for which *Wilhelm Meister* provided the model in his generation.

The primary appeal of the romantic mood to a young man suffused with the sense of boundless yet still undefined powers lay in its exaltation of self-consciousness as the divine element in man and its endorsement of the obsessive cultivation and interpellation of that self-consciousness as the source of truth, the spring of art, and the means of revealing the identity in and through which the terms of relation to the external world were to be negotiated. At the centre of romantic preoccupation lay the nature and nurture of 'genius', the unique spirit immanent in the individual, the recognition and materialisation of which in art and action set the goal of life. The theme can never have been remote from the young Disraeli, whose father spent his literary life compensating for the feebleness of his own creative talent by rummaging among the qualities and quirks of others' genius in volumes sufficiently in tune with the fashion of the age to bring him the admiration of Byron. To define and demonstrate his genius was the first object of Disraeli's early writing: his novels were about his self, less because that was all he knew than because he needed to know it to the full. The principal works of 1826–33, *Vivian Grey*, *The Young Duke*, *Alroy* and *Contarini Fleming*, were all about young men venturing on the Odyssey of self-realisation.

How far they can be taken as autobiography is a question much discussed. The answer depends on understanding the function which their romanticisation of their author's inner life performed. Disraeli was trying not to describe his personality but to find it, and to fashion it through the play of intellect and will upon a self extruded and objectivised so that work could be done on it. If the novels were, as he said, 'the secret history of my feelings',[8] it was history as a process, rather than simply a record, of development, in which he was trying on alternative versions of himself and exploring the potential of different roles. It was no accident that, as in *Wilhelm Meister*, metaphors of the theatre were constantly present. The novels were Disraeli's theatre workshop of the personality, where his sense of limitless aspiration and universal talent could strut the stage in anything fetching that he found in the property basket, pausing in long soliloquies to muse on where its real nature and true embodiment lay.

Role-playing was a standard technique of romantic, as indeed of adolescent, self-discovery, but it involved a degree of naive exposure to the audience which rendered especially vulnerable the still callow feelings, immature conceptions and unrefined techniques of someone like Disraeli. For protection, he began to employ the distancing irony, closer perhaps to the German than to the English strain of romanticism, through which the romantic ego might avoid too unambiguous an identification with, and too premature a commitment to, any of the guises it assumed. Even in *Vivian Grey*, 'as hot and hurried a sketch as ever yet was penned', to use his own description of its first instalment,[9] Disraeli was employing the conceits that enabled him simultaneously to cajole and to mystify the reader. The rapid flow of invention, aphorism and philosophical disquisition in satirical, knowing, not-to-be-taken-in-on-any-account vein, is suddenly interrupted by passages which flatter the reader into complicity, inviting him inside the illusion, showing him the stage machinery, and leaving him unsure whether anything the author says is to be taken seriously. 'I find this writing not so difficult as I had imagined', Disraeli cheerfully interjects in *The Young Duke*. 'I see the only way is to rattle on just as you talk ... I use my pen as my horse; I guide it, and it carries me on.'[10] It was not easy to discern what was the horse and what the rider. If the purpose of whisking the reader confidentially behind the scenes was partly ingratiation – almost a demand for approbation – and partly sheer high-spirited delight in the display of the author's cleverness, it was also evasion, a refusal to be pinned down too precisely to any element of the patter and the pose through which the possibilities of being were tried out. It is not surprising that this technique caused Disraeli from the first to be thought trivial and insincere.

It was in fact an integral part of his attempts to evolve out of himself the self-knowledge on which alone sincerity could be grounded. Disraeli was engaged in the process of *Bildung* familiar to continental romanticism, but not acclimatised in England, the recognition and the development of that true nature which formed his destiny. 'What we want', says his creation, Contarini Fleming, 'is to discover the character of a man at his birth, and found his education upon his nature'; an echo, perhaps, of Wilhelm Meister's 'this harmonious cultivation of my nature, which has been denied me by my birth, is exactly what I long for most'. In *Contarini Fleming*, dismissing moral philosophy as 'a delusion fit only for the play of sophists in an age of physiological ignorance', Disraeli argued for the acquisition of knowledge of human nature through 'demonstration', not 'dogma': the avenue to truth lay through personal experience and reflection. Truth resided in personal authenticity: Disraeli did not need to wait for Nietzsche's injunction, 'become that you are'. The process of self-development did not consist in a struggle with original sin according to the fitness routines of some philosophical or religious creed, but in the location, liberation and manifestation of what one was already destined to be, and, in potential, already was. 'I believe', says Contarini, 'in that Destiny before which the ancients bowed ... Destiny is our will, and our will is our nature.'[11] *Bildung* thus conceived set Disraeli apart from the ideal of character-

19

building, seen as the strenuous cultivation of dogmatically prescribed moral qualities, which, even if its narrowness was readily apparent to men like J. S. Mill and Matthew Arnold, was about to set the dominant moral tone of society. The antipathy between Disraeli and Gladstone could almost be defined as *Bildung* versus character, consciousness against conscience; and it is easy to see why, from the standpoint of the latter, Disraeli's moral stance was to seem loose, flippant and self-indulgent, as it did not in the after-glow of the Regency or in the frame of the romantic movement. Disraeli in his twenties was assiduously cultivating a style that was to render him quickly and rather curiously out-of-date among the respectable middle-aged, while at the same time making him instantly recognisable and appealing to successive generations of youth.

It would be wrong to dismiss the role-playing of the personality in course of definition as a set of fantasies of wish fulfilment, though wish fulfilment there was. It represented as much a rehearsal as a surrogate for actual performance. 'Poetry is the safety-valve of my passions – but I wish to *act* what I *write*', Disraeli insisted.[12] Yet action posed in acute form the problem of the terms on which the romantic consciousness could transact with the external world and transcend the physical limitations which obstructed the realisation of its vision. It was here that the continental influence upon Disraeli's mind was shot through with revolutionary implications. Romantic sensibility was inevitably corrosive of established order. The free expression of genius which it exalted defied conventional bonds of morality and taste; the criteria it established related to the authenticity and integrity of experience and behaviour rather than to social restraints. At odds on principle with the moral constriction and aesthetic poverty of conventional living, romantics cherished their status as outsiders as the mark of their spiritual aristocracy: in making Contarini Fleming leave university to lead a robber band of fellow students in a castle, Disraeli was subscribing to the common self-congratulatory collocation of romantic artist and outlaw. He was doing so, however, in the bitter knowledge that the heroic days of outlaws in castles were dead, and that the creeping miasma of bourgeois civilisation offered little in the way of fitting opportunity to their romancers. The French Revolution and the

Napoleonic wars – Disraeli was born in the year in which Napoleon crowned himself emperor of the French – had shattered the old moulds and, in George Steiner's words, 'quickened the pace of felt time', opening up limitless prospects of achievement to youthful genius. If Byron was the poetic hero of the romantics, Napoleon was their genius of world-historical action, master of France at thirty-three, of Europe at thirty-seven. Yet the age of Napoleonic cataclysm was over, the 'great ennui', as Steiner puts it, had set in, and ardent young men with no apparent chance of stamping their genius on the world were left to stalk in frustration 'through the bourgeois city like *condottieri* out of work. Or worse, like *condottieri* meagerly pensioned before their first battle.' Disraeli, in *The Young Duke*, compared his own sense of frustrated powers to the young Bonaparte's. 'View the obscure Napoleon, starving in the streets of Paris! What was St. Helena to the bitterness of such existence? The visions of past glory might illumine even that dark imprisonment; but to be conscious that his supernatural energies might die away without creating their miracles – can the wheel, or the rack, rival the torture of such a suspicion?'[13]

Disraeli was not starving, and the pangs of confined ambition were a standard ingredient of romantic agony, but the sense of poor employment prospects for genius was real enough. What to some degree relieved, as it fed upon, the tension between unbounded aspiration and limited opportunity, between the force of inspiration and the obduracy of things, was the power of the romantic vision to transcend mundane reality and recreate the world in its own terms. Via Madame de Staël, Disraeli knew enough of Kant and the post-Kantian idealists to be aware how perception might fashion the object perceived, how it was, as he summarised it in his youthful notes, 'understanding which gives laws to exterior nature and not exterior nature to it'.[14] 'The world', Novalis had written, 'must be romanticised.' Behind the apparent certainties of the external world, beneath the surfaces of seemingly intractable reality, the creative vision discerned mysteries, deeper meanings, hidden forms, giving it an occult knowledge which it was the business of art to suggest, less by direct statement than through the 'hieroglyphs' which achieved a symbolic transliteration of the poetic perception. The transcendental imagination could not of itself materialise Disraeli's ambition or dematerialise his circumstances, but it could endow him with the sense of a capacity and a mission equal to his cravings by assimilating him into the ranks of those supreme beings of preternatural insight, the poets, who, as they were the divinely inspired interpreters, must also be the unacknowledged legislators of mankind.

The trouble was that Disraeli was determined not to be unacknowledged. The 'continental' and 'revolutionary' mind needed not only the sense of spiritual election but also the world's accolade – and quickly. The literary production of his twenties was the medium not only of the realisation of the personality but also of its strident claim on the public's attention. His first essay turned out a disaster. *Vivian Grey* manages in parts to be a lively enough caper through the scenes of youth, but pace and invention flag too often, the characters are cardboard, the conversations mostly flat, and the incident frequently preposterous (it is characteristic of the author's weakness for melodrama that when, at the end of volume three, Vivian Grey declares his love for Violet Fane, she promptly has a seizure and dies). Intrigued at first by what was thought to be the work of a man of fashion (for the book was published anonymously), the critics tore it apart once they found that they had been beguiled by a boy, and figures like Murray whom Disraeli had incautiously caricatured were offended. 'I was ridiculous. It was time to die', as Disraeli put it, recycling the experience (for he left little unused) in *Contarini Fleming*.[15]

He had no intention of dying, but the disappointment, coming on top of the *Representative* fiasco, and the continued fretting of a teeming mind and a burning but unsatisfied ambition on a constitution not naturally robust, probably contributed to the illness which largely removed him from circulation between the summer of 1827 and the latter part of 1829. The nervous exhaustion and depression from which he seems to have been suffering were real and harassing, but they ministered nicely to the demands of romantic ennui and the tendency of the romantic artist to luxuriate in a spiritual crucifixion to which he brought his own cross and nails. Disraeli did not choose psychiatric illness, but it is hard not to think that he was too interested in it wholly to resist it. The exploration of disturbed states of mind, even to the embracing of madness, was one of the means of access to the inner mysteries of human nature which the romantic consciousness sought to apprehend. Besides, the material could be stored up for later literary exploitation. In *The Young Duke*, *Contarini Fleming* and *Alroy*, Disraeli was to draw from the mental whirlpool of these two, half-lost years of his life to evoke the disorientation and terror of the ego unsure of its identity and its destiny, objectivising itself for its own inspection, testing the personality close to destruction. Alroy is distracted by the conflict between his dreams and aspirations and the terms of his real existence: 'What am I? ... I know not what I feel – yet what I feel is madness.' 'I was not always assured of my identity, or even existence, for I sometimes found it necessary to shout aloud to be sure that I lived', says Contarini Fleming, 'and I was in the habit very often at night of taking down a volume, and looking into it for my name, to be convinced, that I had not been dreaming of myself.' Contarini collapses, but gets no help from the doctors, being 'bled, blistered, boiled, starved, poisoned, electrified, galvanised', until at length he shakes off a half-fascination with the idea of dying and realises that his exhaustion of forces is a necessary consequence of his psychological disposition.[16]

Disraeli, like Contarini, needed a change of scene and a sea voyage. The obstacle was debt, one of the triggers of his depression and a prime reason for his reclusion. By November 1829, he could visit London only incognito 'from fear of the Philistines', the sheriff's officers set on by his creditors. An excursion on filial affection in *The Young Duke* contains a wry skit on his need for his father's financial indulgence: 'What though, at this most fatal moment, I am drawing a most unhappy, a most unexpected, and a most unreasonable bill, and at the shortest date! I grant it all – yet pity! pardon! pay!'[17] In fact, he dared not reveal the extent of his difficulties to Isaac. To help finance the travel on which his mind was now set, he borrowed from the solicitor Benjamin Austen, a family friend, whose wife, Sara, had helped him in the publication of *Vivian Grey*. He had journeyed with the Austens to Switzerland and northern Italy in late 1826, when he had been rowed at night on Lake Geneva by Byron's boatman, Maurice, to the accompaniment of a grand romantic storm.

His other method of raising money was, as usual, to hack for it, this time by dashing off *The Young Duke*, 'delightfully adapted to the most corrupt taste', he told the publisher, Colburn, ' … which will set all Europe afire and not be forgotten till at least 3 months'. Published in 1831, while he was out of England, it was another exploration of a young man's progress, this time with the advantages of rank and wealth, more mature in style than *Vivian Grey*, though not much less fantastical. The whirl, the glitter and the emptiness of fashionable society are well caught – 'this glare, and heat, and noise – this congeries of individuals without sympathy, and dishes without flavour' – and the vignettes typical of Disraeli's finished manner are already beginning to flicker across the page, for instance Lord Squib's waist, 'where art successfully controlled rebellious Nature, like the Austrians the Lombards'. Disraeli refers to his tale as 'our skiff', protests that he is writing the book merely for fun, and was to tell his sister that he 'never staked any fame on it', yet a good deal of his more serious feeling is present, as he follows his protagonist through the theatre of struggle which constitutes social life and dilates on the 'blunder' (a characteristic word at this time) that is youth unfashioned by experience and undisciplined by self-knowledge. All the same, the sententiousness, even if relieved by irony, constantly teeters on the edge of absurdity, as with Disraeli's recommendations (he was not yet twenty-six) on the conduct of life from thirteen to twenty-two. From thirteen to nineteen, 'you may gain some acquaintance with every desirable species of written knowledge'. 'No man', however, 'should read after nineteen'. From then onwards, it was to be 'action, action, action. Do every thing, dare every thing, imagine every thing. Fight, write, love, sport, travel, talk, feast, dress, drink. I limit you to three years, because I think that in that period a lively lad may share every passion, and because, if he do, at the end of that period he will infallibly be done up.'[18]

Disraeli had hardly accomplished the half of this stimulating agenda, but *The Young Duke* emphasised how 'done up' he already felt. 'I write with an aching head and quivering hand; yet I must write, if but to break the solitude, which is to me a world quick with exciting life. I scribble to divert a brain, which, though weak, will struggle with strong thoughts, and lest my mind should muse itself to madness.' The world is 'slipping through my fingers. My life has been a blunder and a blank, and all ends by my adding one more slight ghost to the shadowy realm of fatal precocity!' The worst was the sensation that his genius might not match the force of his ambition. 'To doubt of the truth of the creed in which you have been nurtured, is not so terrific as to doubt respecting the intellectual vigour on whose strength you have staked your happiness.'[19]

Travel would not only constitute an adventure which might dissipate this melancholy, it might also offer an alternative avenue of self-realisation. If the million remained a dream and the genius was suspect, something might be done with the blood that had hitherto seemed so commonplace. Up to that point, Disraeli had shown no recorded interest in his origins. On tour with the Austens in 1826, when, at Ferrara, he saw a Jewish ghetto for the first time, his passage close to Cento, whence his grandfather had set out for England, produced no more than a glancing 'which perhaps you remember' in a letter to Isaac (who had never seen the place). Yet by 1830 he had begun to work on the life of the twelfth-century Jewish hero, David Alroy, and in one of his authorial intrusions into *The Young Duke* had spoken explicitly of the contribution of 'full many an Eastern clime and Southern race' to his blood.[20] The object of the grand tour for which he was struggling to find the cash was the Near East, and more especially Palestine, by way of southern Spain. No doubt there was a tribute here, as in the oriental affectations of Lord Alhambra in *Vivian Grey*, to the romantic taste for those climes that Napoleon's Egyptian expedition had opened up to European power politics and Byron's travels in Greece and the Levant to the poetic sensibility. But that was not all: Disraeli was looking already beyond the immediate Italian antecedents of his family to the historic cradle of his race to find nobility in his blood.

In May 1830 he sailed from Falmouth on a journey of seventeen months that took him via Gibraltar, southern Spain and Malta to Albania, Greece, Constantinople, Jerusalem and Egypt, and formed a decisive epoch in his life. Disraeli revelled in the East. Its scenes, manners and people fed the appetite for the brilliant, gaudy, sensual, extravagant and bizarre which had already been exhibited in *The Young Duke*, and prompted a stream of sparkling letters home which are the brightest and freshest production of his writing and the source of much colour for his subsequent novels. His excitement began already in

Spain, where his flashing vignette of Cadiz – 'Figaro is in every street, and Rosina in every balcony' – was offered (for he was never one to waste a good thing) to three separate correspondents. Its high point came, perhaps, in Albania, just undergoing a ferocious 'pacification' by its Turkish overlords, for whose army Disraeli had thought of volunteering. The letter to his father in which he describes his night carouse with an Albanian chief is one of the most vivid in the language, and passed directly into *Contarini Fleming*. He slipped with abandon into the indolent ease of Ottoman life as he encountered it, telling Benjamin Austen: 'I find the habits of this calm and luxurious people entirely agree with my own preconceived opinions of propriety and enjoyment.' He relished the brilliance of its colours and display, to which he hastened to contribute: 'with the united assistance of my English, Spanish and fancy wardrobe', he says, 'I sported a costume in Yanina [the Albanian capital] which produced a most extraordinary effect on that costume loving people. A great many Turks called on purpose to see it.'[21]

The barbaric side of the Orient was no less fascinating. It did not trouble Disraeli to congratulate on his suppression of the Albanian revolt the ruthless grand vizier of the Ottoman empire, Reshid Mehmet Pasha, 'an approved warrior, a consummate politician, unrivalled as a dissembler in a country where dissimulation is the principal portion of their moral culture ... who as the Austrian Consul observed, has destroyed, in the course of the last three months *not* in war, "upwards of four thousand of my acquaintance"'. On the contrary, he told Austen of 'the delight of being made much of by a man who was daily decapitating half the province'. He embraced experience on its own terms, not seeking to judge this new civilisation by the morality of the one he had left. 'I could not help viewing this extraordinary man with great interest and curiosity', says Contarini Fleming of his audience with the grand vizier, who had just treacherously massacred the rebel beys. 'A short time back, at this very place, he had perpetrated an act, which would have rendered him infamous in a civilized land, the avengers meet him, as if by fate, on the very scene of his bloody treachery, and – he is victorious. What is life?' The moral relativism which Disraeli derived from an ambiguous background, an eclectic education, and a commitment to the authenticity of feeling was reinforced by his stunning encounter with the East. As he had Cadurcis put it in his novel, *Venetia*: 'Truth at Rome is not the truth of London, and both of them differ from the truth of Constantinople. For my part, I believe every thing.'[22]

In August 1830, from Granada, Disraeli told his mother that he still could not stand any mental exertion: 'the moment that I attempt to meditate or combine, to ascertain a question that is doubtful or in anyway to call the greater powers of intellect into play, that moment I feel I am a lost man'. By the end of November, however, he was writing from Athens: 'I feel an excitement which I thought was dead'. Hot climes, sea breezes and shifting scenes routed his hypochondria. Travel of course carried the risk of other ailments. 'Between us', wrote the rake and expert on whist, James Clay, who had become his travelling companion at Malta and was to be a lifelong friend, 'we have contrived to stumble on all the thorns, with which (as Mr. Dickens, the Winchester Porter, was wont poetically to observe) Venus guards her roses.' Disraeli's encounters with Venus led to a course of mercury, the usual specific for venereal disease. That aside, he returned to England in October 1831 'in famous condition', as he told Austen, bringing as a trophy Byron's former servant, Tita (picked up by Clay at Malta), whom he installed in his father's service at Bradenham, the country house in Buckinghamshire to which the family had moved from Bloomsbury Square in the summer of 1829.[23]

From afar, he had followed in the newspapers the progress of the parliamentary reform bill that was agitating the country, and his interest in politics had been quickened. The life of action beckoned more urgently, now that he had recovered his health. Yet for a time literature continued to run alongside politics as an arena for the manifestation of genius and the realisation of the self. The reaching back towards origins already evident before his voyage now became more conspicuous. The heroes of his works had hitherto been young Englishmen uncomplicated in their antecedents, if not in their feelings and desires. The enchantments of the Near East and the extended sense of his ancestry which his travels had helped to develop now encouraged Disraeli to experiment in his self-definition with a different kind of protagonist. In 1832 and 1833 respectively, he published *Contarini Fleming* and *Alroy*, the hero of the first a youth of noble Italian ancestry, of the second a prince of medieval Jewry, a sequence that was to be continued with Ferdinand Armine, scion of an 'illustrious and fallen race', in *Henrietta Temple* in 1837.

If Disraeli had staked nothing on *The Young Duke*, he staked everything on *Contarini Fleming*. Characteristically, he was aiming at the top: nothing less than the definitive treatment of 'the poetic character', a subject which was 'virgin in the imaginative literature of every country', or so he was to assert in the revealing preface to the 1845 edition, by implication brushing aside Byron's *Don Juan* and Wordsworth's *Prelude*. He did not quite brush aside Goethe, who was said to have admired *Vivian Grey*, and he acknowledged *Wilhelm Meister* as an imperfect forerunner in the study of the development of the poetic consciousness. *Contarini Fleming* was enough of a *Bildungsroman* in the German mould for Heine later to characterise it as 'a strange, wild book, of the kind I might have written myself'.[24] As 'a psychological autobiography', to take its sub-title, the work constitutes Disraeli's final and most candid delineation of his own growth processes through the figure of a hero whose name deliberately embodies that mingling of northern and southern strains which it was now his need explicitly to recognise and to explore. As a novel, it altogether lacks the vivacity, the light-hearted, tongue-in-cheek, show-them-the-works impetuousness of his earlier productions. His purpose was too serious for his style, which did not easily carry profundity, even at the rare moments when his meaning approached it. The liveliest passages, taken more or less verbatim from his letters, were those which swept Contarini through the scenes of his recent travels. The book hardly functions as a novel in the usual sense, with plot, incident and interplay of character; it becomes a spiritual Odyssey with pictures, and in parts merely a sketchbook with random ideas jotted in the margins. The philosophical disquisitions, the analyses of thought and feeling which are the point of the exercise are flat and uninspired. Disraeli had overreached himself. He could never admit it, confiding to his diary in 1833: 'I shall always consider "the Psych" as the perfection of English Prose, and a chef d'ouvre [*sic*]'; and reissuing the work in 1845 with the defiant statement that he found on critical examination that it had 'accomplished his idea'. In a way it had. He had worked auto-analysis almost out of his system – 'I shall write no more about myself', he confided to his diary in 1833 – and had achieved a kind of catharsis of the agonies of his striving for self-realisation. He had not, however, achieved recognition as the supreme psychoanalyst of genius, nor even commercial success. Murray sold only 614 copies of the first edition, and the profits were £56. However much Disraeli might snap that none of them had 'the slightest idea of the nature or purposes of the work', he knew that its critics had a point and that the highest range of literary achievement might lie beyond his powers.[25]

The prospect of great literary achievement was still tempting enough, however, for a couple of final assaults on the peak. In *Alroy*, in 1833, he announced that he had discarded verse on account of its limitations and invented a new style: the novel was couched in a pretentious poetic diction which irresistibly invited parody, and it gave full rein to Disraeli's Arabian nights complex in its rapturous evocation of the ornate richness and splendour of oriental life, and its taste for prophecies, visions and magical happenings. Through its hero, a prince of the Jewish captivity who redeems his departure from the purity of his faith and the mission of his nation by his martyrdom, Disraeli played out in fantasy what he called his 'ideal ambition': the translation of which into his British life he could not yet perceive. More ambitious still was his turning his mind to the continental and revolutionary themes which might answer the 'unconquerable desire, which now seems near at hand, of producing something great and lasting', as he put it to Austen in November 1833, answering the latter's demand for repayment of a loan by tapping him for another for the sake of world literature. Disraeli had concluded that 'all great works that have formed an epoch in the history of the human intellect have been an embodification of the spirit of their age ... Since the revolt of America a new principle has been at work in the world to which I trace all that occurs. This is the *Revolutionary* principle, and this is what I wish to embody in "*The Revolutionary Epic*".' He claimed to have conceived the idea of the poem on the plains of Troy, 'Standing upon Asia, and gazing upon Europe', seeing the two continents as 'the Rival Principles of Government that at present contend for the mastery of the world', the aristocratic on the one hand and the revolutionary and democratic on the other. He could not carry it out and never finished the work. Few people can have struggled through the published version of *The Revolutionary Epick* in its entirety. When it fell still-born from its poetic stilts, Disraeli must have known that the game was up. Supreme literary talent was not his, and he lacked the patience and the application to go on trying to cultivate it. He had promised in the preface to the *Epick* to bow to the decision of the public, 'for I am not one who finds consolation for the neglect of my contemporaries in the imaginary plaudits of a more sympathetic Posterity'. The pangs of creation, too, seem again to have endangered his health. Action was better for the system than the sedentary musings of authorship, its rapid results more suited to his nature than the grinding disciplines of literary development. 'I am never well save in action', he told Lady Blessington in October 1834, 'and then I feel immortal.'[26] He would go on writing, with less lofty aim (and, perhaps for that reason, better success), but the full exhibition of his genius must take place elsewhere. Disraeli was adaptable: if it was necessary to scatter a different set of pearls before a different kind of swine, he would do it. Henceforth he would concentrate on politics.

2

THE THEATRE OF POLITICS
1832–1837

BY THE time *The Revolutionary Epick* appeared, in March 1834, Disraeli had made his bow in fashionable society, stood twice for parliament at High Wycombe, and begun his grand romantic affair with Henrietta Sykes. Society, politics and love, but especially the first two, required new forms of composition between his genius and the external world, as the personality discerned and shaped in the crucible of introspection moved from self-definition to self-presentation and self-assertion in a larger theatre. Disraeli had to develop a social persona and a political stance, and, as he struggled for recognition in public roles, he had to elaborate the means by which his newly developed sense of ancestry and his cosmopolitan consciousness could be reconciled with the English life he sought to lead. Genius must be accommodated to the *genius loci*.

In February 1832, Disraeli took lodgings in Duke Street, St James's, in the heart of the West End, and began his penetration of metropolitan society with the help of his friend, the novelist and politician, Edward Lytton Bulwer. Older friends from the family's Bloomsbury days, like the Austens, now began to fade into the background, though indebtedness if nothing else obliged Disraeli to maintain touch with Benjamin Austen until he could finally pay him off in May 1837. His social progress was chronicled in self-congratulatory detail in his letters to his sister, Sarah, in whom he found that constantly admiring and affectionate 'audience' (his own term for her) that his nature demanded. In the novel *A Year at Hartlebury or the Election*, which she and her brother published in 1834 under the pseudonyms of 'Cherry and Fair Star', Sarah wrote: 'In this country where the art most sedulously fostered is the art of making a connection, numerous are the established means of arriving at the great result. A public school, a crack college, the turf if

31

you are rich, are all good in their way – but to travel on the Continent is a highly esteemed mode.'[1] Brother Ben had only travel of all those requirements, and not much in the way of acquaintance to show for that. As an author of some slight repute and a budding politician, he gradually extended his circle, but entry into the high society he had visualised in his imagination in *Vivian Grey* and *The Young Duke* would not come quickly. The world around Bulwer or the household of the gorgeous Lady Blessington and her lover, the dandy, Count Alfred D'Orsay, were intellectually and spiritually agreeable but socially on the margin of respectability, which was where Disraeli was, too, as his blackballing at his father's club, the Athenaeum, indicated.

Disraeli moved in society with a manner consciously designed to protect against the mockery to which a too naive revelation of his immature feelings and designs had exposed him in his literary sallies. It was designed, too, to protect him against bores and intellectual inferiors. 'I have not gained much in conversation with men', he noted in September 1833, ' ... I make it a rule now never to throw myself open to men ... I am always exhausted by composition when I enter society, and as I never get anything in return, I do not think the exertion necessary.' He tended thus to be reserved in company, until he chose, or was stimulated, to let loose the flow of sparkling, sarcastic conversation, to the brilliance of which observers testify, but of which they have left us few samples. Disraeli was beginning to assume the mask which was to contribute to his reputation as a 'mystery man', whose real sentiments, motives and beliefs lay hidden behind an impassive exterior. To some extent, it was the mask of the dandy. Disraeli was attracted to the construction of the personality as an aesthetic pose, not least when it came to the cultivation of a striking appearance. His friend Meredith's description of him just before he left for the East in 1830 sums it up: 'B.D. to dine with me. He came up Regent Street, when it was crowded, in his blue surtout, a pair of military light blue trousers, black stockings with red stripes, and shoes! "The people", he said, "quite made way for me as I passed. It was like the opening of the Red Sea, which I now perfectly believe from experience. Even well-dressed people stopped to look at me." I should think so!' Yet the finished affectation of the dandy, which his friend D'Orsay exemplified, was in the end too detached and artificial a persona with which to pursue the wordly success that was now more than ever Disraeli's aim, and, as Lord Blake points out, he did not possess quite the required coolness to carry it off: an ardent temperament and an inner insecurity broke through in the occasional very undandified explosion of emotion and assertiveness.[2]

So it seems to have been in the early stages at least of the love affair on which he embarked in the spring of 1833 with Lady Henrietta Sykes. Unusually for a man, Disraeli liked women. He liked them older than himself, married, and willing to give him the maternal embrace which he seems to have lacked as a child. 'There is', he says in *Vivian Grey*, 'no fascination so irresistible to a boy, as the smile of a married woman', and it is possible that he was the lover of Sara Austen, who assisted with the birth of that novel. Almost certainly he performed that office in 1832 for Clara Bolton, the wife of a fashionable physician who had treated him. His affair with Henrietta Sykes was a liaison of a different kind. She had nothing of the intellectual pretensions of her predecessors, and on that score was inclined to wonder what Disraeli saw in her: 'How I wish I was very clever for your sake', she wrote, ' ... I have just sense enough to feel my deficiency & to wish we were more on a par.' What she did have was a bold, voluptuous beauty, a passionate and mettlesome nature, and a willingness to play the maternal role, signing herself 'your Mother' and referring to Disraeli as 'my child'. This was the child's last free romantic gesture. 'When we first love', he had written in *The Young Duke*, 'we are enamoured of our own imaginations.' It is hard to dispute Lord Blake's verdict that he was in love with the idea of being in love as much as with Henrietta, and that he was too egoistical and calculating a carver of his career to support her importunities beyond the point at which his romantic vision of her, or rather of the two of them, began to fade. Still, it was the only passion of his life and consuming while it lasted, and its end in late 1836 hurt more than over-cynical interpretations of his nature would allow, if we believe his description of his state to D'Orsay: 'As a man of the world, you will perhaps laugh at me and think me very silly for being the slave of such feelings, when perhaps I ought to congratulate myself that an intimacy which must have, I suppose, sooner or later concluded, has terminated in a manner which may cost my heart a pang but certainly not my conscience. But it is in vain to reason with those who feel. In calmer moments, I may be of your opinion; at present I am wretched.'[3] He was also disreputable. Henrietta's husband, Sir Francis Sykes, seems to have been remarkably complaisant – he was friendly enough with Disraeli for the three of them to spend a month together at Southend with the Boltons (Clara having graduated from being Disraeli's mistress to being his) – but he finally lost patience when his wife moved on into the arms of the fashionable portrait painter, Daniel Maclise, possibly via those of another friend of Disraeli, Lord Lyndhurst (musical beds was a not uncommon pastime in the circles in which Disraeli now moved). Henrietta's resulting social disgrace did not entail Disraeli's, but his family's Buckinghamshire neighbours did not soon forget his introduction of his mistress together with Lord Lyndhurst to his parents' home at Bradenham on two occasions in 1835. These events gave a lasting colour to his reputation.

So did the debts which were the most constant companions of these years. The overheads of pseudo-Byronic living were heavy, and a large part of Disraeli's correspondence is concerned with the shifts and devices necessary to meet them, through a constant flurry of bills and promissory notes and borrowings at up to 40 per cent, and schemes for making a fortune at a stroke by seeking the British agency for the proposed Paris–Boulogne railway or promoting a loan to the Swedish government. Going out in society was occasionally made impossible by the fear of being 'nabbed'. 'I was glad to find the Sheriff's officer here among my staunch supporters', wrote Disraeli at the Maidstone election of 1837, 'I suppose gratitude.'[4] Not the least attraction of parliament was the immunity from arrest it conferred during sessions.

Railway speculation and the money market aside, there were two routes out of the morass. The first, as usual, was to throw off a couple of novels, *Henrietta Temple* and *Venetia*, published in 1836 and 1837 respectively, followed in 1839 by a verse tragedy, *Alarcos*, set in thirteenth-century Castile, which was at least an improvement on the *Epick*, though Macready declined to produce it. The novels resumed the familiar theme of growing up to which Disraeli seemed continually compelled to recur, partly to analyse what had gone wrong in his own youth, partly to hold on to the receding excitements of what it was like

34

to be young (even if unhappy).

In *Henrietta Temple* he capitalised as usual on recent experience with a faintly embarrassing story of love at first sight, in which emotional turmoil is closely keyed to meteorological disturbance, and a hero whose surface glitter covers some lack of the genuine and sincere pursues a heroine who is more an assemblage of womanly qualities than a woman, though her style of expression closely evokes the real Henrietta. Even the debts are pressed into service, as Ferdinand Armine meets Mr Bond Sharpe, gets arrested for debt, and sees the inside of a sponging-house – perhaps Disraeli's talisman against the ever-present threat of the real thing. The vein of autobiography, however, was almost extinct, and in *Venetia* disappeared, as Disraeli made his genuflection to the figures of Byron and Shelley. Monypenny suggests that in his choice of heroes he was demonstrating that, even if he had by then become a Conservative hopeful, his romantic genius was not to be confined within the ordinary bounds of his party's outlook and sympathies, but the tale's moral that happiness lies in being true to nature and natural feelings is not pressed in any unconservative way and hardly contradicts the markedly conventional moral scheme of *Henrietta Temple*. The book reads more like Disraeli's last respects to at least some of the romantic models of his youth. Perhaps, too, it was part of the farewell which he seemed to be bidding in these years to the great turmoil of creative aspiration which had once racked him. He had conceived *Alarcos*, he told its readers, 'rambling in the Sierras of Andalusia', at that time of life 'when the heart is quick with emotion, and the brain with creative fire; when the eye is haunted with beautiful sights, and the ear with sweet sounds; when we live in reveries of magnificent performance, and the future seems only a perennial flow of poetic invention'.[5] His tone, already at thirty-four, was elegiac and nostalgic: that ferment was past.

'As men advance in life', we read in *Henrietta Temple*, 'all passions resolve themselves into money. Love, ambition, even poetry, end in this.' Though well enough received, his latest novels could only mitigate Disraeli's financial difficulties. The other way of getting money was to marry it, and so satisfy the desire for companionship and the need for cash at one stroke. However much Disraeli enjoyed bachelorhood – 'my sweet liberty, and that indefinite future, which is one of the charms of existence', as he put it on the eve of abandoning it – he seems to have been easily prone to what he described as 'that melancholy which after a day of action is the doom of energetic celibacy'. Writing *The Young Duke*, he had remarked carelessly: 'no doubt there is great pleasure in a well-regulated existence, particularly if no children come in after dinner'. By the time of *Henrietta Temple*, the tone was less flippant. 'A female friend, amiable, clever, and devoted, is a possession more valuable than parks and palaces; and, without such a muse, few men can succeed in life, none be content.'[6] His chance came in March 1838 with the death of Wyndham Lewis, his colleague in the representation of Maidstone, where he had been returned to parliament in the previous year.

With Wyndham Lewis's widow, Mary Anne – 'a pretty little woman, a flirt and a rattle; indeed gifted with a volubility I sho[ul]d think unequalled, and of which I can convey no idea', as he described her on their first meeting in 1832 – Disraeli soon proceeded from admiration to intimacy. His motives were those which he frankly expounded to her in the supremely egotistical letter he wrote in February 1839, when, feeling that her delay in consenting to their marriage was exposing him to ridicule and ignomi010, he angrily charged her with degrading 'a bird of heaven' and evoked the retribution to come when she would recall with remorse 'the passionate heart that you have forfeited, and the genius you have betrayed'.

I avow [he wrote] when I first made my advances to you, I was influenced by no romantic feelings. My father had long wished me to marry; my settling in life was the implied, tho' not stipulated, condition of a disposition of his property, which would have been convenient to me. I myself, about to commence a practical career, wished for the solace of a home, and shrank from all the torturing passions of intrigue. I was not blind to worldly advantages in such an alliance, but I had already proved, that my heart was not to be purchased. I found you in sorrow, and that heart was touched. I found you, as I thought, amiable, tender, and yet acute and gifted with no ordinary mind; one whom I co[ul]d look upon with pride as the partner of my life, who could sympathise with all my projects and feelings, console me in the moments of depression, share my hour of triumph, and work with me for our honor [*sic*] and our happiness.[7]

Mary Anne had just thrown Disraeli out of her house after calling him 'a selfish bully', but his wounded and desperate tone may not have been due entirely to a lover's tiff. His debts would prevent his facing the next election, and the loss of his seat and parliamentary privileges would leave him defenceless against his creditors. He now knew Mary Anne's fortune to be considerably less than he had at first supposed, but she could still offer security as well as sympathy. The breach that provoked his effusion lasted only a day. They were married on 28 August 1839.

Probably on that day, Disraeli wrote to William Pyne, the solicitor on whom he relied to juggle his debts: 'Mrs. D. is aware that I am about to raise a sum of money, but is ignorant of the method'. He was never entirely frank with her about his financial straits, and may not have been entirely faithful, though there is no conclusive evidence. He was right, all the same, in looking forward to his marriage as 'that epoch in my life which will seal my career – for whatever occurs afterwards will I am sure never shake my soul'. If the pressure of creditors and the need to work some mysterious 'great business' which would alleviate it continued, Mary Anne was able to pay election expenses and outstanding debts to the tune of £13,000 in the first two years of marriage. More important, as her husband put it in one of his wedding anniversary odes, she 'Brought faith & solace to the Mournful life / Fortune had ever crossed'. Disraeli gained, as he wrote in August 1842, not only 'all those worldly accidents wh: make life desirable', but 'that peace of mind & consequent physical health wh: render it even delicious'. His craving for constant affection, admiration and attention was answered. With Mary Anne as hostess in her Grosvenor Gate mansion, he was now able to advance his career by giving political dinners. His married status did something to diminish the air of raffishness that had hung around him, and went down well with the electors at Shrewsbury in 1844: 'my domestic character', he reported to Mary Anne, 'does me a great deal of good'.[8] He even felt able to act as a marriage counsellor to his friends.

There were costs of this bourgeois domesticity and of approaching middle age. With the raffishness and the melancholy went some of the jaunty panache and the restless self-searching that had given interest to Disraeli's youth. He did not regret the change, which was essential to his further advance, and his gratitude to Mary Anne issued in an attachment and a loyalty which ensured that for the rest of his career the swiftest route to his enmity would be to ridicule or slight the vivacious, shrewd, courageous and touchingly absurd woman who was his wife. Hers was now the inspirational force. 'She is, as you know, a heroine', he wrote to D'Orsay in December 1841, 'and as I have ceased to be a hero, it is fortunate that one of us has some great qualities.'[9] The words suggest, like those of the preface to *Alarcos*, a consciousness of fading vision. Yet politics might still offer a heroic role.

'Playing at Parliament' had been a favourite boyhood pastime, and from the age of fourteen or so Disraeli displayed a fascination with historical figures like Wolsey, who had risen from humble origins to great political power. For Vivian Grey, power was the object for which 'men, *real* men, should alone exist'. Absorbing through historical example and his reading of Bacon the Machiavellian approach to politics, the young Disraeli could be in no doubt about the role of cunning, ruthlessness and self-mastery in the attainment of such power. Robert O'Kell has urged persuasively that, as he moved towards active political engagement in the early 1830s, he sought to work out in his writings – notably *Contarini Fleming*, the satire *Ixion in Heaven*, published in 1832, and *Alroy* – the tension which perturbed the brains and churned the stomachs of his fictional heroes between the promptings of worldly ambition on the one hand and the impulse towards sublime spiritual purity on the other. He came finally to an acceptance of the costs entailed for his conception of himself by the corruption of his nature which success in the world must involve, while yet holding off the inevitable contamination through a certain ironic self-distancing from the values of the society he sought to conquer. It was like Disraeli to try to have it both ways, but the inner struggle, if there really was one, was always unequal. It was the headlong dash at success by Vivian Grey that had portrayed his own 'active and real ambition', as he noted in 1833. In any case, the desire for power and success could easily be moralised and a career in the world be sanctioned as the necessary antidote to selfish and unproductive egoism. Contarini Fleming, like Wilhelm Meister, is finally persuaded that, having nurtured his genius, he must employ it in action for 'the amelioration of his kind', and upon his initial desire to devote himself to the study and creation of beauty supervenes the feeling that it may be his lot at no distant date to take part in the political regeneration of his country.[10]

Disraeli was leading his hero to this conclusion just as the Reform crisis was moving towards its *dénouement*, and was pressing John Murray to be sure to publish the novel before the election contest he expected shortly to fight. His launch into politics was precipitated by his sense that the Reform struggle had thrown the country into the kind of turmoil, and might lead to the kind of political upheaval in which an ardent young spirit of superior power might enjoy opportunities of rapid ascent unthinkable in settled times. For a young Napoleon who had had the misfortune to miss the French Revolution, this was the next best thing. Recapturing his first Wycombe election in the novel *Hartlebury*, he described how the hero, Bohun, who combined 'a fine poetical temperament, with a great love of action', was prompted by the Reform bill to return from foreign travel to an England seen from abroad as gripped by anarchy and tumult. 'At the prospect of insurrection, he turned with more affection towards a country he had hitherto condemned as too uneventful for a man of genius': he felt 'all was stirring'. Despite his ambition, Bohun had 'too great a stake in the existing order of things to precipitate a revolution', but 'he intended to ride the storm, if the hurricane did occur'. This seems a faithful transcription of Disraeli's outlook. 'The times are damnable', he told Austen in November 1831, just after his return from the East. 'I take the gloomiest views of affairs, but we must not lose our property without a struggle. In the event of a new election, I offer myself for Wycombe.'[11]

'If the Reform Bill pass', was the condition of his candidature as announced to his father.[12] In the sense that the enlargement of the electorate by a measure of parliamentary reform would open up the constituencies to men like himself, without favour or connection in the established political world, Disraeli was naturally a reformer. A chance vacancy, however, meant that he found himself standing for the borough of High Wycombe, a few miles from the family's Bradenham home, in June 1832, before the Reform bill had passed, and thus on the old footing of election by the handful of burgesses. A Reform stance was still indicated, since the borough corporation and the local people had shown themselves strongly in favour of the bill, but the Whig majority in the corporation found a solid Reform candidate in the prime minister's son and secretary, Charles Grey, so that Disraeli, who had opened his canvass of the borough in January by cheerfully soliciting all parties, now had to look for support to the Tories and to Radicals resentful of the corporation's privileges and hostile to Grey as a representative of the aristocracy. This situation was repeated in December when, the Reform bill having passed, he fought the seat again on the new ten-pound householder franchise, against two Whigs, Grey and Smith.

In these circumstances, his platform and his associations were necessarily eclectic. 'Toryism is worn out, and I cannot condescend to be a Whig', he told Austen in June, announcing that he would stand 'on the high Radical interest'. The condition of the Tory party was certainly not such as to render it attractive to a trainee politician on the make, and Disraeli was careful to avoid identification with it by refraining from joining the Conservative and Carlton clubs. Nevertheless he put some surreptitious Tory credentials in his pocket by attacking the foreign policy of the Grey ministry in his *England and France: a Cure for the Ministerial Gallomania* published anonymously in April, and his agent at Wycombe, John Nash, as well as being his father's solicitor, was the local man of business of the duke of Buckingham, whose son, Lord Chandos, led the county's Tories. As for the Whigs, he would have condescended to them if they had listened to his friend Bulwer's urging to let him run unopposed. He told Sarah in April that, with the *Gallomania* in hand, he was 'sure of a Boro' if the Tories ultimately succeed, w[hi]ch I doubt, and have a fair chance the other way', adding that '[I] really do not care about it, as I am more desirous of writing than ever' (which, with *Contarini Fleming* still awaiting the critics' verdict and *Alroy* on the stocks, may have been genuine).[13] However, with the Tories in a trough and the Whigs standing aloof (because he lacked noble birth, he complained at Wycombe in December), Radicalism was a natural holding position.

A great deal of ingenuity has been expended, as it was by Disraeli himself, in reconciling his early Radical flourishes with his subsequent

Tory professions. Much of it has been wasted because of a failure to grasp the nature of the Radicalism with which Disraeli was operating. This was not the straightlaced, doctrinaire, utilitarian, nonconformist Radicalism of the 'Birmingham heroes' like Attwood and Scholefield, none of whom Disraeli found 'above par' when he met them in May 1832. As W. H. Greenleaf has noted, it was 'in the guise of a popular or philanthropic (as opposed to a Benthamite or philosophical) radical of a sort best represented perhaps by Cobbett, Burdett, or Sadler' that Disraeli opened his political account. Sir Francis Burdett was one of the leading Radicals (O'Connell and Hume were the others) to whom Disraeli's friends unsuccessfully applied for endorsement of his candidature. A supporter of equal electoral districts, annual parliaments and a direct taxation franchise, he adopted a 'patriot' posture which linked him to the 'country' opposition ideology of the late seventeenth and early eighteenth centuries; he described his political creed as that of a Tory of the reign of Queen Anne, and owed a substantial intellectual debt to Lord Bolingbroke. Disraeli, who was later to describe him as a Jacobite who had been mistaken for a Jacobin, had no need to look further for a model of a political stance combining popular sympathies with Tory traditions in opposition to Whig exclusiveness, and possessing the added attraction of a certain careless social distinction: Byron's description of Burdett as the only reformer in whose company a gentleman would be seen was to be echoed in Disraeli's 'the greatest gentleman I ever knew'.[14] Radicalism of this high-toned, independent and sometimes eccentric kind was an ideal vehicle for the first political forays of a youngster who had yet to find a political connection and a parliamentary seat.

In his October address to the electors of Wycombe, Disraeli declared for the standard Radical objects of secret ballot and 'those old English and triennial parliaments of which the Whigs originally deprived us', and he was soon assimilating both to old Tory tradition by citing the support of 'Sir William Wyndham and my Lord Bolingbroke'. His stance was that of a man of the people, dedicated to promoting the improvement of the condition of the lower orders, but the lower orders, even under the new franchise which governed his second contest, had few votes. Beaten by twenty to twelve in June, he went down again in December, polling 119 against the 140 and 179 respectively of Grey and

Smith. All the same, he enjoyed it hugely. The opportunity for dramatic self-presentation that elections offered answered to a fundamental impulse of his nature. 'At length', says Contarini Fleming of his childhood passion for the theatre, 'I perceived human beings conducting themselves as I wished.' Politics for Disraeli was always the most fulfilling form of theatre. In *Hartlebury*, he recreated, with an actor's eye and self-complacency, the vivid scenes of his first electoral adventure, even to bringing his hero, Bohun, 'who was a perfect master of stage effect', out on to the portico of the *Rose*, to commemorate his own address from the portico of Wycombe's *Red Lion*, where he had used the eponymous beast as a prop. In the election, declares Bohun, 'I feel I live'; and so did Disraeli.[15]

Over the next four years, his twistings and turnings in search of a seat added a good deal to his reputation for insincerity, not to say cynicism. His observations at Wycombe on such touchy topics as the protection of agriculture by the laws imposing duties on imported corn, and the abolition of slavery, seem to have been carefully modulated to avoid annoying either the local agriculturalists or the marquess of Chandos, who was chairman of the Society of West India Planters and Merchants; and immediately upon losing his second contest in December he sought to stand alongside Chandos in the Buckinghamshire county election as a supporter of the agricultural interest, 'the only solid basis of the social fabric', withdrawing, however, on the appearance of another candidate to second Chandos in the Tory cause. In March and April 1833, though he never went to the poll, he was presenting himself as a Radical and anti-ministerial candidate at Marylebone, reproducing his populist Wycombe platform, while hoping again that the Whigs might let him in unopposed. By June 1834, expecting that the political crisis created by the resignation of three ministers from the Whig cabinet would lead eventually to the triumph of the 'Ultra-Liberal party', he was cultivating, via Lady Blessington's salon, the leader of that wing, Lord Durham, and looking for closer contact with the Irish leader Daniel O'Connell. 'The Tories', he told his sister in July, 'are lost for ever.'[16]

Yet it was precisely at that moment that, at Henrietta's dinner table, he struck up acquaintance with the former Tory lord chancellor,

Lyndhurst, to whom he was soon to attach himself as a kind of political secretary. It was the right time to hedge his bets. In the immediate aftermath of the passing of the 1832 Reform bill, it had seemed likely that the Tories would be out of power for a long period, and that the real political struggle would lie between the ministerial Whigs and the Radicals, whose dominating personalities were Durham and O'Connell. By the end of 1834, however, Sir Robert Peel's coming into office as prime minister signalled the revitalisation of what was now increasingly called the Conservative party. Disraeli was still trying in November to get Durham to help him into parliament as a Radical, but more and more he was turning to Lyndhurst, Chandos and the duke of Wellington. Writing to Lyndhurst in December, he sought to play the two sides off against each other. Durham, he alleged, had offered him a seat and was urging him not to side with the Tories: 'I wd. sooner lose with the Duke and yourself than win with Melbourne [the late Whig prime minister] and Durham, but win *or* lose I must – I cannot afford to be neutral. How then, my dear Lord, am I to act?' Within weeks he was fighting his third and last contest for Wycombe, with his old Tory and Radical coalition and £500 from the central Conservative office, delivering to the electors on 16 December a speech (printed as *The Crisis Examined*) which was so patently aligned to the position Peel was about to take in his Tamworth manifesto that it is impossible to resist Richard Davis's conclusion that he must have had advance knowledge of the latter through Lyndhurst.[17] Conveying the news of his narrow defeat to Wellington on 7 January 1835, he described himself as having fought 'our battle'. As the Radicals and O'Connell's Irish coalesced with the Whigs against Peel's government early in 1835, so the vista of a powerful, independent Radicalism faded, Disraeli's connection with Durham lost its attraction, and between the Whigs whom he had consistently vituperated and the Tories whose fortunes in the country were on the mend the choice was straightforward. 'A Whig is like a poet, born not made', said Sir Francis Baring, adding: 'It is as difficult to become a Whig as to become a Jew.'[18] Disraeli was unlikely to break into that tight circle; more opportunity for 'new men' lay with the Tories, whose chief was now openly parading himself as one such, 'the son of a cotton-spinner'. In April 1835, Disraeli appeared at the

Taunton by-election as the official candidate of the party which he was to inhabit for the rest of his life.

As yet, he had only taken rooms in the Conservative party. To convert it into a permanent residence for his genius required the extensive rearrangement of its furniture which he undertook in the next dozen years, as he reinterpreted its nature and its mission in terms which both accommodated his previous professions and laid the foundation for the realisation of his present aspirations. Disraeli's politics, as he elaborated them in the 1830s and 1840s, were the politics of denization, through which his 'continental' and 'revolutionary' mind sought to put down roots and fashion a satisfying role for itself, in Britain, where chance had located it, and in the Conservative party, where circumstance had lodged it. Their development was a special case of the exercise of the transformational power of the romantic vision to dissolve the surface texture of mundane reality and reveal beneath it the magical world of hidden forms and occult forces, through knowledge of which alone the master-spirit could achieve its mission to guide the destinies of men and nations. It was a case, too, of the not uncommon retreat from the exhilarating but in the end lonely and terrifying extremes of romantic egoism into a search for the reassurance of a settled place in time and space, in history and in society, in a secure tradition and in a native land.

'I co[ul]d rule the House of Commons, altho' there wo[ul]d be a great prejudice against me at first', Disraeli had confided to his diary in 1833. 'It is the most jealous assembly in the world. The fixed character of our English society, the consequence of our aristocratic institutions renders a *career* difficult.' That career could not flow from the unstudied inheritance of a native tradition or from a hereditary connection with either of the major parties. As Disraeli had invented his social, so he had to invent his political persona almost from scratch. Some tinge of Toryism may have been caught from a father whose vindication of the character of Charles I had earned him a DCL from the university of Oxford, but according to Disraeli's later reminiscences, his father 'not only never entered into the politics of the day, but ... could never understand them'. 'I am not in a condition', Disraeli told the Commons in 1846, 'to have had hereditary opinions carved out for me and all my opinions, therefore, have been the result of reading and thought.'[19] They were also the result of his need to formulate the terms in which his penetration and domination of England's aristocratic institutions could be achieved.

In these politics of settlement, Disraeli's starting point was necessarily his physical location on the map. 'My politics are described by one word, and that word is ENGLAND', he wrote early in 1832 in his 'very John Bull book', as he described it to Sarah, *England and France*. His strident assertion of Englishness suggests a sharp awareness of how easily his credentials in that sphere could be questioned. In many respects, by the 1830s, the assimilation of the D'Israeli family into English life might have appeared almost complete. From being a minor metropolitan literary celebrity, Isaac had become, with the move to Bradenham, a Buckinghamshire country gentleman. His family was accepted at a certain level of county society and his eldest son became in 1836 a justice of the peace for the county. Benjamin's affection for Bradenham was deep: it provided a kind of rootedness in English soil as the Bloomsbury of his adolescence had not done and the round of fashionable London salons could not do. 'Write to me about Bradenham, about dogs and horses, orchards, gardens, – who calls, where you go', he had enjoined his sister from Gibraltar in 1830.[20] Yet in temperament, in consciousness, in aspect he remained a stranger and a sojourner. The quality of strangeness, the tinge of exoticism mattered little, indeed constituted a valuable part of his stock-in-trade, when he was pursuing the materialisation of his genius in literature and dandyism. In entering into politics, however, he altered the nature of his relationship to the society which he inhabited.

Claiming a place in the councils of the realm was not like claiming a place in its circulating libraries. The assertion of a role in public life meant exposure to the hostile scrutiny of opponents and rivals and the mocking appraisal of crowds who would naturally seize on any trait that could be exploited to deride and marginalise this unconventional aspirant to office and honours in a sphere less open (because taken more seriously in England) than that of literature or fashion. Here, the alien tint conferred by Disraeli's Jewishness, by his romantic flourishes, and by his oriental affectations, would constitute less a resource of his own repertoire than a weapon in his enemies'. The cries of 'Shylock' and

'Old Clothes', which met him on the hustings at Maidstone in 1837, were evidence that his Jewishness in particular would be employed against him, however little he resembled either Shakespeare's hostile stereotype or the one which Charles Dickens was just about to produce in the character of Fagin. Lord Blake's remark that the tiny Jewish minority in Britain was far from a size to attract persecution is correct, but it needs to be taken in conjunction with his observation that Disraeli was far from reproducing the reserved, prudent, inconspicuous respectability of the elite of Anglo-Jewry in his day – and of his own family.[21] Keeping his head below the parapet was not Disraeli's way: his instinct was to advance to the storm of the great world with all possible flamboyance, and that activated against him in virulent form prejudices that the more discreet and circumspect might hardly face. It did not matter that he was a baptised Christian. He was perceived as a Jew, and Jewishness in a racial if not in a religious sense was readily ascribed to him by those who thought to rebuff his pretensions to a role in English public life by assimilating him to an unfavourable stereotype, and occasionally by those who wished to claim him as a champion of his race. His own sense of Jewishness, stimulated by his Eastern tour and manifested in *Alroy*, had not yet attained its final, deliberately challenging form, but the problem of composition between it and the place he inhabited was rendered more urgent by the public assertion and exposure which entry into politics entailed.

The definition of his politics as simply English was the almost enforced response. If he could hardly define himself as simply English, he could at least sublimate the alien strains in an expressly English frame of thought and feeling. 'Although full many an Eastern clime and Southern race have given me something of their burning blood, it flows for thee!', runs his apostrophe to England in *The Young Duke*. An ostentatious patriotism alongside a freebooting Radicalism was the obvious starting-point for an ambitious adventurer with no connection among the country's political elites. The politics of Englishness meant confiding in 'the genius of the people', and governing in accordance with the national character formed by 'particular modes of religious belief, ancient institutions, peculiar manners, venerable customs, and intelligible interests', as he put it in *England and France*.[22]

That, he contended, was precisely what the Whigs were failing to do. From the moment they shut him out at Wycombe, he attacked them as an anti-national party, an exclusive and doctrinaire caste, which had incongruously combined with agitators and extremists in the Reform crisis to destroy the aristocratic principle of government which had hitherto prevailed in England. In *Hartlebury*, where his hero, Bohun, immediately sees that the Reform bill is a device of the Whigs to entrench themselves in power, Disraeli gave full vent to his spleen against the dissenting 'low Whig' electorate, which had rejected him with all that 'intense predisposition of enmity, which cold-blooded, calculating, unsympathetic, selfish mortals always innately feel for a man of genius, a man whose generous and lively spirit always makes them ashamed of their dead, dunghill-like existence'. The only way to break the power which the Whigs based on the 'oligarchy of the High Street' was to accept that, the aristocratic principle being beyond revival, it was necessary to advance to the democratic and to 'expand the Whig constituency into a national constituency'. The heroic role of introducing true national and popular government Disraeli reserved, of course, for himself. 'Great spirits may yet arise', he declared in April 1833, in his aptly titled pamphlet, *What is He?*, 'spirits whose proud destiny it may still be, at the same time to maintain the glory of the Empire, and to secure the happiness of the People!'[23]

In *What is He?*, Disraeli conjured up the vision of a junction of Radicals and Tories, of the kind he had fostered at Wycombe, in that tempting vehicle for an independent adventurer, a national party. The idea was obvious enough, but it seems to have owed something to that extensive reading in his father's library which, he liked to claim, had freed him from conventional misconceptions about the development of English politics and parties and given him insights denied to his contemporaries. In politics as in literature, Disraeli's originality was limited. He sought models, and he found one for a political career transcending the shackles of established parties in the figure of Viscount Bolingbroke, whose 'country' opposition to the Whig oligarchy of the early eighteenth century offered a convenient precedent and vindication for his combat against the Whiggery of his own day. Bolingbroke too had believed in the power in public affairs of those superior intellects who, he wrote, 'engross almost the whole reason of the species; who are born to instruct, to guide, and to preserve; who are designed to be the tutors and the guardians of human kind'. He too, as Disraeli interpreted him in the *Vindication of the English Constitution*, had been 'opposed to the Whigs from principle, for an oligarchy is hostile to genius', and had incurred the charge of inconsistency by his display of 'that vigilant and meditative independence which is the privilege of an original and determined spirit'.[24]

By the time he published the *Vindication*, in December 1835 however, Disraeli had discovered, as he supposed Bolingbroke to have done, that the idea of a new party, 'that dream of youthful ambition in a perplexed and discordant age', was 'destined in English politics to be never more substantial than a vision'. He had accepted the necessity of accommodating his genius to one of the two great historic alliances, and with it the need to strike out a line which would achieve a satisfying rhetorical reconciliation of 'vigilant and meditative independence' with a party allegiance. 'In politics', as he put the problem to the Tauntonians, 'there can be no refinements. He who aspires to be a practical politician must in this country be a party man: he who is a party man must act entirely with his party ... Hence a compromise of opinions is a necessary consequence of public life.' Refinements, however, were Disraeli's speciality. Twitted with the incongruity between his previous Radical roistering and his new Conservative colours, he launched, both in his Taunton polemics and in the *Vindication*, into a remarkable reconceptualisation of the party he had only just joined, designed not only to harmonise his political past and present but to insinuate him into the very heart of Toryism as the detached and contemplative observer who could reveal to the party the true meaning of its history and the true path of its future. The ghostly mentor, once more, was Bolingbroke, who, forced, like Disraeli, to choose between the Whigs and the Tories, had 'penetrated their interior and essential qualities', had grasped that it was a choice between oligarchy and democracy, and, having taken the Tory side, had from that instant, through his writings, 'eradicated from Toryism all those absurd and odious doctrines which Toryism had adventitiously adopted', and 'clearly developed its essential and permanent character'.[25]

It was under that spiritual aegis that Disraeli set out in the *Vindication* the programme of regenerating the Tory party by returning it to its true traditions that he was to represent to a correspondent almost forty years later as being his life's work.

In the conduct of the Tory party at this moment, it appears to me that there are three points to the furtherance of which we should principally apply ourselves: First, that the real character and nature of Toryism should be generally and clearly comprehended: secondly, that Toryism should be divested of all those qualities which are adventitious and not essential, and which, having been produced by that course of circumstances which are constantly changing, become in time obsolete, inconvenient, and by the dexterous misrepresentation of our opponents even odious: thirdly, that the efficient organisation of the party should be secured and maintained. The necessity of the third point has already been anticipated by the party; but they have blundered in the second, and totally neglected the first.[26]

Disraeli made up for this alleged neglect with a rapid review of British history since the Glorious Revolution, designed to characterise the two parties in the manner which his relation to each required. The Whigs, 'a small knot of great families who have no other object but their own aggrandisement, and who seek to gratify it by all possible means', backed up by the nonconformists and '"the money interest", the fungus spawn of public loans', had done their utmost, ever since their accession to a near-monopoly of political power at the Hanoverian succession, to establish their oligarchical control by the subjection of the great institutions – crown, church, universities, municipal and commercial corporations, the magistracy and local government – which made Britain a nation rather than a mass of individuals looking up to a centralised despotism as the sole fount of wealth and honour. 'The rest of the nation – that is to say, nine-tenths of the people of England', Disraeli asserted, 'formed the Tory party, the landed proprietors and peasantry of the kingdom, headed by a spiritual and popular Church', which constituted 'the national party ... the really democratic party of England', devoted to the defence of those institutions which alone could safeguard the liberties of the people against Whig designs.[27]

This was Disraeli's first essay in a technique of radical inversion which he was to use more than once to effect a conceptual transformation of his relation to the world about him. For almost half a century before 1830, the Whigs, in opposition, had been proclaiming themselves the defenders of the people's liberties against an exclusive, corrupt and bigoted Tory establishment. Having no intention of languishing, in a 'democratic age', on the anti-popular side, Disraeli, joining the Tory party, simply reversed the stereotypes. Yet the fact that it was exaggeratedly partisan and polemically convenient does not mean that his version of the development of parties was necessarily as absurd as Whig historiographical tradition would have it. If it depended rather heavily on intoning the magic names of Sir William Wyndham and Lord Bolingbroke, Disraeli's version of eighteenth-century national and popular Toryism has been made to seem less fanciful by Linda Colley's showing how Tories, excluded from place and profit before 1760 and substantially dependent on the more open constituencies, might 'identify themselves at least rhetorically with the socially and politically dispossessed' in a common hatred of the Whig regime.[28] Whig designs may have been less sinister than Disraeli chose to paint them, but the social exclusivity of the Whigs and their taste for the rewards of public power and employment were hard to overstate. The Whig core was small: thirty-nine noble families between them provided 162 of the Whig-Liberal members of parliament between 1832 and 1885. Earl Grey in 1830 provided government places for eight of his nearest relations and friends; and it was Gladstone, as much an outsider to the tight Whig circle of consanguinity as Disraeli himself, who remarked in 1855 that the 'prizes' of public life were 'air, light, heat, electricity, meat and drink and everything else to that which meets at Brooks's'. Disraeli's historical view of party was far from disinterested, but it was also far from implausible.[29]

It stood, moreover, in the tradition which had come to him from Machiavelli via Bacon and Bolingbroke, of looking into the past to discover both the type of pristine political virtue and the causes of its present corruption. In a diary of 1821, Disraeli had quoted from Bacon: 'Reduce things to the first institution, & observe wherein and how they have degenerated; but yet ask counsel of both times: of the ancient what is best: of the latter time what is fittest.' History was the key to the analysis and the remedy of present discontents. Disraeli's style of political thinking was of a piece with the vogue among both Radicals and conservatives in his youth for seeking to ground their arguments less in the abstract formulae of political philosophy than in the right understanding of national spirit and national tradition as conferred by the study of the past. While Radicals like Burdett had evoked the ancient or Anglo-Saxon constitution to support their demands for manhood suffrage or annual parliaments, conservatives, anxious to deprive them of the powerful support of prescription and patriotic nostalgia, had criticised their historical postulates and, following Bolingbroke and Hume, had turned for their model to the system of liberties established by the Glorious Revolution.[30] Disraeli couched his views in the latter strain, as might have been expected of the godson of the antiquary Sharon Turner, one of the leading historical critics of the Radical notion of the Anglo-Saxon constitution, but it was easy for him to find common ground with Radicals in calling for devices like the ballot and short parliaments as the only way to break the grip achieved by the Whigs through their rigging of the electoral system in 1832, just as Bolingbroke and Wyndham had done in opposition to the consolidation of Whig oligarchy after 1715. The idea of a 'national' coalition of the excluded and oppressed against a usurping aristocratic clique which was corrupting the ancient constitution, was a natural weapon to employ against the governments of Grey and Melbourne as against the supremacy of Walpole, and it served to rid the Tories of the taint of being an anti-popular party as it had done in Bolingbroke's day to deflect the charge of Jacobitism.

It served also to accommodate Disraeli's Radical and Tory professions in a stance capable both of supplying the intellectual consistency which he needed to feel – as much for self-esteem as for self-defence – and of embodying the Englishness which he was anxious to assert. There were admittedly some inconvenient flaws. The coalescence of Radicalism with the Whigs against Peel's short-lived Conservative ministry, which was driven from office in April 1835, made it impossible for a young Tory aspirant to go on vaunting Radical associations (even if Burdett was now supporting Peel) or playing with Radical proposals. Disraeli had to explain that measures like triennial parliaments and the ballot, which it had been necessary to advocate as the means of keeping an

anti-national government in check, were no longer needed now that the
true national party he had been endeavouring to promote had emerged
with the revival of Toryism 'under the guidance of an eloquent and able
leader'. Yet, despite minor embarrassments, the idea of Toryism and its
place in English history which he elaborated in the course of 1835 was
to provide his political standing ground for the rest of his career. It
enabled him to claim for his party the cause at once of conservatism and
of democracy. In a letter to a Taunton supporter in July, which was
intended for publication, he wrote:

I hold one of the first principles of Toryism to be that Governmt. is instituted
for the welfare of the many. This is why the Tories maintain national institutions, the objects of which are the protection, the maintenance, the moral, civil,
and religious education of the great mass of the English people: institutions
which whether they assume the form of churches, or universities, or societies
of men to protect the helpless, and to support the needy, to execute justice and
to maintain truth, alike originated, and alike flourish for the advantage and
happiness of the multitude. I deny that the Tories have ever opposed the
genuine democratic or national spirit of the country; on the contrary they have
always headed it ... The more popular the constituency, the stronger the
Tories will become.[31]

The popular, not to say populist, line was carried to the point of
asserting in the *Vindication* that 'Toryism, or the policy of the Tories,
being the proposed or practised embodification, as the case may be, of the
national will and character, it follows that Toryism must occasionally
represent and reflect the passions and prejudices of the nation, as well
as its purer energies and its more enlarged and philosophic views.' In
the context, this was in part a neat device to excuse what Disraeli
regarded as the excessively repressive character of Toryism during the
French wars and its 'dangerous liberality' in the 1820s, by ascribing
both to the function of echoing the 'national voice'. More generally,
however, it opened the way to almost any degree of manoeuvre in the
interest of maintaining political stability or securing political power. 'A
statesman', Disraeli had already told the Wycombe electors when
revealing to them his new-found commitment to Peel's policies in
December 1834, 'is the creature of his age ... The people have their
passions, and it is even the duty of public men occasionally to adopt

sentiments with which they do not sympathize, because the people must have leaders.'[32]

The credo worked out in 1835 Disraeli called his 'Primitive Toryism', the realisation of the essential and historic nature of the party, stripped of accidental accretions and 'obsolete associations' through that power of penetrating beneath the surfaces of reality which only a detached and cerebral observer of British politics, 'unconnected with its parties, and untouched by its passions', as he described his young self, could truly possess. In the clarity of the outsider's perception which enabled him, as he claimed, to show the party its destiny, lay his only right to lead it. Yet the heights could not be scaled by essay-writing, even if Peel, with faint ambiguity, declared himself impressed by the 'original force of argument and novelty of illustration' of the *Vindication*. Disraeli devilled in political work for Lyndhurst (the *Vindication* was in large measure a tract to justify his patron's hostility to the Municipal Reform bill in the Lords), gained election to the Carlton Club in March 1836, and in June was the only non-member of parliament to be invited by Chandos to a dinner for the leaders of both Houses; but he was still merely a suitor for a seat. Not until the general election of July 1837 was he returned for Maidstone in tandem with Wyndham Lewis, as 'an uncompromising Adherent to that ancient Constitution, which once was the boast of our Fathers, and is still the Blessing of their Children'.[33]

3

THE THEATRE OF PARLIAMENT
1837–1846

FROM September 1842 to January 1843, the Disraelis made an extended visit to Paris, where they moved in a brilliant society, and Disraeli was exhilarated by the deference paid by the *salons* to intellect and wit, even if, as he would note in *Coningsby*, the French dined off cold plates. The high points of the visit were Disraeli's intimate conversations with King Louis Philippe, to whom, probably in November 1842, he presented a memorandum in which he offered himself as the 'influential member' who might restore what he now regarded as the proper understanding and amity between England and France by inducing the House of Commons to deliberate on the condition of relations between the two countries. Professing 'that knowledge of the actors & motives of the political world of England wh. years of thought & action & intimate intercourse with the chiefs of parties can alone give', he suggested that, as Sir Robert Peel's ministerial majority included forty to fifty 'agricultural malcontents', so 'ano[the]r section of conservatives members [*sic*], full of youth & energy, & constant in their seats, must exercise an irresistible control over the tone of the Minister. Sympathising in general with his domestic policy, they may dictate the character of his foreign.' A 'gentleman' had already been solicited to form a party of 'the youth of England' which could assume the task, and the writer was ready to plan a 'comprehensive organis[atio]n of the Press of England', and to exercise 'the same general supervision that Ld. P[almerston] now exercises over the Anti-Gallic press'. These schemes, Disraeli reassured his royal reader, 'may perhaps seem vast, but they are not visionary'; on the contrary they were 'even to the minutest element necessary to their success digested & matured, and it is believed that the influence & intellect of an indiv[idua]l can at this moment carry them into effect'.[1]

Complete with its broad hints about the large expenditure entailed by the leadership of a parliamentary party, this reads like the prospectus of an international confidence trickster whose panache was in danger of outrunning his plausibility; but it was designed to bolster Disraeli's confidence rather than to abuse Louis Philippe's. Its fantasy of power over a House of Commons where he was still a maverick backbencher, of command of a public opinion which knew him mainly as a minor novelist, and of international influence where he had not even acquired a national standing, reflected Disraeli's frustration with the meagre yield of his first five years in parliament and his need to transcend the limitations of his immediate circumstances by the exciting force of his imagination. To Mary Anne in February and March he had written of his feeling of political isolation and of her 'approbation & delight' as being the sole object and support of his continuing his labours. The mood, it is true, was promptly lightened by what he triumphantly represented as a caning of Palmerston in the course of an attack on the deficiencies of the consular service; but the fact remained that his start in political life had failed to live up to the exigencies of his ego.[2]

It was not that he had done badly, simply that he had not done brilliantly. The fiasco of his maiden speech in December 1837, when an inflated style and manner made him an easy target for a body of Radicals and Irish determined to put him down, was gradually overcome, as he took the tone of the House of Commons and learned to win a hearing by carefully prepared discourses soberly delivered. Making only four speeches in 1838, he was averaging one a month in 1839 and venturing provocative opinions on controversial subjects like Chartism. Yet he remained something of a curiosity and a marginal force in politics. It is not surprising that, as he told Sarah in February 1838, he was taken up by 'two of the greatest ruffians in the house', the Irish members Somers and Dillon Browne, who had 'taken a sort of blackguard fancy to me': he and they cohabited on the shadier fringes of parliamentary life.[3] His raffish reputation and his debts stuck to him, the latter despite Mary Anne's resources. If the petition against his election at Shrewsbury in 1841 had succeeded, and he had lost the seat to which he had just moved from Maidstone, it seems that arrest at his creditors' suit would have been a real possibility.

However useful he might make himself as a parliamentary skir-
misher when the Conservatives were in opposition, such a figure could
hardly expect advancement when they came into office. But Disraeli
did, or at any rate he begged Peel for a post when the latter was forming
his government in September 1841, following the Conservative victory
in the general election of the summer. His ambition was quite unreal-
istic. It is true that up to that point his relations with his leader had
verged on the cordial. Peel had been decently affable to his odd recruit
and had done what a leader should to support him in his first parliamentary forays, not least during the ordeal of his maiden speech,
'cheering me repeatedly, which is not his custom', as Disraeli himself
reported. It was however unlikely that relations between the two men
would prosper. The son of a Lancashire cotton master whose family
arms included a bee volant and a shuttle, with the motto 'Industria',
was a world removed from the adventurer dogged by the rumour of
past dissipation and the reality of present debt. The leader whose
official experience went back to 1810 must have been startled to receive
in March 1838 an offer from one of its most junior members to write for
anonymous publication 'a species of Manifesto of the views and principles of the Conservative Party'.[4]

Disraeli, for his part, might have no difficulty in following the
Tamworth line of defence of established institutions coupled with, in
his own words of December 1834, 'those considerable changes firmly,
but cautiously, prosecuted in our social system, which the spirit of the
age demands, and the necessities of the times require', but he could not
admire a leader who seemed to him to lack the inspiration and the elo-
quence to breathe life into the dry bones of prudent amelioration. Peel's
immense grasp of business and lucidity of exposition were not har-
nessed to any vision to which he could lift his supporters' eyes. His
major speech of January 1837 at Glasgow, Disraeli told Sarah, was, as a
composition, 'both solemn and tawdry; he cannot soar, and his attempts
to be imaginative and sentimental must be offensive to every man of
taste and refined feeling'. Disraeli's party allegiance to this chief could
never be cemented by personal sympathy. In any case, Disraeli meant
absolute fidelity to no leadership except his own. In March 1839 he
assured that other egregiously loose cannon, David Urquhart: 'As

regards the trammels of party, I believe there is not a man in the house, whose seat renders him more independent of them, than my own.'[5]

Even though he had accepted the necessity of operating from within one of the established parties, Disraeli could not quite dismiss the beguiling notion of forming a new one. Of the soap bubbles he blew for Louis Philippe's admiration and his own encouragement, the agreeable dream of his heading his own body of 'the youth of England' had a touch of substance behind it. In October 1842, two young Conservative members, George Smythe and Alexander Baillie-Cochrane, had visited him in Paris to discuss the prospect of the three of them acting together, along with another young member, Lord John Manners, in the next parliamentary session. This was the beginning of Disraeli's considered involvement in 'Young England'.

He neither started the group nor baptised it. Its origins lay in the Cambridge of the late 1830s, where Manners and Smythe, already close friends at Eton, had embarked on a romantic reaction against the heartless, materialistic utilitarianism of the age which, with some infusion from the Oxford movement, inspired them with an alternative vision of a society given spiritual vitality by a revivified faith and church, and communal solidarity by the acceptance of mutual responsibility between classes. Their gaze lingered on the supposed glories of the medieval church, the feudal system and the pre-Hanoverian monarchy as sources of order, unity and social justice, to an extent that sometimes led them into a ridiculous idealisation not only of the substances but of the forms and ceremonies of the imagined past, but their impulses were generous and their talents not mediocre. In an epoch when national self-realisation and regeneration were being promoted by romantic revolutionaries under such names as Young Italy or Young Germany, it is not surprising that they and their friends acquired the label of 'Young England', which was being used to signify the moving spirits of the rising generation at least as early as 1837. Smythe knew Disraeli through the latter's acquaintance with his father, Lord Strangford, which went back to 1832. There was a clear affinity between their ideas and, indeed, their personalities: the younger man was already a sufficiently accomplished wit, rake and cynic to have no difficulty in catching the drift of the elder. The more earnest and virtuous Manners, son of the duke of Rutland, was in a very different category, but still open to Disraeli's charm, and when he, Smythe and their friend Baillie-Cochrane entered the House of Commons in 1841, it was natural for the three of them to gravitate towards Disraeli on the back benches. By March 1842, Disraeli was preening himself on being 'leader of a party – chiefly of the youth, & new members',[6] and the result of the Paris negotiation was a close parliamentary association with the three younger men over the next two years, with occasional support from half-a-dozen figures on the periphery of the group.

In parliamentary terms, Young England was an agreeable fling, the last lark of Disraeli's springtime, with no political weight. It lacked concerted policy, and fell apart after a couple of sessions, even before Smythe deserted the flag by accepting minor office from Peel at the beginning of 1846. However much Disraeli enjoyed it, he took care not to be too far compromised by some of its more provocative fancies, for example Manners's fascination with the virtues of the pre-Reformation church: 'This I shall quietly soften down', he told his wife in August 1844, on finding some of his Shrewsbury constituents alarmed about 'Popery, Monasteries & John Manners'.[7] Its place in his development was as a stimulus and a sketch for the transition appropriate to his years and situation, from the reckless parade of his own youthful ambition to the intellectual formation of the aspiring youth that was coming up behind, in a bid to seize the political future by capturing the minds of those who would shape it.

Manners and Smythe were only twenty-four in 1842 and Baillie-Cochrane twenty-six. Disraeli relished the sensation of moulding the outlook and directing the political debuts of his young aristocrats. It nourished his own sense of youthfulness, wafted into his middle-aged nostrils the intriguing scents of the public-school and university world which had been denied him, and fed his need to feel powerful when he was powerless. It no doubt evoked, too, a piquant parallel with Bolingbroke's inspiration of Lord Cornbury and his circle of young aristocrats. Disraeli would have relished these things all the more had he known (perhaps he did) that the fathers of Manners and Smythe were engaging in anxious correspondence about the influence exercised over their sons by 'the arts of a designing person'. But the design was grander than to create a coterie: it was to inform a nation. Picking up something of Manners's medievalism and Smythe's admiration of Laud and Strafford, he wove it into his own tapestry of English history, translated his friends into the characters of a novel, and set out to supply the comprehensive vision of England's state and England's necessities which could guide the country's youth and establish his own title to direct the country's fortunes. 'A great man', he declared in *Coningsby*, 'is one who affects the mind of his generation.'[8]

Since it was by the power of the word and the idea that he must transform the Conservative party and the country, and his place within them, it was natural for Disraeli to turn again to literature. Having failed to carry parliament by storm, he set out to capture public opinion by sap and to save the nation by psychoanalysis. The three novels of the years 1844 to 1847, *Coningsby or: The New Generation*, *Sybil or: The Two Nations*, and *Tancred or: The New Crusade* (to give them their full and significant titles), show him, as in the *Vindication*, shifting the focus of his creative introspection from the individual to the collective plane, and attempting nothing less than a *Bildungsroman* of the English nation – an anatomy of its political growth, an analysis of its present discontents, and a prospect of its future regeneration. In so doing, he followed a not unusual pattern of romantic evolution, turning away from the limitless extension of the self, subversive of all forms and conventions, into the infinite but ultimately terrifying and isolating spaces of total freedom, to seek instead the reassurance and the rooting of personality in the sense of finite place, settled tradition, organic community and shared belief, commonly derived from an idealised version of the past but summoning all the energies of great spirits to maintain and assert it in a corrupt and confused present. Disraeli evidently felt that the task of locating and materialising the collective identity was sufficiently analogous to that of discerning and realising the individual self for his professed mastery of the latter to serve as a token of his fitness for the former. It can hardly have been due entirely to the impulse to capitalise on the success of new works to sell old ones that in 1845 he addressed explicitly to 'the new generation' a second edition of *Contarini Fleming*, his paradigm of the individual's self-search, just when he was, in *Coningsby* and *Sybil*, conducting the nation's.

Indeed, in *Coningsby*, published in 1844, the two forms of psychological study are yoked. The development of the hero's mind is the vehicle for the examination of the collective soul and the awakening of the collective consciousness of youth. As the instrument with which to open up a vista of the political state of the nation and a review of the responsibilities of its coming generation, however, young Henry Coningsby lacks the substance of real flesh and blood. Despite the sparkling vignettes of minor characters at which Disraeli was now adept, the book is about ideas rather than people to the extent that it has often been regarded as the first political novel. Much the same might be said of *Sybil*, published in the following year, where the heroine is an ideal type, the hero is once more a device for linking the scenes and arguments which supply the real matter of the book, and the liveliness and humanity of the composition again depend on the supporting cast. It is a tribute to Disraeli's matured powers as a writer that both novels somehow survive and flourish as novels, even though the goal of the creative force which animates them is not the delineation of character or story but the integration of Disraeli's fully realised genius into its inexorably given surroundings, by asserting its supereminent role in confronting the great national tasks the nature of which only its superior vision can define and the accomplishment of which only its superior inspiration can guide. Disraeli was trying on the mantle of the artist as legislator, testing the force of Balzac's dictum that the writer was a prince because he shaped the world.

In levelling the artist's preternatural perception at the political and social condition of England, he turned first to history, not simply because, as he said in *Sybil*, 'it is the past alone that can explain the present', but because he needed to construct the past in such a way as to offer himself a future. English history was at present, he told his readers, 'a complete mystification'. 'The influence of races in our early ages, of the Church in our middle, and of parties in our modern history, are three great moving and modifying powers, that must be pursued and analysed with an untiring, profound, and unimpassioned spirit, before a guiding ray can be secured.' As in the *Vindication*, he sought to use the dynamite of historical revision to blast the stony face of Whig oligarchy and give the Tories a mission of national salvation to perform and a tradition with which to perform it. This time, however, he reached back beyond the Glorious Revolution (now seen as a Whig coup) to find in the plunder of the monasteries, in other words, in the spoliation of the lands intended for 'the education of the people and the maintenance of the poor', the origins of the power that had enabled the great Whig families to visit upon the nation the 'triple blessings of Venetian politics, Dutch finance, and French wars'; that is to say, had enabled them to reduce the monarch to the impotent condition of a Venetian Doge (Disraeli here employing a metaphor that went back at least to the late seventeenth century) and to charge the industry and labour of the country with an impressive national debt incurred in conflicts profitable to their own interests and connections but ruinous to the nation.[9]

It was these depredations which at least in part accounted not only for the political decay which Disraeli saw about him but for the social chaos of which he attempted a dramatic panorama in *Sybil*. Drawing on the report of the Children's Employment Commission and other blue books, the debates on the factory bill of 1844 and his own visits to the north of England in 1843 and 1844, he rendered in vivid scenes and poignant description the condition of the working masses which at that moment stood at the centre of national attention. He touched on the conditions of factory labour, on children's employment and the system of butties or middlemen in the mines, on working-class housing and sanitation, on the impact on family life of children's and women's labour, on incest, infanticide and infant mortality, and on men's alienation from their work, and even, when the hero of *Sybil* was warned against crediting a book 'that statistically proved that the general condition of the people was much better at this moment than it had been at any known period of history', foreshadowed by a century what historians have dubbed the standard of living controversy. Yet his main purpose was to throw into drastic relief the sharp divide and perilous antagonism between classes which concentration of wealth and power on the one hand and proliferation of misery and bondage on the other were producing, a cleavage which, in *Sybil*, Walter Gerard describes as one between 'masters and slaves' but Disraeli himself more memorably presents as that between the 'two nations' of rich and poor.[10]

If the causes of this potentially fatal fissure were essentially long-term, running back to the robbing of the people's patrimony at the Reformation, if not to the imposition of the Norman yoke at the Conquest, as Gerard is made to suggest, there were also more proximate reasons. Since the Reform act, Disraeli alleged, 'the altar of Mammon has blazed with triple worship. To acquire, to accumulate, to plunder each other by virtue of philosophic phrases, to prepare a Utopia to consist only of WEALTH and TOIL, this has been the breathless business of enfranchised England for the last twelve years, until we are startled from our voracious strife by the wail of intolerable serfage.' The 'philosophic phrases' which lay behind this frantic and ruthless materialism were mainly those of the utilitarian school, whose 'mechanical' philosophy Disraeli traduced just as contemptuously as Carlyle. In a bright little satirical fantasy, *The Voyage of Captain Popanilla*, published in 1828, he had ridiculed Popanilla's efforts to reform his fellow citizens of the Isle of Fantaisie on utilitarian lines, so that 'instead of passing their lives in a state of unprofitable ease, and useless enjoyment, they might reasonably expect to be the terror and astonishment of the universe; and to be able to annoy every nation of any consequence'; and in the *Vindication* he had attacked utilitarianism as based on a contracted and unreal view of human nature, elevating to an overriding criterion of judgement a self-interest defined in the most crudely materialistic terms. The result of the rampant and conscienceless individualism so encouraged was necessarily to dissolve society by atomistic competition in which the few must prosper at the expense of the many. As the utopian socialist Morley puts it in *Sybil*: 'There is no community in England; there is aggregation; but aggregation under circumstances which make it rather a dissociating than a uniting principle.' Without community of purpose there was no society: 'men may be drawn into contiguity, but they still continue virtually isolated'.[11]

The language of *Sybil* is so reminiscent of the characterisation that Hegel had given some twenty years earlier of 'civil society' (not least in England) running riot under the influence of an unbridled and acquisitive individualism, and generating as its own nemesis a division between a wealthy few and a deprived and alienated proletariat, as to remind us that Disraeli was picking up, albeit not much above the level of dinner-table talk, one of the great European debates of modern times. How or whether, especially in the swarming life of the expanding cities, an organic and stable community could be sustained or formed, when old bonds of locality, traditional authority and religion had been loosened, and the impersonal cash nexus was replacing the sense of reciprocal duties and responsibilities that was sometimes held to have obtained between upper and lower orders in the past, was a question canvassed in this age of accelerating demographic, industrial and urban growth with all the urgency arising from the knowledge that revolution might be the price of inability to answer it. Throughout Europe the economic difficulties and social distress of the 1840s, and in Britain Chartism, the first mass movement of the working classes, kept it on the boil. Lorenz von Stein, following Hegel, published his analysis of the class struggle and of the development of the proletariat as a revolutionary class in 1842. There is no reason to think that Disraeli had direct knowledge of these German works, but his promiscuous intellect usually picked up a dose of whatever was going the European rounds, and in any case the subject, in less philosophic form, was equally a commonplace at home.

Social cleavage was a constant theme of thinking politicians. Disraeli's own declaration to his Shrewsbury constituents in August 1844 that there was 'something rotten at the core of our social system', when in a country as wealthy as Britain the working classes, 'the creators of wealth, were steeped in the most abject poverty, and gradually sinking into the deepest degradation', echoed Gladstone's words to his wife in August 1842: 'This is a time when we may reflect on the thorough rottenness socially speaking of the system which gathers together huge masses of population having no other tie to the classes above them than that of employment.' The famous metaphor of the two nations was hardly novel either when it appeared in *Sybil*. Heine's play *William Ratcliff* had spoken in 1822 of 'two nations ever at war, the well fed and the hungry'; and nearer home Disraeli's friend W. B. Ferrand, in December 1843, two months after he had entertained the Disraelis in Yorkshire, was speaking of the country's being divided into 'two classes – the very rich and the very poor'.[12]

There was thus little if any originality in Disraeli's embrace of the condition of England question, even if his talent produced an exceptionally vivid image of it. Yet he was not just packaging topicality for the circulating libraries. The avoidance of social disintegration formed for him both the most fascinating problem of modern politics and the most promising vehicle for his own career as a politician with ideas. The politics of catastrophe were instinctively attractive to him. As social and political upheaval had unpinioned the wings of the young eagle, Napoleon – that 'volition that vanquished the world'[13] – and had looked for a moment like giving the young Disraeli an exciting ride on the tiger of revolution in 1832, so the crisis of emergent industrial and urban civilisation offered the prospect of ascendancy to the great man who could grasp its nature and perceive its remedy. In metaphorically splitting the nation into two, Disraeli offered himself the commanding role of making it one again.

The role could be assumed only by the man of pre-eminent genius who understood the laws of human evolution and those 'mysteries of predisposition', the fathoming of which in the individual psyche Disraeli, in his preface to the new edition of *Contarini Fleming*, acknowledged to have been the achievement of *Wilhelm Meister*, and which he now intended to elucidate for the consciousness of the nation. Nations, he had asserted in the *Vindication*, had characters, like individuals, formed by nature and fortune, and, like individuals, ascertained by self-examination principles of conduct which they took for their guidance on the basis of their proven efficacy. That was all the theory that the construction of lasting political institutions and the exercise of statecraft required. Like the social question, the idea of national character was inhaled with the intellectual atmosphere of the day: 'the laws of national character' formed for John Stuart Mill 'by far the most important class of sociological laws', and for many of his contemporaries a convenient means of explaining, or constructing, the superiority over other nations which they believed or wished themselves to possess.[14] Yet Disraeli's title to instruct the English nation (he seldom said 'British', preferring so far as possible to ignore the existence of Celts) could not rest on unimpeachable hereditary membership of it, when the nation was defined less in terms of a constitution and a law to which anyone might subscribe, and more in terms of a distinct character formed by time and experience which minorities and immigrants might be thought incapable of sharing or acquiring. To lecture on English character and destiny to the English, he had to rely, not on the instinctual knowledge, or prejudice, of the native, but on the peculiar insight of the stranger. The special perception of the outsider was his passport to being accepted as an insider, at least for the purposes of politics; detachment was the precondition of effective intervention, aloofness of intimacy.

It was this paradox that Disraeli rendered imaginatively in the figure of Sidonia, the mysterious Jew who appears in *Coningsby* to form the political understanding of the hero and his friends. Commanding untold resources (the Rothschild parallel is made more explicit in *Tancred*), in touch with 'all the clever outcasts of the world', but devoid of all known human affections, having 'exhausted all the sources of human knowledge', Sidonia is almost pure intellect, gifted with 'that absolute freedom from prejudice, which was the compensatory possession of a man without a country'. Sidonia was not Disraeli, but in making him the intellectual mentor of the young nobleman, Henry Coningsby, Disraeli tried out one form of resolution of the problem of how he himself was to operate in the aristocratic environment of high politics. He was approaching his fortieth birthday when *Coningsby* appeared, and the catalogue declaimed by Sidonia of men who had already achieved fame by that age suggests, like his remark to D'Orsay in 1841, that he felt that the power of heroic youth had slipped beyond recall. If he was to rule England, it might have to be as the superior intelligence shaping the beliefs and counselling the steps of the rising generation, as he was already doing in Young England. Sidonia was a *modus operandi* for imposing himself on a world to which he did not precisely belong, the world in which it took him two years to progress from 'My dear Lord' to 'My dear Lord John' in writing to Manners. It was the translation of the role of romantic hero from the sphere of direct action to that of almost occult influence, where the master spirit figured as Victor Hugo's magus or as the Carlylean seer, a guiding light to a confused world in its 'dark pilgrimage through the wastes of Time'. Time, Disraeli asserted on the last page of *Sybil*, was bringing to the English mind some inkling of the truth of those views on the parties and the people which had brought him so much incomprehension and misrepresentation. Their vindication in action must depend on 'the energy and devotion of our Youth'. 'We live', he wrote, 'in an age when to be young and to be indifferent can be no longer synonymous. We must prepare for the coming hour. The claims of the Future are represented by suffering millions; and the Youth of a Nation are the trustees of Posterity.'[15]

The notes of this clarion call were, however, more uncertain than they sounded. It was not at all clear that aristocratic youth, even as idealised in Henry Coningsby or in Egremont, the hero of *Sybil*, rather than as personified by George Smythe and John Manners, was up to the job of supplying the heroic tool of Disraeli's heroic conceptions. Nor was it clear that it would gratefully accept the situation advertised with the deference due to the superior faculties of its mentor, or that he would find it easy to support the position of official subordination and social inferiority for which even the consciousness of a genius ruling behind the scenes would scarcely compensate. In *Sybil*, in tones of bitterness which suggest he saw a parallel, however strained, with his own career, Disraeli portrayed through the case of Burke the sort of shabby treatment that the pre-eminent mind that tutored aristocratic politicians might expect from its patrons – as well as (in a half-hint of what he was to do to Peel) the revenge it could execute. Both in *Coningsby* and in *Sybil*, his attitude to the traditional ruling class was deeply ambiguous. It was as though the need to suck up entailed a compensatory urge to spit out. If Coningsby and his circle and Egremont are set up as ideal types to personify the generous spirit and noble ambition that Disraeli's notion of national regeneration required, a large part of the flesh-and-blood upper crust portrayed in the two novels is represented as a thoroughly bad lot, from the wasters de Vere and Mountchesney, who, having 'exhausted life in their teens', have nothing left but to 'mourn, amid the ruins of their reminiscences, over the extinction of excitement', to the hard, mean, narrow Lord Marney, domineering over his miserable tenantry in their insanitary hovels, and the overweening earl de Mowbray, whose great Norman title conceals the founding of the family's fortunes by a waiter in a St James's club who made a killing in India by cornering the rice market in time of famine.[16]

Of course the dissection of corruption was necessary to point up the urgency of renewal, and to open the way for the man of *virtù* (in Machiavelli's sense of the term) who would restore health to the state, but it was savage enough to have the ring more of radical destructivism than of conservative renovation. In *Sybil*, Disraeli not only conjured up via Walter Gerard the familiar Radical picture of a people for centuries oppressed by the Norman yoke, but used the ousting of Gerard's family from its ancestral estate as a metaphor for the dispossession of its birthright of a whole population. His description of the rise of the Greymount family to the earldom of Marney, beginning with its engorging the Marney abbey lands in return for its avidity in stripping the monasteries to the profit of Henry VIII, is acid enough to prefigure Joseph Chamberlain's jibe four decades later about aristocratic fortunes founded on 'the services which courtiers rendered kings'; and his lampooning of the Whigs' profiteering from 'Dutch finance and French wars' on the back of 'a fettered and burthened multitude' anticipates by a dozen years Bright's lashing of British foreign policy as a system of outdoor relief for the upper classes. Perhaps the worst thing about the English upper classes from Disraeli's point of view was the lack of interest in ideas and of respect for intellect which he pointedly contrasted with the flattering attentions which he had found paid to those things in the salons of Paris. His view of the relation of ideas to the average nobleman's skull was wryly conveyed in Lord Monmouth's response to the strange political notions revealed to him by his grandson, Coningsby: 'You go with your family, sir, like a gentleman; you are not to consider your opinions like a philosopher or a political adventurer.'[17] Even Coningsby's ideas are hardly his own: they have to be injected into his sluggish Saxon arteries by Sidonia.

Disraeli sometimes rebelled at the prospect of being intellectual bagman to this dullard class. The depth of his resentment at the practical necessity of laboriously currying its condescending favour flashed out when he made Egremont turn on Ladies St Julians and Firebrace, the scheming political hostesses of *Sybil*: 'you fine ladies, who think you can govern the world by what you call your social influences: asking people once or twice a year to an inconvenient crowd in your house; now haughtily smirking, and now impertinently staring, at them; and flattering yourselves all this time, that, to have the occasional privilege of entering your saloons, and the periodical experience of your insolent recognition, is to be a reward for great exertions, or, if necessary, an inducement to infamous tergiversation'. That from the Disraeli who a few months later, in one week of July 1845, would be going to Lady Salisbury's ball on Tuesday, the marchioness of Lansdowne's party on Wednesday, Baroness Brunnow's Ball on Friday, and Lady Palmerston's assembly on Saturday.[18]

The consciousness of genius by itself was not enough to armour Disraeli's pride against the humiliations of having to court the attention of a class to which he did not belong and which he could not always respect. He bolstered it by taking out membership of a racial elite and a natural aristocracy prouder and more select than the nobility of England. Sidonia, the incarnation, if not of Disraeli, then of Disraeli's sense of intellectual power, is an aristocrat twice over, a scion of an ancient and noble Spanish family and the child of a race to whose creativity everything of importance in the modern civilisation of the west is to be traced.

A necessarily intriguing subject for one of Disraeli's origins, race was also by the 1840s a leading principle by which Europeans sought to organise the picture of historical development, to explain and to validate the variations of national character and the gradations of social class, and to forge or reinforce the solidarities which religion or nationalism only imperfectly supplied. Racial polemicists were usually the slaves of some defunct anthropologist, and Disraeli took the classification of races which he employed in Coningsby from the natural history of the Göttingen professor and craniometrician Blumenbach, 'the Newton of physiology' as he called him, published between 1790 and 1811. In Blumenbach's division of mankind into five races, the Jews figured in the Caucasian category, which included all the ancient and modern European peoples, except Finns and Laplanders, and many of the Asian; but Disraeli added to this model, as he revealed in reply to some criticisms with an anti-Semitic tinge which appeared in The Morning Post, the assertion in the mouth of Sidonia that the Jews enjoyed a special status in this 'first and superior class' as the sole Caucasian strain to remain 'pure and unmixed'. It was that purity which gave them their ability to survive all persecutions and constituted their title to look the nobility of England or anywhere else in the eye. 'An unmixed race of a first-rate organisation are the aristocracy of Nature.' It made no difference that among the Hebrew communities of the world Sidonia had in general found 'the lower orders debased; the superior immersed in sordid pursuits': 'the living Hebrew intellect' remained unimpaired and continued to cast its profound influence over the affairs of a Europe which had derived from it 'the best part of its laws, a fine portion of its literature, all its religion' and much of its musical talent, as Sidonia explained in the course of reciting to an open-mouthed Coningsby a litany of powerful Jews in politics, warfare and the arts.[19]

Having thus neatly inverted the usual relation of superiority between the Jew and the gentile host community, Disraeli also inverted the relation of patronage between himself and his hopeful young noblemen by admitting them more or less as honorary Jews: Sidonia accepts Coningsby as a fellow Caucasian whose race is 'sufficiently pure'. But, given Disraeli's astringent if not actively hostile and resentful view of the nobility as a class, it was not only, or even primarily, from its ranks that the natural aristocracy could be recruited that was to regenerate England under the inspiration of one of the aristocrats of nature. The vigour of the old blood was too much abated. 'There is no longer in fact an aristocracy in England', we hear in *Sybil*, 'for the superiority of the animal man is an essential quality of aristocracy.' New sources had to be tapped when, as Coningsby was forced to realise, 'Brains every day become more precious than blood.'[20]

In *Coningsby*, it is the independent and upright manufacturer, Millbank, who is made to call for recognition of a 'natural' or 'essential' aristocracy in 'the government of those who are distinguished by their fellow-citizens'. The bohemian in Disraeli liked to jibe at the mediocrity of bourgeois existence ('for the middle class', he noted waspishly, 'marriage often the only adventure of life'), and the snob in him at the mean manners and low conceptions of the shopkeeping class and the sort of Radical paladin it favoured – Joseph Hume, he remarked, 'can neither speak nor write English; his calligraphy reminds one of a chandler's shop, and his letters resemble a butterman's bill'. When, in one of his radical sallies in the Commons, in 1840, he declared that 'the aristocracy and the labouring population form the nation', or when, addressing his Shrewsbury constituents in May 1843, he defended the preponderance of the landed interest against the Anti-Corn Law League and assumed that his hearers had no wish to be 'turned into a sort of spinning-jenny, machine kind of nation', he seemed to consign the middle classes altogether to the dark. Yet he knew that nothing could be done without the middle classes, and, his education having been enlarged by his visit to the north in the autumn of 1843, his tone was more carefully managed by the time he published *Coningsby*. In Shrewsbury, he even had to come to terms with the shopkeepers, 'whom I wish most to please', he told Mary Anne during a canvass in August 1844, when he acknowledged the manufacturing interest as 'the primary source of our wealth and greatness', and found himself 'the *tradesmen's member* – so I don't trouble myself much about the pseudo aristocracy, & less about the real'. The reality of aristocracy as a faculty of command rather than a quality of blood might lie in any social situation: even in describing in *Sybil* the brutal tyranny of the small masters over their apprentices in the lock-making town of Wodgate, Disraeli acknowledges the masters, however coarse, as 'a real aristocracy: it is privileged, but it does something for its privileges'.[21]

It was still easier to recognise the strain of natural aristocracy in Millbank and in the paternalistic factory owner, Trafford, in *Sybil*, who 'recognised the baronial principle, reviving in a new form'. When he comes to write of the pulsating industry of the north and midlands, Disraeli is gripped not only by the hideousness of its social consequences but also by the power and grandeur of its achievement. The fact that he pursued a conventional conservative critique of modern industrialism, or rather of the corrosion of the social fabric by the pitiless individualism which drove it, should not lead to the assumption that he was anti-modernist or reactionary. He responded with excitement to the romance of the vast liberation of productive energy and development of human and material resources which, on one side of its Janus face, the transformational genius of capitalism offered. This new bustling, smoky, glaring, clangorous world was no less an object of wonder than the old: 'rightly understood, Manchester is as great a human exploit as

Athens' – and Disraeli was happy, in October 1844, to star at the annual soirée of the Manchester Athenaeum. The monuments of the new age were no less impressive than those of former times: Coningsby finds himself among 'illumined factories with more windows than Italian palaces, and smoking chimneys taller than Egyptian obelisks'.[22] Disraeli's were not the politics of cultural despair or negative nostalgia. The industrial was as thrillingly creative as any other revolution, and the men who directed its course were princes of their age.

Disraeli may not have known how Hegel had turned from the landed aristocracy to the middle orders to perform the function of identifying themselves with that universal life of the state through which alone the conflicts and divisions of an atomised civil society could be overcome, but he can hardly have been unaware of the idealisation of the middle classes as the representative class of society propagated by Guizot, whom he had met in London and Paris, as by James Mill in England. His retrospect of the true Tory tradition in *Sybil* gave high place to Shelburne, 'the first great minister who comprehended the rising importance of the middle class, and foresaw in its future power a bulwark for the throne against "the Great Revolution families"' (that is, the Whigs), an example that he held Pitt to have followed. Millbank and Trafford emerge much better from his novels than most of the titled aristocrats. Their natural aristocracy, however, represents, not a force of unreconcilable antagonism to old blood, but a necessary transfusion of new, which Edith Millbank's marriage to Coningsby symbolises. Economic growth, Disraeli recognised just as much as Marx, could create new and powerful classes, but he assumed that in England they would assimilate rather than overwhelm, writing of 'the Manufacturer, who ... aspires to be "large-acred", and always will, as long as we have a territorial constitution; a better security for the preponderance of the landed interest than any corn-law, fixed or fluctuating'.[23]

The assimilation of the working classes was a different matter. Egremont immediately recognises the natural aristocracy of the mill overseer Walter Gerard and his daughter, Sybil, with whom he falls in love, but the Gerards turn out to be dispossessed gentry. Disraeli knew little enough about the lower orders, but he did his best in *Sybil* to give a realistic and sympathetic portrayal of them, which was not without its successes. If he ever wrote a genuinely moving passage, it is that on the sufferings of poor children in the factory town of Mowbray. He possessed understanding enough, however, to recognise the absurdity of representing working-class life as uniformly and unrelievedly grim: as P. J. Keating has pointed out, one of the few gleams that penetrates the dedicated gloom of the Victorian industrial novel is Disraeli's bright sketch of working-class relaxation in the 'Temple of the Muses' in *Sybil* – in that department he had more grasp than Mrs Gaskell.[24] If he made a lurid melodrama out of their initiation ceremonies, he respected the power of organisation revealed in the trade unions, and he was impressed by the Chartist movement, in which the open-air, torchlight dramatisation of mass politics appealed to the romantic fancy. His sociology was developed enough to differentiate between, on the one hand, relatively prosperous but brutalised mining communities and, on the other, the 'reading and thinking population of the factories'. His portrait of the havoc wreaked by the 'Hell-cats' of Wodgate on the rampage is balanced by his account of the rigorous discipline of a couple of thousand striking Lancashire operatives seeking relief from the lady of a local estate, which anticipates by two decades Gladstone's admiration of the self-control of the same population under the privations of the cotton famine. If he poked a little gentle fun at the aspirations of the 'Shoddy-Court Literary and Scientific', which took in 'three London papers; one *Northern Star* and two *Moral Worlds*', he had no fear of the spread of knowledge and political awareness among the working classes, even displaying a marked indulgence towards the involvement of their women in political discussion. He noted that many of the working class came under sound Jewish influences: the wretched people of Marney found spiritual solace in 'little plain buildings of pale brick with the names painted on them, of Sion, Bethel, Bethesda; names of a distant land, and the language of a persecuted and ancient race; yet such is the mysterious power of their divine quality, breathing consolation in the nineteenth century to the harassed forms and harrowed souls of a Saxon peasantry'. Still better, some of them read his novels, to judge by the request from the Leeds Mechanics' Institution (which claimed 1,100 members) that he should 'allay a fierce contention' by telling the discussion class where to place the stress in pronouncing 'Sybil'.[25]

All the same, it was the destiny of the working classes to be guided by their natural superiors. If Disraeli had thought since 1832 that it was necessary to recognise that the democratic principle had effectively replaced the aristocratic in politics, that animated him to the task of offering leadership to the people, but not to acquiescence in manhood suffrage or anything else that would deliver an unchecked supremacy into inexperienced hands. His attitude could not avoid condescension. If Chartism was treated as the product of real grievances, it was equally regarded as a futile effort of emancipation by the politically naive. 'The people are not strong', Egremont tells Sybil, 'the people never can be strong. Their attempts at self-vindication will end only in their suffering and confusion.' They have nothing to do but to stick it out, until Disraeli and Young England have educated the higher classes to their social responsibilities and they find 'property acknowledging as in the old days of faith, that labour is his twin brother; and that the essence of all tenure is the performance of duty', as Coningsby puts it, to Lord Monmouth's signal distaste. Then they can be winched up the scale of improvement. 'The future principle of English politics', Egremont explains to Sybil, 'will not be a levelling principle; not a principle adverse to privileges, but favourable to their extension. It will seek to ensure equality, not by levelling the Few, but by elevating the Many.'[26] At the end of *Sybil*, the social problem is not resolved but eluded by abruptly elevating a few of the Many as a sort of payment on account: Sybil and her father are suddenly restored to their ancestral lands, and Dandy Mick and Devilsdust, the two sparky and enterprising young operatives who have provided much of the vivacity in the portrait of working-class life, become successful capitalists.

Disraeli had run out of ideas, dramatically and politically. He had to agree with Manners that the ending of *Sybil* was a mess: 'We call up spirits from the vasty deep, but they are sometimes too vital to get rid of at the end of a third volume.' The diagnosis of the condition of England in *Coningsby* and *Sybil*, if in large part derivative, was often acute and telling, but the prescription was written in a hand so runic that no one could tell what it meant, not even Disraeli himself. So far as any kind of

was not only derivative but shallow. As Marx and Engels would note in 1848, in an oblique reference, at once contemptuous and grudgingly appreciative, in the *Communist Manifesto*, there was a void at the centre.[29] The last page of *Sybil* turned, it remained a riddle quite what the people of England were to adore and to obey, the glitter of the author's intelligence apart.

Adoration, in any case, was limited by circulation. *Coningsby* and *Sybil* initially sold only about 3,000 copies each. Even though the number of readers was, of course, much larger, Disraeli was not going to conquer public opinion and political power by that route alone. He still had to work through the parliament the representative character of which he had impugned and the party which had failed to promote him. The double yoke almost exhausted him. 'I have never been thro' such a four months, & hope never again', he told his sister after finishing *Sybil* on the last day of April 1845. 'What with the House of Commons wh: was itself quite eno' for a man & writing 600 pages, I thought sometimes my head must turn.'[30]

Whether his exertions could turn the head of the Conservative party was very doubtful. *Sybil* evoked the vision of Disraeli's ideal Tory party, the party of Bolingbroke and Wyndham, rising once more 'to bring back strength to the Crown, liberty to the subject, and to announce that power has only one duty – to secure the social welfare of the PEOPLE'; but *Coningsby* had been largely devoted to demonstrating that that party and its principles had been replaced by a 'Conservative Cause' under which 'the crown has become a cipher; the church a sect; the nobility drones; and the people drudges'. Disraeli's slanging of the party he inhabited was just as caustic as his slanging of the nobility whose parties he frequented – when he was asked. In the two novels, he developed the true Tory tradition, as he had proclaimed it in the *Vindication*, around the figures of Bolingbroke, Shelburne and the younger Pitt, and the guiding precepts of commercial freedom and alliance with France, reinforced in the early and genuine Pittite system by extension of the franchise and Catholic relief. This brisk appropriation of what most people thought of as liberalism should easily have accommodated Peel, and indeed Disraeli recognised the liberal Toryism of the later 1820s, in which Peel had figured largely, as belonging to the canon. But if imagination governed mankind, Peel was not the man for the job, and in any case Disraeli wanted it for himself. In *Coningsby*, Peel's Tamworth manifesto was scorned as an 'attempt to construct a party without principles' (Disraeli forgetting the skilful defence of expediency with which, in *The Crisis Examined*, he had hurried to associate himself with the Tamworth line); his idea of Conservative government was derided as 'Tory men and Whig measures', and the Conservative party under his leadership was denounced for its incapacity to conserve, that is, to protect in their full vigour the national institutions of crown, lords and church by which alone the liberties and privileges of the people could be sheltered from Whig tyranny.[31]

By this time it was hard to see Disraeli as belonging to Peel's Conservative party. Despite the rebuff of his pretensions to office in 1841, he had not at once come out against the government, and Young England had functioned as a ginger rather than a splinter group. Yet his stance had always been relatively independent. In part, perhaps, from a desire to assert consistency, but also from predilection, he had maintained his radical leanings even when in a tiny minority and given credibility to some of his earlier rhetoric. He admired Oastler's Tory radicalism, and in 1840 told Charles Attwood: 'I entirely agree with you, that "an union between the Conservative party and the Radical Masses" offers the only means by which we can preserve the Empire. Their interests are identical; united they form the Nation.' He continually lambasted the new poor law, which, he said, 'announces to the world that in England poverty is a crime'. While he could not accept its aspirations to real political equality and popular sovereignty, he expressly sympathised with Chartism's feeling that an 'ancient constitution' which had protected the liberties and privileges of the people was being undermined by such arbitrary innovations as the new poor law and the new police, under the aegis of a 'monarchy of the middle classes' more interested in cheap and centralised government than in popular welfare. In 1844-5, Young England was supporting the Chartists' champion in the Commons, Duncombe, in frustrating a new master and servant bill which would have facilitated the imprisonment of strikers and in revealing the opening of correspondence at the Post

Office, and Disraeli was receiving the gift of his works from Thomas Hodgskin, the socialist economist and pioneer of the labour theory of value, and was impressing with his 'friendliness and lack of affectation' the Chartist Thomas Cooper, just out of gaol, and recommended to him by Duncombe for help in finding a publisher. The Chartist leader Feargus O'Connor, whose correspondence Disraeli apparently consulted when writing *Sybil*, said in December 1844 that he 'looked on Young England as coadjutors to a certain extent', and was prepared to recommend that some of the Chartists' best speakers should be selected to 'meet them, in a friendly spirit, and instruct them'.[32] None of this consorted very easily with an official Conservatism more anxious about public order than popular rights, and Young England's support (Smythe excepted) of Ashley's bill to secure a ten-hour day for factory children ranged it against a government which saw the stimulation of economic growth rather than the imposition of restrictive legislation as the way to improve the condition of the people. Disraeli had already lost the Conservative whip at the beginning of 1844, having in the previous August criticised the government's Irish and Near Eastern policies in terms which drove Peel to conclude, with an explicit nod to the 'country' opposition tactics of the previous century, that disappointment had made him 'independent and a patriot'.[33] *Coningsby*, begun in the autumn of 1843, widened the breach.

Disraeli and his friends, however, formed only a fraction of the prime minister's increasing difficulties with his following. Peel's problem was that Disraeli's allegation that he had denatured the old Tory party was at best only half true. So far was he from having imposed his liberal brand of Conservatism that the election of 1841 gave him a strongly agrarian, protectionist and protestant majority whose suspicions were soon roused by his drive towards freedom of trade and confirmed by his proposal in 1845 to increase the state's support for the Roman Catholic seminary at Maynooth in Ireland. His ineptitude in personal relations and contempt for the judgement of his backbenchers in contrast to his own vast official expertise, his tendency to see the party merely as the necessary support of the executive and to bully it into toeing the government line, as over Ashley's factory bill and the sugar duties question in 1844, made things much worse, but it was his measures, not his manner, that mattered: corn laws and Catholics would have tripped the most dexterous of liberalising leaders. Disraeli might have supported him on both issues. He had held up to Tory admiration in August 1843 Charles I's policy of conciliating the Irish Catholics, and in *Coningsby* had approved Catholic relief as part of the true Pittite system. As for commercial freedom, he had celebrated its long Tory pedigree when endorsing in the summer of 1842 Peel's reduction of the tariff, including the duties on corn, and had made it a central feature of the great Tory tradition delineated in *Sybil*.[34] Yet he had two sets of reservations about the application of the principle, which could readily be employed to justify opposition to a leader with whom his relations had become hostile when the latter moved towards the completion of free trade and the total abolition of the system of protective tariffs on imported wheat, which since the Napoleonic wars had shielded British farming against the effects of a European glut, but by the mid-1840s was arguably doing no more than penalise the British consumer in a time of general shortage.

The first reservation, a staple of criticisms of free trade through the century and beyond, was that liberalisation of trade could not be unilateral; unless reciprocal arrangements were negotiated with her trading partners, Britain would render herself dangerously vulnerable to foreign competition by abolishing her import duties. Already in 1843, Disraeli, citing Friedrich List, had pointed to the nationalist school of political economy increasingly influential on the continent, and warned that Britain should not 'fight against hostile tariffs with free imports'. The second consideration was more fundamental. In underpinning the prosperity of British agriculture, the corn laws were seen as vital to the stability of the landed interest, on which, at both central and local level, the ordered government and social cohesion of the country could be argued to depend. Whatever the deficiencies of its practical operation in the hands of the class he chastised in *Coningsby*, Disraeli firmly maintained that the 'territorial constitution' of England, basing political power and social influence on a secure landed proprietary, was the foundation of the stability and greatness of the nation. In an extensive exposition of his political outlook to his Shrewsbury constituents in May 1843, he insisted that what he cared about was not this or that level of tariff, but 'the preponderance of the landed interest', by which he meant not merely the great landed proprietors:

I am looking in that phrase ... to the population of our innumerable villages, to the crowds in our rural towns: I mean that estate of the poor which, in my opinion, has been already dangerously tampered with; I mean the great estate of the Church ... I mean also by the landed interest that great judicial fabric, that great building up of our laws and manners, which is, in fact, the ancient polity of the realm.[35]

That it was the apparent object of the Anti-Corn Law League to use an economic change to subvert that interest and bring about a political revolution was a sufficient reason for resisting it – indeed Peel himself was inhibited by dislike of the League's political agenda from announcing his conversion to its economic principle.

Despite his careful assumption at Bradenham of some of the attributes of a country gentleman and county magistrate, and his successful soliciting of a deputy-lieutenancy in April 1845, Disraeli was an odd champion of the landed interest, but identification with it offered possibilities for his political advance. Peter Jupp has suggested that this was a period at which the landed interest, battered since the age of Pitt by the assaults of other forms of power – ministerial, bureaucratic, commercial, industrial and intellectual – was beginning to reassert its dominance of the political system through control of the machinery of party.[36] Disraeli could be virtually certain by 1843 or 1844 that he was not going to be taken up by the neo-Pittite meritocracy of middle-class origin represented by Peel, and the rising W. E. Gladstone, whose strenuous ethic of character and public duty was so hostile to his cultivation of sensibility and instinct of public performance. His future in the Conservative party must depend on their displacement by other forces, as his attacks on their brand of Conservatism in *Coningsby* implicitly acknowledged. The fulcrum from which to move them was supplied by Peel's decision at the end of 1845 to repeal the corn laws, less to deal with Irish famine than because of a conviction that they must go the way of all outmoded obstacles to the freedom of the country's trade.

Disraeli had little independent political weight to apply to the lever. The Conservative backbench revolt against Peel in the corn law debates of 1846 and in the country could perfectly well have proceeded without him. In the surge of agrarian disaffection which had been welling up for years through the agricultural protection societies and had now found an acceptable Commons leader in Lord George Bentinck, he was a marginal figure, though he tagged along, as one who had been active in the Royal Bucks Agricultural Association under the 'farmers' friend', Chandos (now duke of Buckingham) since 1834, and had urged its assumption of a political role. If, however, downright, irascible, immensely laborious Bentinck admirably personified bucolic indignation, he was a wretched speaker, and in a parliamentary system the agricultural interest could not be defended in dumb show. 'In the lobby', Disraeli had told Sarah after his speech against repeal of the corn laws in 1838, 'all the Squires came up to shake hands with me, and thank me for the good service. They were so grateful, and well they might be, for certainly they had nothing to say for themselves.' Disraeli had plenty to say for himself, and he had already demonstrated the power of his derisive wit to unsettle Peel. It was that that made him one of the leaders of the anti-repeal section in the Commons in 1846. He put the basic case (against total repeal rather than for protection as such) well enough, repeating his preference for Pitt's policy of expanded trade on principles of reciprocal advantage, as continued by Liverpool, Huskisson and Peel himself, and supporting the preponderance of agriculture as the natural concomitant of the territorial constitution, but he was not the warmest or most plausible champion of what he had described in *Coningsby* as 'fiscal arrangements, some of them very impolitic, none of them very important'.[37] His real significance was to bring to a crescendo the work he had begun in 1845 of undermining Peel's hitherto commanding authority in the house, partly by a ridicule to which Peel was unduly sensitive, partly by pressing home, as already over Maynooth, the charge of betrayal to which he was more sensitive still.

Disraeli on loyalty to party was a brazen performance, but it was undeniable that Peel had broken faith with the overwhelming commitment to agricultural protection of most of the Conservative constituencies in 1841, and Disraeli turned the issue into a serious constitutional point. A parliamentary system of government, he contended, could only be organised in a manner to command the confidence of the public through party and through the fidelity of parties and their leaders to the professions on the basis of which they had sought the votes of the electors: 'it is only by maintaining the independence of party that you can maintain the integrity of public men, and the power and influence of Parliament itself'.[38] This elevation of party was an almost necessary concomitant of Disraeli's altering situation. Without root or close connection in the established political elite, he could look for advancement only as the servant of party, however irksome that service might be. By 1846 he had long ceased to be a fringe follower of a high-minded but exclusive clique of 'official men' which would never take him in, and was becoming a spokesman of what was rapidly turning into a new, protectionist party. It did not matter that he did not believe in protection. Party was the stirrup by which he must mount.

When Peel's corn law bill passed its third reading in the Commons by 98 votes on 15 May 1846, two-thirds of its supporters were Whigs or Radicals; only 106 Conservatives voted for it, and 222 voted against. Six weeks later, the votes or abstentions of vengeful protectionists defeated the government on an Irish coercion bill, and Peel resigned. With an eye to his place in any combination that might offer, Disraeli had been busying himself with the prospects of a new ministry bringing Whigs and protectionists together on the basis of some compromise on the corn duty, but Russell, whom he had curiously flattered in *Coningsby*, was recalcitrant and followed Peel in office at the head of a purely Whig administration. Disraeli's future lay with the squires in opposition.

4

A LEADING PART, 1846–1865

'Onward I feel my way', wrote Disraeli in his customary wedding-anniversary ode to his wife in August 1846, turning aside for a moment from

> 'the blaze of factious senates ... where the prize
> Is power o'er the powerful, & to sway
> The race that sways the World.[1]

To a man just arriving in his prime on the front bench of a substantial party, the power for which Vivian Grey thought *real* men should alone exist must have shimmered enticingly in the nearer distance. Yet as Disraeli felt his way towards it, the mirage would constantly recede. From the rapid results college of his youth, he was matriculating, at the onset of middle age, into a university of life where promotion would be slow, rewards meagre, performance jealously appraised, and colleagues often intractable.

Not the least of the obstacles in his path was the chequered reputation left over from his bravura youth. In December 1834, Lord George Bentinck had dismissed out of hand the suggestion that Disraeli might be his running mate at King's Lynn in the impending general election. Just two years earlier, the (probably unfounded) conviction that Disraeli, for his own profit, had lured his younger brother into bad company, had created a deep prejudice in the mind of Edward Stanley, heir to the earldom of Derby, who in mid-1846, now in the House of Lords, emerged as the leader of the Protectionists in parliament. Close collaboration against Peel seems to have removed Bentinck's antipathy, but Stanley's took longer to evaporate, if it ever entirely did, and the doubtful odour that had brought Disraeli the distrust of those who were now his leaders lingered in the nostrils of those who were called upon to be his followers in the protectionist cause.

Even as he prepared to attack Peel, Disraeli had sought to acquire the copyright of *The Young Duke* in order to suppress the work – a foretaste of the attempt he was to make in the collected edition of his novels in 1853 to exorcise the youthful sallies and solecisms which consorted unhappily with the grave respectability which the Victorians had come to expect of a statesman. He knew that to be a spokesman of the agricultural interest he must obscure past indiscretions and avoid fresh extravagances. When he took his seat on the Protectionist front bench, the old flamboyance of dress and manner was distinctly curbed. At the same time, he sought to merge into landed society by substituting for the guise of an essentially metropolitan political professional that of a country gentleman and a county member. He could not achieve this from his own resources. It was mainly £25,000 of Bentinck family money that in 1847–8 set Disraeli up as a squire and supplied him with the property qualification needed for a county seat by enabling him to purchase Hughenden Manor, just outside High Wycombe. At the general election of 1847, having cleared his intention with Lord Chandos, heir to the local magnate, the duke of Buckingham, he peremptorily deserted his Shrewsbury constituents and was returned without a contest as one of the three members for Buckinghamshire. His election address and speeches were clearly designed to emphasise his identification with the landed and agricultural interest, dilating upon 'the cause of the Territorial Constitution of England, as the best and surest foundation for popular rights and public liberty, imperial power and social happiness', and contending that the 'maintenance of the agricultural industry of the Country is the necessary condition of the enjoyment of that Constitution'. Staking out his position in 'the great struggle between popular principles and liberal opinions, which is the characteristic of our age', he declared his support for local self-government against 'enervating' centralisation, and for all measures to improve the condition of the working classes, 'by lessening their hours of toil – by improving their means of health – and by cultivating their intelligence'.[2]

'It seems impossible', Disraeli had told Manners a year earlier, 'that I ever cd live anywhere except among the woods & turfy wilderness of this dear county, wh:, tho' it upset Charles 1st., so exhausted its progressive spirit in 1640, that it has now neither a town, nor a railroad.' Settlement in Hughenden and in the county seat represented the final form of his physical rooting. In 1860 he would write of his return for Buckinghamshire as 'the event in my public life, wh. has given me the greatest satisfaction'. The seat was a comfortable one for nearly thirty years, if not quite as carefree as Disraeli implied in telling Lady Janetta Manners at the end of his life that 'during that time I scarcely ever received a letter from a constituent, certainly never answered one'. Yet there were strict limits to Disraeli's plausibility as a knight of the shire, not least in the minds of those local opponents who saw him in 1847 as obtruded onto the county by the duke of Buckingham's influence, on a qualification of '£900 a year purchased within the last nine weeks'. They would have been more sceptical still had they known about the use of Bentinck money to endow the Protectionists' most skilful debater with the appropriate background. Disraeli was being hired, rather as Lord George Bentinck had originally contemplated hiring the services of a good lawyer to make the case he himself could not adequately articulate. He was explicit enough about the nature of the transaction, reporting to his wife that in negotiating for a favourable arrangement he had explained to Lord Henry Bentinck that 'it wd. be no object to them & no pleasure to me, unless I played the high game in public life; & that I cd. not do that witht. being on a rock'.[3]

Perhaps it was his consciousness of the relations of dependence he was assuming that prompted the vigorous assertion of independence he made in the Buckinghamshire election. The claim would have sounded impudent had his circumstances been better known, but in his own fashion he had already done something to substantiate it. At the very moment that the funds were being assembled and the electoral interest solicited to enable him to blend into the Protectionist ranks as a landed proprietor and a county member, he was broadcasting to the world, in *Tancred*, published in March 1847, a set of opinions calculated to outrage, when they did not merely bewilder, almost every man on the Protectionist benches, opinions which he defiantly repeated in the debate on Jewish disabilities in December 1847 (when he could easily have recorded a silent vote), reinforced in the preface to the 1849 edition of *Coningsby*, and, as though to make sure that there should be no mistaking him, incorporated two years later in a chapter of his biography of Lord George Bentinck so blatantly irrelevant to the subject that the next one had to begin with the nonchalant admission: 'The views expressed in the preceding chapter were not those which influenced Lord George Bentinck.'[4]

Tancred or: The New Crusade completed the investigation of the political, social and spiritual condition of England begun in *Coningsby* and *Sybil*, but the fact that it was written in large part and published while Disraeli was making the quick costume change from freebooting backbencher to Protectionist leader, suggests that it should be seen not only as the finial to his enterprise of teaching his contemporaries what to think, but as an oblique definition of the terms on which he was prepared to take service on the front bench. Its provocations were the measure of his sensitivity to the sacrifice of independence that his advancement required him to accept. With it, he approached as nearly as he could to an imaginative resolution of the question of how a Jewish outsider, as he necessarily appeared, could impose his claims on the aristocracy and gentry of England, while at the same time he suffered their patronage and sometimes their disdain. *Tancred* was the final working out in fictional metaphor of that conceptualisation of the relationship which Disraeli needed to entertain, partly as an operating technique, but still more as a condition of psychic security.

The novel followed the device of *Coningsby* and *Sybil* in analysing contemporary malaise in such a way as to create a tutelary role for the outsider of genius, who, precisely by virtue of being an outsider, with the special insight that comes from obliquity of view, can supply the diagnosis and the nostrum to effect a cure. Once again, the vision of the seer and the wisdom of the magus are transmitted to the rising generation through the education of a young aristocrat, Tancred. Sidonia reappears as philosopher and mentor. His man, Baroni, the factotum he lends Tancred for his travels, is a Sephardic Jew from Cento, home of Disraeli's forbears. If there is here the flicker of an ironic recognition of the lackeying side of Disraeli's functions among the English elite, it is firmly subordinated to the implication that it is the master who depends on the servant: 'If anything can save the aristocracy in this levelling age, it is an appreciation of men of genius.'[5]

Whereas Coningsby was guided to perceive the key to England's political dilemmas in the right understanding of her history, and Egremont the solution of her social strife in the acceptance by the rich of their responsibilities towards the poor, Tancred is despatched on an altogether more grandiose mission, to discover the meaning of duty and faith at the epicentre of Christian civilisation, Jerusalem itself. His difficulty is to discern any satisfactory and sustaining principle in the order of things which he is born as a nobleman to uphold. Criticising the policy that 'confounds the happiness with the wealth of nations', he asks:

where is the art? ... Art is order, method, harmonious results obtained by fine and powerful principles. I see no art in our condition. The people of this country have ceased to be a nation. They are a crowd, and only kept in some rude provincial discipline by the remains of that old system which they are daily destroying.[6]

With this formula (complete with the Hegelian metaphor of the crowd), Disraeli drew his readers once again into the current of the debate on how to generate a sense of collective moral identity in societies riven by individualist ethics and rationalist obsessions. 'Enlightened Europe', he wrote, 'is not happy. Its existence is a fever, which it calls progress.' The liberal and rationalistic creed of progress, contemptuous of the past, complacent in its Eurocentric ignorance, evoked one of Disraeli's most slashing assaults:

Progress to what, and from where? Amid empires shrivelled into deserts, amid the wrecks of great cities, a single column or obelisk of which nations import for the prime ornament of their mud-built capitals, amid arts forgotten, commerce annihilated, fragmentary literatures and populations destroyed, the European talks of progress, because, by an ingenious application of some scientific acquirements, he has established a society which has mistaken comfort for civilisation.[7]

Spiritual renewal depended on a return to the sources of the faith which had inspired the west. Tancred fails to find guidance in his perplexity from the Church of England, and Sidonia tells him why.

Your bishops here know nothing about these things. How can they? A few centuries back they were tattooed savages. This is the advantage which Rome has over you, and which you can never understand. That Church was founded by a Hebrew, and the magnetic influence lingers ... Theology requires an apprenticeship of some thousand years at least; to say nothing of clime and race.

What Tancred needs to do is to 'penetrate the great Asian mystery'. The clime in which he must seek the answer to his question, 'What ought I to DO and what ought I to BELIEVE', is the Holy Land; the race through whose intermediary alone he can approach the great Asian mystery is the Jewish.[8]

Clime does not prove very helpful, except in giving Disraeli the chance to use up his Palestine material and indulge his taste for eastern exoticism. Tancred on tour is a trial. Disraeli's real talent was for English social satire, not for pseudo-oriental mysticism, and the promise of the novel's sparkling opening on the mysterious quarter between Piccadilly and Curzon Street is sadly belied by the pilgrim's guide to the Holy Land which follows. Tancred is no more than a vapid vehicle for his creator's ideological obsessions: when he tells Sidonia 'I require a Comforter', one wishes that the great spider of 'Sequin Court' would supply that very article. Since he is quickly led to understand that God does not generally speak to Europeans, it is hardly surprising that the revelation vouchsafed to him on Mount Sinai is somewhat perfunctory. The solution of the problems of modern Europe, he learns, requires a return to 'eternal principles'. 'The equality of man can only be accomplished by the sovereignty of God ... Cease, then, to seek in a vain philosophy the solution of the social problem that perplexes you. Announce the sublime and solacing doctrine of theocratic equality.' It is never made clear what this gnomic utterance means. Presumably it is intended to offer as a panacea for the ills of western society the Judaic notion of the theocratic state in which rich and poor are united in God, but how the model is to be translated into European terms Disraeli does not indicate. Nor does he become less Delphic when he has Tancred and his ally, the emir Fakredeen – who plots his grand political combinations under 'the two greatest stimulants in the world to action, Youth and Debt' – dream of beginning in the Near East a movement to introduce 'a new social system, which was to substitute the principle of association for that of dependence as the foundation of the Commonwealth, under the sanction and superintendence of the God of Sinai and of Calvary'. Under this leadership, the forces of Syria and Arabia are to reassert the spiritual supremacy of Asia in arms. 'We wish to conquer the world, with angels at our head, in order that we may establish the happiness of men by a divine dominion, and, crushing the political atheism that is now desolating existence, utterly extinguish the grovelling tyranny of self-government.'[9]

With the proclamation of this cryptic crusade, the novel runs downhill to an unsatisfying conclusion, or, rather, lack of conclusion. Tancred, Disraeli told Lady Londonderry on Boxing Day 1846, had 'turned out a much more troublesome & unmanageable personage than I anticipated'. The end of the book maroons him in Jerusalem: it is hard to see how he could have gone home. To relate in any convincing way his new-found eastern illumination and the performance of his hered-itary functions as a leader of the English nation was beyond his creator's power. Disraeli had simply lost control of his grandiose philosophical project of demonstrating to Europe the solution of its conflicts and con-fusions through the transcendent spiritual inspiration of Asia. The chosen messenger had no decipherable message, unless it was, as in *Coningsby*, that social and political reconstitution, the building of com-munity out of conglomeration, depended on the power, not of the politician to manipulate elites, but of the genius to mobilise masses. Tancred concludes that the age of 'management' in politics is past: 'there are popular sympathies, however imperfect, to appeal to; we must recur to the high primeval practice, and address nations now as the heroes, and prophets, and legislators of antiquity'. 'High primeval practice' was a formula as empty as it was meant to be evocative. The 'great Asian mystery' became a standing object of ridicule to those who could see nothing in *Tancred* but the great Disraelian mystification.[10]

So far as there is a coherent principle in *Tancred*, it arises not from the spiritual inspiration of an eastern clime but from the spiritual ascen-dancy of an eastern race. 'All is race; there is no other truth', says Sidonia, pressing home the teaching of *Coningsby*. Once again, the racial primacy conferred on the Jews by unmixed blood is asserted, the origin of Christianity in their peculiar genius for religion stressed.

Disraeli levels his lance at the heart of Christian anti-Semitism by dismissing the doctrine of Jewish guilt for the death of Christ, through the medium of Eva, the beautiful Jewess with whom Tancred falls in love, symbolically prostrating English nobility at once before the spiritual influence and the sexual fascination of the mysterious other. If, Eva asks, the crucifixion, as a necessary prelude to the atonement, was a pre-ordained part of the divine plan, 'Where then was the inexpiable crime of those who fulfilled the beneficent intention? ... We have saved the human race, and you persecute us for doing it.' *Tancred* reinforces the contention of *Sybil* that 'Christianity is completed Judaism', the New Testament 'only a supplement'. As Eva summarises it: 'half Christendom worships a Jewess, and the other half a Jew'.[11]

The startling twenty-fourth chapter of *Lord George Bentinck* combines with this racial patenting of monotheistic truth the assertion of a special racial affinity with conservative and anti-egalitarian values.

The Jews represent the Semitic principle, all that is spiritual in our nature. They are the trustees of tradition, and the conservators of the religious element. They are a living and the most striking evidence of the falsity of that pernicious doctrine of modern times, the natural equality of man ... cosmopolitan fraternity ... a principle which, were it possible to act on it, would deteriorate the great races, and destroy all the genius of the world.

(What would happen, Disraeli wondered, if the citizens of the United States were to mingle with their coloured populations?) Adding to religious reverence and pride of blood 'the faculty of acquisition', it is clear that 'all the tendencies of the Jewish race are conservative. Their bias is to religion, property, and natural aristocracy.' Only if gentile statesmen were too stupid to see this would persecution and exclusion drive them to punish 'ungrateful Christendom' by exercising their talents in the leadership of the 'secret societies' which Disraeli (in 1851) rather curiously pictures as having engineered the continental revolutions of 1848.

If there was a hint of threat in this last argument, echoing Sidonia's warning in *Coningsby* that denial of full civil rights was pushing English Jews, though natural conservatives, to associate with 'the leveller and the latitudinarian', it was not necessary for Disraeli, in Britain, to follow Marx by subsuming the emancipation of the Jews under the revolutionary liberation of all the oppressed. Britain he contrived to regard almost as a cultural colony of Israel, the history of its liberties, literature and laws, as well as its religion, suffused with Hebraic inspiration. 'Vast as the obligations of the whole human family are to the Hebrew race', he asserted in *Tancred*, 'there is no portion of the modern populations so much indebted to them as the British people.' In the Holy Land, where Tancred kneels, 'words had been uttered, and things done, more than thirty centuries ago ... which influenced his opinions and regulated his conduct every day of his life, in that distant and sea-girt home, which, at the time of their occurrence, was not as advanced in civilisation as the Polynesian group or the islands of New Zealand.' Saxon and Celt are reminded in *Lord George Bentinck* that 'they daily acknowledge on their knees, with reverent gratitude, that the only medium of communication between the Creator and themselves is the Jewish race'. The formation and the future of the British nation are linked to the lays of ancient Israel. The seventeenth-century conquest of constitutional and religious freedom that was increasingly becoming an ideological prop of the mid-Victorian sense of England's destiny is transposed into a Hebraic key. 'It was "the sword of the Lord and of Gideon" that won the boasted liberties of England; chanting the same canticles that cheered the heart of Judah amid their glens, the Scotch, upon their hill-sides, achieved their religious freedom.'[12]

As the Jewish mind has inspired the great achievements of the British past, so, Disraeli implies, can it supply the pattern for the preservation of national character and national cohesion in the future. The secret of what elevates a crowd into a community lies, like everything else, in race. 'A Saxon race, protected by an insular position', the British rank, for Sidonia, alongside the Arabian tribes in the 'first and superior class' of the racial hierarchy, even if they cannot emulate the purity of blood which establishes the ultimate aristocracy of the latter. The only important European community still governed by the 'traditional influences' which form the sole alternative to military force, as Disraeli represents it in *Lord George Bentinck*, in the aftermath of the revolutions of 1848, Britain must take her cue from the Semitic hostility to false doctrines of natural equality if she wishes to emerge triumphant from 'the great contention between the patriotic and the cosmopolitan principle which has hardly begun, and on the issue of which the fate of this island as a powerful community depends'.[13]

That the religious and racial ideas of *Tancred* and *Lord George Bentinck* were too shallow and contrived to be other than an anti-climax to the great project begun in *Coningsby* and *Sybil* of anatomising the political, social and spiritual condition of the English nation seems not to have occurred to Disraeli, whose capacity for distinguishing between pseudo-profundity and the real thing, at least in his own work, was slight. The set of notions embodied in the three novels of the 1840s would constitute his stock-in-trade to the end of his life, retailed with hardly any variation and complacently held up in his 'General Preface' to the collected edition of his novels in 1870 as an intellectual *chef d'œuvre*. By the time of *Tancred*, however, the ambition to create an impressive intellectual system was less urgent than that other motive of the trilogy, the need to resolve the contradictions of Disraeli's situation in English life in order to make possible that 'power o'er the powerful' which beckoned him on. Taking England under the wing of Israel and asserting the pre-eminence of the natural aristocracy of race and genius which conferred his patent of nobility was Disraeli's way of establishing his qualification to lead. Yet, aiming to fuse the Jewish identity he had determined to acknowledge with the Christian conferred on him by baptism, the operation in fact suspended him precariously between the two.

The political prominence into which Disraeli stepped in 1846 rendered much more acute the problem of how a parvenu of Jewish antecedents was to operate in a Christian polity. Whatever he said or did, he would be seen as a Jew by Gentiles. 'He bears the mark of the Jew strongly about him' was Lady Salisbury's diary entry after meeting him at the Londonderrys in 1837. *Punch*, of the malevolence of which he was already complaining in 1844, responded to his rise by at once caricaturing him in the Jewish stereotypes of old-clothes dealer and itinerant cheapjack. Yet it was not only the fact that he could not avoid the attribution of it that determined Disraeli to embrace Jewishness in a form which would convert the brand of inferiority into the mark of aristocracy. Once he began to doubt, as he seems to have done by the end of the 1820s, that his bid for the universalism of supreme creative genius, a means perhaps of transcending his Jewish origin, was going to succeed, he in a sense fell back on the universalism conferred by membership of what he contrived to see as an ancient and indestructible race and a universal spiritual culture. Doing so involved a reaction against his upbringing which was perhaps the final form of his assertion of adult independence. He was not, he wrote in 1853, 'bred among my race, & was nurtured in great prejudice against them. Thought, & the mysterious sympathy of organisation' (that is, his psychological make-up) had led him to adopt different views. From 1827 he was plunged in the reading of Jewish history and literature which would supply the theme of *Alroy*: the journey to the Holy Land which followed was the symptom, rather than the trigger, of an embrace of origins in what Philip Rieff has aptly characterised as a kind of home-sickness.[14] The relation of his Jewish home to his English was the question which his political advance compelled him to face.

The temptation to evade it struck him at least once, just after his entry to the House of Commons, in December 1837, when he voted against an attempt to remove the obligation on those taking municipal office to subscribe an oath, the form of which excluded such practising Jews as David Salomons or Moses Montefiore, both of whom were then prominent figures in the affairs of the City of London. 'Nobody looked at me and I was not at all uncomfortable, but voted in the majority (only of 12) with the utmost sangfroid', he told his sister. What he subsequently came to feel about this way of seeking to be comfortable by passing unremarked was scathingly conveyed in his description in *Tancred* of Mlle de Laurella, who

felt persuaded that the Jews would not be so much disliked if they were better known; that all they had to do was to imitate as closely as possible the habits and customs of the nation among whom they chanced to live; and she really did believe that eventually, such was the progressive spirit of the age, a difference in religion would cease to be regarded, and that a respectable Hebrew, particularly if well dressed and well mannered, might be able to pass through society without being discovered, or at least noticed. Consummation of the destiny of the favourite people of the Creator of the universe![15]

Inconspicuous conformity was not Disraeli's style, and his pride in the sense of chosenness which he felt both as a romantic and as a Jew ensured that he would repulse the sort of strenuous assimilation into the host society which, driven by self-hatred, involved performing an amputation on one's own identity. His attitude could not be that of the grandmother of whom he wrote that she 'had imbibed that dislike for her race which the vain are too apt to adopt when they find that they are born to public contempt'. Whatever the backslidings of his family in the matter of Jewish self-esteem, he was determined by the 1840s to claim its links with the most noble families of Israel, discovering in the Sephardic snobbery of aristocratic origins the 'blood' which Vivian Grey had placed alongside the million and the genius as the prerequisites of success. His portrayal of the D'Israelis, in the memoir of his father published in 1849, as the descendants of a Hebrew family forced out of Spain by the Inquisition at the end of the fifteenth century, and his fascination with their connection with the great Lara clan of Aragon, stretched their genealogy further than the evidence would readily bear, but it supplied part of the equipment with which he faced out the English aristocracy and justified his assumption of the crest bearing the castle of Castile which appeared at Shrewsbury in 1841.[16]

In the end, however, Disraeli's assertion of aristocracy derived less from the contriving of a great family than from the proclamation of a great race. The tendency of his cultivation of Sephardic snootiness was, perhaps designedly, to distance him from the Ashkenazim who constituted the great majority of European Jewry, much of it living in conditions that he found sordid or demeaning; but racial pride could be nothing if it was not comprehensive. He admitted to Monckton Milnes in 1844 that 'the Germans', even if they did not rank 'high in blood', were now 'the most intelligent of the tribes'; and, while making in *Lord George Bentinck*, like Sidonia in *Coningsby*, what he called a 'full admission of the partial degradation of the Jewish race', he sought to avoid the posture of embarrassment into which well-to-do Anglo-Jewry was often thrown by its poorer brethren who lent themselves easily to hostile stereotypes of the Jew. Jews figured disproportionately among the 'vile' of the great cities (a statement for which he adduced no evidence), but it was precisely their ability to survive the worst conditions that demonstrated the tenacity of a superior breed.

Conceive [Disraeli enjoined the reader of *Tancred*] a being born and bred in the Judenstrasse of Hamburg or Frankfort, or rather in the purlieus of our Houndsditch or Minories, born to hereditary insult, without any education, apparently without a circumstance that can develop the slightest taste, or cherish the least sentiment for the beautiful, living amid fogs and filth, never treated with kindness, seldom with justice, occupied with the meanest, if not the vilest, toil, bargaining for frippery, speculating in usury, existing for ever under the concurrent influence of degrading causes which would have worn out, long ago, any race that was not of the unmixed blood of Caucasus, and did not adhere to the laws of Moses.

Blood and the law, or at least Jewish blood and the Jewish laws, will conquer all: 'the other degraded races', we learn in *Lord George Bentinck*, 'wear out and disappear; the Jew remains, as determined, as expert, as persevering, as full of resource and resolution as ever ... Obdurate, malignant, odious, and revolting as the lowest Jew appears to us, he is rarely demoralised.'[17]

If, in all this, Disraeli appeared as a vindicator rather than a leader of what he chose to consider in some fashion as his people, he none the less at moments dreamed the dream of being the prince who would lead them out of the captivity. In *Alroy*, in 1833, strangest of the psycho-dramas through which he endeavoured both to find and to fashion his identity, he had used Jewish history of the twelfth century to construct an allegory of the tension he felt between the lofty attraction of the pure messianic and national vision of his recently discovered people and the less spiritual temptations of worldly conquest and dominion.'What am I?', asks David Alroy, torn by the conflict between his dreams and aspirations and the real terms of his existence as the prince of a captive people. He finds relief from inner turmoil in leading his people in a successful revolt, only to be gripped by the ambition to found a far-flung empire based on religious toleration, which brings him into fatal collision with the high priest, Jabaster, prophet of the 'national' and theocratic vision of establishing the pure rule of the Mosaic law in an exclusive Hebrew state centred on the rebuilt temple of Jerusalem. Overwhelmed by rebellion, invasion and treachery, Alroy finally redeems what he has come to recognise as his abandonment of the true path by submitting to martyrdom rather than deny his mission and renounce his faith, leaving his deeds to be sung for the inspiration of the future by some Jewish bard, 'his fancy fired with the national theme'.

If the novel embodied Disraeli's 'ideal ambition', as he said it did, it was seemingly to be an Alroy less compromised in his integrity as a Jew. The ideal might not be attainable, or relevant, in the conditions of English politics, but that it lingered, however abstractly, in Disraeli's mind is suggested by his conversation with his young intimate Lord Stanley (the 24-year-old elder son of his party chief) in January 1851. As they walked in Lord Carrington's park near Wycombe, he spoke of the restoration of the Jews to Palestine. Stanley's diary (as revised by its author in 1855) records his remarks:

The country, he said, had ample natural capabilities: all it wanted was labour, and protection for the labourer: the ownership of the soil might be bought from Turkey: money would be forthcoming: the Rothschilds and leading Hebrew capitalists would all help: the Turkish empire was falling into ruin: the Turkish Govt would do anything for money: all that was necessary was to establish colonies, with rights over the soil, and security from ill treatment. The question of nationality might wait until these had taken hold. He added that these ideas were extensively entertained among the nation. A man who should carry them out would be the next Messiah, the true Saviour of his people. He saw only a single obstacle: arising from the existence of two races among the Hebrews, of whom one, those who settled along the shores of the Mediterranean, look down on the other, refusing even to associate with them. 'Sephardim' I think he called the superior race.

'His manner', Stanley recollected, 'seemed that of a man thoroughly in earnest; and though I have many times since seen him under the influence of irritation or pleasurable excitement, this is the only instance in which he ever appeared to me to show signs of any higher emotion.' Some debate has centred on the question of whether such hints of Disraeli's inner consciousness justify his being described as a proto-Zionist. They are certainly enough to show that the Zionist dream was within his range of sympathy, and they were enough for Theodor Herzl, starting his newspaper, *Die Welt*, to place Disraeli's name first in a proposed series of literary profiles of 'representative exponents of the Zionist idea'.[18]

In whatever form Disraeli might conceive the national and messianic vision, however, there was always a void at the centre. The difficulty in his espousal of Jewishness was that it necessarily excluded the religion which informed Jewish life, or at least devalued it into a mere formative stage of Christianity. Baptised at the age of twelve-and-a-half, on the verge of full entry into the Jewish community, Disraeli had only a slender knowledge of Jewish religious practice, and, if he disliked his family's tendency to be ashamed of Jewishness, he followed his father closely in regarding Judaism with a jaundiced eye. When it came to religion, Isaac D'Israeli was a sceptical, even scoffing, *philosophe* of the eighteenth century. In *The Genius of Judaism*, published in the year of *Alroy*, he anticipated many of the views his son was to express, savaging 'the degrading servitudes, and the bewitching superstitions of rabbinical Judaism', which had kept 'the national genius stationary and unchangeable' and excluded the Jews from 'the great family of mankind', and imploring the Jews to 'begin to educate their youth as the youth of Europe, and not of Palestine'. 'The Christian', Isaac contended, 'exults in the completion of that Judaism which the Hebrew contemplated as perfect at its divine institution ... Christianity and Judaism rest on the same foundations.' After this, it comes as no surprise to find Benjamin mocking rabbinical Judaism in his rendering, in *Alroy*, of the conversation between rabbis Zimri and Maimon on 'the treatise of the learned Shimei, of Damascus, on "Effecting impossibilities"':

'I never slept for three nights after reading that work', said Rabbi Maimon. 'It contains twelve thousand five hundred and thirty-seven quotations from the Pentateuch, and not a single original observation.'
'There were giants in those days', said Zimri; 'we are children now.'
'The first chapter makes equal sense, read backward or forward', continued Rabbi Maimon.
'Ichabod!' exclaimed Rabbi Zimri.
'And the initial letter of every section is a cabalistical type of a king of Judah!'
'The temple will yet be built', said Rabbi Zimri.[19]

Both father and son were grappling with the central problem of European Jewry in the early nineteenth century, that of the terms on which, emerging from the ghetto as it still was over much of the Continent, it could be integrated into modern European society and find the means to translate into a modern idiom the Jewish mission of messianic redemption. Both wanted to strip out of Judaism those aspects which appeared to them as farcical relics of a barbarous age and hence obstacles to modernisation and acceptance. Disraeli's approach strongly resembled the operation of romantic transformation which he had attempted to perform on the past and principles of the Tory party, purging obsolete excrescences in order to create a new model tradition within which he could more comfortably operate; and in this sense he and his father had much in common with the effort of contemporary Reform Judaism to achieve re-entry from the outer space of messianic expectation into the mainstream of modern European history by emphasising all that was universal and timeless, as opposed to all that might be seen as particularist, archaic and irrational, in Jewish life and thought. The Berlin-centred movement known as Wissenschaft des Judentums and some German rabbinical reformers of the 1830s and 1840s were tending to dilute the particularity of Jewish history by fusing it into the history of the progressive self-realisation of the human spirit as a whole. In this, however, vital and continuing as they might think the contribution of Judaism to be, they risked delivering themselves into the hands of those sympathetic but patronising Christian thinkers like Wilhelm von Humboldt, who saw Judaism as only a stage of spiritual evolution and the Jewish people as possessing its importance in world history through its contribution to the development of Christianity.

Disraeli was anxious to assert rather than blur Jewish particularity, as the basis of his own status among 'the nations of the world', but it could not be religious particularity (as opposed to the Jewish genius for religion), since he was a Christian in a formally Christian polity, so that it was into the Humboldt position that he naturally fell. It was to Christ that the Jews owed their fame, he declared in *Lord George Bentinck*, a thought developed in a private jotting of the 1860s:

I look upon the Church as the only Jewish Institution remaining ... If it were not for the Church, I don't see why the Jews should be known. The Church was founded by Jews, & has been faithful to its origin. It secures their history & their literature being known to all Xdom ... The Jews owe everything to the Church, & are fools to oppose it.

As Christians were in some sense the product of conversion by Jewish ideas, so Jews should now convert to Christianity. It was persecution, Disraeli alleged in *Lord George Bentinck*, that had deterred most of the Jewish race from believing in the most important portion of their religion, but, as 'the converted races' became more humane in their behaviour towards Jews, he looked forward to the latter's embracing Christianity.[20]

Collapsing the differences between Judaism and Christianity helped Disraeli, as it helped some other baptised Jews, like Heine, to operate in a Christian frame without explicit repudiation of Judaism. It enabled him to universalise the genius of Judaism and to inject it into the main arteries of western civilisation as Sidonia injected his mind-stretching notions into the sluggish blood of young English aristocrats. 'Assuming that the popular idea of Inspiration be abandoned, & the difference between sacred & profane history relinquished', he wrote in 1863, 'what would be the position of the Hebrew race in universal History, viewed with reference to their influence on Man?' This was the theme that always fascinated him, and he thought of offering £500 or £1,000 for the best essay on it, the judges to be Gladstone, A. P. Stanley and himself. It is a pity that the competition never took place, for the judging would have been piquant. Its proposed terms, however, underline the extent to which Disraeli fell in with the tendency to subsume Judaism under the spiritual and cultural development of humanity as a whole, and to attenuate its specificity even in asserting its historic primacy. The point was sharply emphasised by the manner of his support for the modification of the oath taken by members of parliament, so as to enable it to be subscribed by practising Jews. The argument he employed in the famous debate of December 1847 made the claim of Jews to the removal of all remaining civil and political disabilities depend, not on the principle of equality of citizens before the law without respect to their beliefs, but on their status as proto-Christians, with a natural right to inclusion in a Christian polity. This radical assimilationism ran clean against the position of Jewish emancipationists (and most of their Christian supporters), who were looking for equal treatment, not absorption, of minorities, and made Disraeli a highly uncomfortable ally. It was rather to Peel, Russell and Gladstone that men like David Salomons turned. As the *Jewish Chronicle* put it in August 1850, Jews asked for justice 'not as a peculiar race, or [on] account of a peculiar religion, but as citizens of the same state. We claim it not upon the ground of the eccentric fiction of one who praises the Jews up to the skies – and he himself a descendant of Jews, but not a Jew.' No wonder that Disraeli told the duke of Newcastle, in February 1849, that he wished 'the Jew Bill' were 'at the bottom of the Red Sea': the question was profoundly embarrassing for him. When, in the following year, he excused the silence of his post-1847 votes in favour of Jewish emancipation by stating that he believed that his opinions on the subject were not shared by a single member on either side of the House of Commons, he might almost have added, 'or by a single Jew'.[21]

Disraeli's treatment of Jewishness perhaps sublimated a touch of the self-hatred he seems to have striven consciously to avoid. As a Christian, he could afford, without obvious violence to his own identity, to indulge his patent dislike for what he, with his father, regarded as the musty and eccentric appurtenances of Jewish faith, even while asserting the spiritual virtue of its central core. His stance, however, placed him in a very ambiguous relationship to the Anglo-Jewish community, for which he appeared as not only a convert to, but a proselytiser for, Christianity, however much he might blur the issue by maintaining that Christianity was Jewish. From 1839 onwards, he was mixing socially with Montefiores and Rothschilds, but neither by origin, wealth or faith did he belong to the Anglo-Jewish elite, and his position became more rather than less anomalous as time went by. He had been baptised at a period when conversion was common, even fashionable, among well-to-do and aspiring Sephardic families, and Lopeses and Bernals and Ricardos sat on the benches of the Christian House of Commons, but, by the time he was pressing Christianity on his contemporaries in *Lord George Bentinck*, the tide was moving the other way. As Todd Endelman has pointed out, conversion was simply unnecessary and Reform Judaism unappealing for the prosperous Jewry of Victorian

England, a respectable, middle-class sect of a kind almost akin to a variety of protestant dissent, which suffered no persecution and little economic or social disadvantage for its faith. With none of the intense pressure to assimilate that affected continental Jewry, conversion and intermarriage became unusual. It is perhaps significant that Disraeli's closest connections in the Jewish community were the Rothschilds, who were something of an exception to the rule, marrying out several of their daughters. Lionel de Rothschild, whose election for the City of London in 1847 had occasioned the great debate on Jewish disabilities, evidently did not mind his friend's referring to him, in *Lord George Bentinck*, as one 'unfortunately believing only in the first part of the Jewish religion'.[22] Others might be less easy-going. Moreover, Disraeli's assumption of Sephardic loftiness would leave him increasingly on the margin of Anglo-Jewish life as the more numerous Ashkenazim took control after mid-century.

In Disraeli's glorification of his origins, the necessary compensation for the devaluation of the Jewish religion rendered unavoidable by his Christianity was the vaunting of the Jewish race. Because he had to have a rock for pride of self and a springboard for his assault on the pinnacles of power, he could hardly follow the logic which would have derived from his absorption of Judaism in Christianity an implicit downgrading of post-biblical Jewish experience. He could not side with Moses Hess in regarding the Jews as having become a 'mummy' because of their rejection of Jesus, or with his father in complaining that 'the Jews have no men of Genius or talents to lose ... Ten centuries have not produced Ten great men.'[23] But the racial bragging into which he was driven only intensified the awkwardness of his relationship to contemporary Jewry.

Race was for Disraeli the principal dynamic of historical development – therefore the factor through which the insight of genius could grasp and act upon historical process – that the class struggle was for Marx, and the Jewish race, with its quality of purity and universality, was the agent of unification and transcendence, the people chosen to lead humanity out of bondage and oppression, whose role Marx transferred to the proletariat. He delighted in unearthing Jews in every sphere of talent and influence, 'another and an[othe]r still', as he would write gleefully to his sister. It was possibly the only subject on which he allowed himself to become a bore, if we follow Cecil Roth's anecdote of Lionel de Rothschild's reply to an enquiry as to what he and Disraeli had talked about at one of their regular encounters: 'The Race, as usual' ('I hope he will prove worthy of his pure and sacred race' was Disraeli's way of congratulating his friend on the birth of a son in December 1845).[24]

There were always Jews who were ready to play his game and to add him to the list, especially when he rose to political eminence, as a Jewish paladin. Already, in 1845, Henri Avigdor was dedicating to him a work published in Paris in reply to an anti-Semitic tract, and receiving an acknowledgement typically laudatory of 'the children of Israel, who baffled the Pharaohs, the Assyrian kings & the Roman Caesars; to say nothing of the Crusades & the Inquisition'. Yet it was obvious that racial assertiveness was risky. Disraeli wondered in *Tancred* why the Jews were reviled and persecuted by peoples that in a spiritual and cultural sense owed them everything, and supposed that it was *because* they owed them everything. Jealousy of the 'oriental intellect' and resentment of the Semitic revelation had brought about the corrosive scepticism of the Enlightenment and the turmoil of the French Revolution. The current state of religion, he suggested in a draft letter of the 1860s, was 'only one of the periodical revolts of the Northern races against Semitic truth, influenced mainly by mortified vanity in never having been the medium of direct communication with the Almighty'.[25]

Oddly, for one with his financial background, it did not occur to him that the animus of the debtors against the creditors was likely to be sharpened by his harping on the extent of their borrowings and by the racial superciliousness that went with it. As he was finishing *Tancred*, the French historian Jules Michelet was warning the Jews (whose country, he sneered, was the London stock exchange) that they were courting trouble by abandoning the prudence of their medieval forbears and exposing themselves in high society and politics. Disraeli's triumphal lists of powerful Jews through the ages, however erroneous, his determination to see the Jewish hand in all the significant twists of European history and all the creative flights of western civilisation, his exultation in the capacity of 'the pure Asian breed' to survive all the persecutions that more mongrel races could visit on it and to outlast its oppressors, could hardly fail to fuel the anti-Semitism that regarded Jews as simultaneously a sinister controlling presence in all the world's back rooms and arrogant intruders in all its front parlours, and saw in their communal cohesiveness and tenacity the measure of an alien racial conspiracy. Within five years of his death, the foremost French anti-Semite, Edouard Drumont, was using him as an authority for the identification of prominent personalities as Jews; within twenty, Houston Stewart Chamberlain was citing with approval his fetish of racial purity, as a lesson the Teutonic races had better learn if they were to repulse the Jewish challenge.[26] In his racial provocativeness, Disraeli was just the kind of Jew, if he was a Jew, that the cautious leadership of Anglo-Jewry, heads usually tucked well beneath the parapet, found embarrassing, if not actually dangerous. To have been chosen by God was an awesome fate. To have been chosen by Disraeli, on his own idiosyncratic terms, and for his own peculiar purposes, was almost as perturbing.

It was hardly less perturbing for the English, whom Disraeli had saluted in the *Vindication* as being in politics 'as the old Hebrews in religion, "a favoured and peculiar people"'. True, attraction towards eastern exoticism and the bibliocentric and millennial character of evangelical protestantism together supplied a certain public to which Disraeli's fascination with Hebrew spirituality and the world-historical role of the Jewish race did not necessarily sound outlandish. While for Coleridge sublimity was 'Hebrew by birth', for exalted evangelicals like Shaftesbury the conversion of the Jews and their restoration to the Holy Land were prime elements in the fulfilment of the divine purpose, in furthering which the English, another people of the book, might readily appear as the destined inheritors of Israel's mission to the peoples of the world.[27] 'All the great things have been done by the little nations', Disraeli wrote in *Tancred*, and it was possible to see, as George Eliot was to see, the Jewish 'national' idea as a model for the British race to copy. The Arabs whose supposed heroic virtues some English liked to admire were, according to *Tancred*, 'only Jews upon horseback'; the militant puritan austerity of the Ironsides, for which there was increasing enthusiasm among the educated classes in mid-century, was inspired, Disraeli pointed out, by the Jewish spirit – 'Philosophically considered', he noted of the Great Rebellion, 'it might be looked upon as the influence of Hebrew literature on the northern mind.'[28]

Yet, even if he was operating among the thinking classes in an atmosphere that might be as often philo-Semitic as anti-Semitic, Disraeli did not look much like an Ironside, and his views on Christianity and the Jewish race, where they were not baffling, were likely to be offensive to the average Anglican Tory. It did not help that he regarded criticism of them as evidence of stupidity, telling Henry Lennox in August 1852 that 'passages [from Lord George Bentinck] denounced as heterodox by English clergymen, who are more ignorant of theology than any body of men in the world (the natural consequence of being tied down to 39 articles, and stopped from all research into the literature which they are endowed to illustrate), are only reproductions from St Augustin and Tertullian'. They were bound to cast doubt in some minds on the nature of his religious belief, and indeed to raise the question of whether he had any of a doctrinally recognisable kind. Lord Stanley would remark in 1861 on his 'open ridicule, in private, of all religions', and, while that may have arisen from taking the habit of irony for the absence of conviction, it is hard to know what, if anything, Disraeli believed in a religious sense. Perhaps there is no more to know than Stanley discovered at Hughenden in 1851, when he found that Disraeli's favourite topic after politics was

the origin of the various beliefs which have governed mankind, their changes at different epochs, and those still to come ... He seemed to think that the sentiment, or instinct, of religion would by degrees, though slowly, vanish as knowledge became more widely spread ... Yet Disraeli is no materialist: he has always avowed his expectation of some form of future existence, though whether accompanied with any consciousness of personal identity with the self of this present life, he thought it impossible to foresee.[29]

As his Christianity might seem insecure, so might his Englishness. The combination of his final diagnosis of England's ills as a European sickness curable only through spiritual regeneration with his insistence that spiritual regeneration was a Semitic prerogative seemed to remove

English destiny into Jewish hands, as it had to do if he was to guide that destiny. It was essential to him to define national identity in terms that only an outsider could perceive and national problems in terms which permitted only an outsider to offer the solution. Toryism itself, in the teaching of Sidonia, turns out to be just a local facsimile of the natural conservatism of the Jewish race, 'copied from the mighty prototype which has fashioned Europe'.[30] In the end, the peculiar cocktail of religious and racial opinions which Disraeli invented left him in a kind of limbo between Christian and Jewish, English and Hebrew worlds. Christians were not inclined to see themselves as fully developed Jews, nor Jews to see themselves as underdeveloped Christians. Disraeli's position in the two spheres of thought and feeling which he had tried to reconcile remained ambiguous for the inhabitants of each, even if his attempted synthesis was sufficient to hold the two sides of his own identity together in some tolerable fashion. In a philosophical sense, he ended up securely tethered in no recognised body of belief or community of sentiment, not so much the wandering as the free-floating Jew.

Neither was he much more securely anchored in the Protectionist party. To the extent that his quirky opinions on race, religion, history and British destiny were expressed in literature, they might slip past the noses of his not very bookish backbenchers. True, Surtees has Soapy Sponge find Jawleyford reading the life of Bentinck, but *Tancred* sold only a couple of thousand copies, and few of them can have landed on the squires' shelves. It was different with Disraeli's speech of December 1847 on Jewish disabilities. It was probably on that occasion that Lord John Russell, to Gladstone, praised the way in which he stuck to his guns, '"tho' he knows that every word he says is gall and wormwood to every man who sits around him and behind him"'.[31] His version of his party's eighteenth-century tradition had omitted its opposition to the Jewish naturalisation bill of 1753, but he could have been in no doubt of its feeling in 1847, when the support afforded him by his leader, Bentinck, a decided liberal in matters of civil liberty, undermined the latter's position and led to his resigning the leadership of a party that seemed able to be governed only by its antipathies and prejudices.

Disraeli's stand was an open defiance of those prejudices and a proclamation that, bought up as a Protectionist spokesman though he might be, his price included the freedom to take his own line on the matters closest to the centre of his feeling and to the construction of his identity.

The Jewish disabilities debate emphasised that Disraeli was utterly unsuitable to lead the party in the Commons, and, by precipitating Bentinck's abdication, ensured that he would. Leading, as he told Manners on Boxing Day 1847, was 'something more than asking a question at 4 o'clock or making a speech at 11. Independent of the knowledge & management of mankind, the great spirit & social position, the even profuse generosity, wh: are required, & were so eminently practised & possessed by G.B.; the mere conduct of correspondence, & reading of blue books & making calculations, demand physical powers of Herculean range.' If Disraeli himself did not entirely meet the specification, he came closer to it than anyone else on the Protectionist benches. The rejection of Peel and his followers had dashed nearly all the brains and recent ministerial experience out of the old Conservative party. Bagehot later explained, with some partisanship, the problem for the squires who were left: 'There is no free trade in the agricultural mind; each county prohibits the import of able men from other counties. This is why eloquent sceptics – Bolingbroke and Disraeli – have been so apt to lead the unsceptical Tories. They *will* have people with a great piece of land in a particular spot, and of course these people generally cannot speak, and often cannot think. And so eloquent men who laugh at the party come to lead the party.'[32]

There was no settled Protectionist leadership in the Commons in the 1848 session, but it was Disraeli who made the speech winding up the session in August, and the sudden death of Bentinck in the following month left him without question the most substantial parliamentary performer on the Protectionist benches. He knew now that he was sufficiently indispensable to be able to dismiss attempts to fob him off with even a nominally subordinate position. When Stanley, who commanded the party as a whole from the Lords, and, like most people, thought that he lacked the social standing and personal influence to lead, called on him to 'give a generous support to a Leader [Herries] of abilities inferior to your own', Disraeli threatened to act independently;

when Stanley then, in March 1849, proposed leadership in the Commons by a triumvirate, yoking him with Herries and Granby, he talked of returning to literature, declaring: 'I am Disraeli the adventurer and I will not acquiesce in a position which will enable the party to make use of me in debate, and then throw me aside.' He did not mean to be exploited by a supercilious aristocracy as he thought Burke had been, and if they regarded him as an adventurer they could hardly expect to succeed with appeals to his magnanimity. In fact, he accepted Stanley's invitation to the first meeting of the proposed triumvirate and acted with Herries and Granby in the session of 1849 without formally accepting the arrangement, knowing that it was, as Lord Aberdeen put it, an affair of 'Sieyes, Roger Ducos, and Napoleon Bonaparte'. Though the system lasted in form for three years, there was little doubt from 1849 that 'Bonaparte' was the real leader. The whip, William Beresford, was far from alone in thinking that Disraeli's ascent would 'bring great obloquy upon a Party, which I have joined from principle, and which has its weight from character'. It made no difference: there was no alternative.[33]

In any case, there was always Stanley, the fourteenth earl of Derby as he became in June 1851, to reassure the nervous. Derby's sometimes flippant and offhand approach to politics as to much else can easily convey the impression of an aristocratic amateur, given over to 'Whist, Billiards, Racing, Betting, & making a fool of himself with either Ladies Emily Peel or Mary Yorke', in Henry Lennox's well known vignette, while Disraeli kept the party in business.[34] In April 1851, just after he had nearly become prime minister and had delivered two grave orations in the Lords and at the Merchant Taylors', Greville found him in the betting room at Newmarket, 'in the midst of a crowd of blacklegs, betters, and loose characters of every description, in uproarious spirits, chaffing, rowing, and shouting with laughter and joking … I don't suppose there is any other man who would act so naturally, and obey all his impulses in such a way, utterly regardless of appearances, and not caring what anybody might think of the Minister and the Statesman, as long as he could have his fun.' This was not Disraeli's style, and neither man found it easy to like the other. Derby had the assured aristocratic position and manners that Disraeli could never possess. He could afford the resigned pessimism about party prospects and the comparative indifference to office that Disraeli, the careerist, found infuriating. He sneered, his son noted, at Disraeli's 'tendency to extremes of alternate excitement and depression'; his subordinate's urgent fascination with the political drama not being in the temperament of the man who, asked on his deathbed how he felt, replied: 'bored to the utmost power of extinction'. Disraeli was not invited to the Stanley seat at Knowsley until December 1853 ('a wretched house', he told Mary Anne), and in August 1854 was complaining to Lady Londonderry: 'As for our Chief, we never see him. His House is always closed; he subscribes to nothing, tho' his fortune is very large, & expects, nevertheless, everything to be done. I have never yet been fairly backed in life.'[35]

Yet in the end Derby did back the strange confederate who had been forced on him by circumstances. His understanding of Disraeli's necessities was shrewd and not ungenerous, if we can rely on the latter's own anecdote of his chief's defending him against the Queen's censure of his conduct towards Sir Robert Peel: 'Madam, Mr. Di. has had to make his position, & men who make their positions will say & do things, wh: are not necessary to be said or done by those for whom positions are provided.' Beneath the insouciance, Derby was a man of exceptionally sharp and rapid intellect, and a brilliant debater, who could play the political game with skill when he chose, and he was enough of a Canningite liberal by origin to share some of Disraeli's aloofness from the narrower prejudices of his followers and on occasion to outdistance his second-in-command in willingness to pursue reforms. The two men were an odd couple, and jokes about 'the Jockey and the Jew' or 'the Derby and the Hoax' came readily to contemporaries, yet their twenty-year partnership somehow worked. It was the Jew, however, who was the jockey, and Derby who was incontestably the owner of the horse. Disraeli was secure in the saddle only as long as he was covered by the near absolute confidence that the party reposed in Derby, as a figure of unimpeachable standing and unquestioned integrity. Without Derby's authority and support, Disraeli had no political purchase. In *Lord George Bentinck*, he asserted that England was not governed by an aristocracy in the usual sense of the term, but by an aristocratic principle. 'The aristocracy of England absorbs all aristocracies, and receives every man in every order and every class who defers to the principle of our society, which is to aspire and to excel.' His pride compelled him to maintain the front of a member of a natural aristocracy, recognised and accepted in virtue of its talents and its achievements. In fact, he was for twenty years Lord Derby's court Jew, surviving at the summit by patient deference to a traditional aristocratic elite which had need of his skills, but for the most part no interest in his ideas or comprehension of his nature. 'You have sketched with the hand of a master, & with the inspiration of experience, those difficult considerations wh: I had only arrived at by many painful months of plodding', was his way, in December 1849, of bowing to his chief's view on tactics for the approaching session, and the tone thus set was to be maintained. Like Burke, like Berryer, the orator whom the French legitimists set up as a country gentleman to voice their case in the chamber, like the converted Jew, Stahl, who led the Prussian conservative party in the 1850s, Disraeli was an upper servant.[36]

Service had its drudgery, to which Disraeli lent himself with an application that belies his reputation for lack of industry. 'I am surrounded by piles of bluebooks', he wrote to Lady Londonderry from Hughenden in December 1849, '& two posts a day bear me reams of despatches; so that my recess of relaxation has combined the plodding of a notary with the anxiety of a house Steward. Pleasant! – & what is called gratified ambition.' Beresford, three months earlier, had been partially disarmed by finding him 'working very hard', dividing the blue-books into classes, and attributing 'Peel's great power and effect in the House to having always had Blue Books by heart, and having thereby the appearance of a fund of general knowledge greater than he really possessed'. There were compensations for this routine slogging. 'One gets into a great many good things (at least what people think good things) by being Leader of the Oppos[iti]on', he reported to Sarah in April 1850, having been asked to the Royal Academy banquet, where 'they took me out of the wits, among whom I sate last year ... & placed me among the statesmen' (and next to Gladstone, who was 'particularly agreeable'). Yet the incidental benefits could hardly outweigh the labour and the anxiety of directing a party on whose confidence and esteem Disraeli could never safely count. 'He strikes me as very zealous in the cause, and as feeling himself completely embarked now with us, and I do trust that he is fully compromised and will remain true', Beresford told the elder Stanley in September 1849, in terms redolent of the dubiety with which Disraeli was regarded by protestant and protectionist partisans. The party not only distrusted Disraeli, it did not share either his obsession with the political contest or his thirst for office. The younger Stanley remarked in May 1850, as he would do into the 1860s, that 'many of the country gentlemen never attend, unless expressly summoned for some particular division'; and in February 1853 he recorded that Disraeli 'complained loudly of the apathy of the party: they could not be got to attend to business while the hunting season lasted: a sharp frost would make a difference of twenty men. They had good natural ability, he said, taking them as a body; but wanted culture: they never read: their leisure was passed in field sports: the wretched school and university system was in fault: they learnt nothing useful, and did not understand the ideas of their own time.'[37]

Disraeli was lonely in his party, intimate with none of its leading figures. He tended to turn for sympathy and companionship to a few of the well-born young, whose minds he could attempt to form and whose talents he could bring on. He conceived a faintly ludicrous fancy for the insubstantial Lord Henry Lennox, giving him *Coningsby* to read and writing to him as 'my beloved'.[38] On an intellectually more serious level, he was in the early 1850s the mentor of the younger Stanley, who found in their walks and talks in the beechwoods above High Wycombe his 'chief political education', and whose journals provide some of the very few gleams of insight that we have into Disraeli's mind in his middle years. Friendships like these helped to make the Tory party a tolerable habitation, but, if politics was the arena of Disraeli's existence, it was from more private spheres that he drew the reserves of strength that sustained the gladiator's nerve.

The family circle that had helped to form his youth had begun to contract. His mother died in 1847, his father in the following year, and Sarah, his 'audience', in 1859. Increasingly, his private life came to be centred on his marriage and on his Buckinghamshire retreat. The reassurance of the former was grounded more in familiarity and habit than in intellectual sympathy and was not free from strains, but it was essential to Disraeli, and Stanley noted 'the gratitude which during many years he has never ceased to evince towards a person to whom he owes much of his success, but whose claims upon him in return are neither slight, nor easy to satisfy'. In the latter he found refuge and recreation every autumn and winter after the intense pressures of the parliamentary session, uninterested, Stanley found, in the usual 'rural pursuits' of the landowning class for which he spoke, but devoted to his library, delighting in his trees and the conversation of his woodmen, and happy in fine weather to pass the day wandering about the neighbourhood. Hughenden supplied the point of physical attachment and emotional repose that Disraeli's spirit needed. If he remained an odd graft upon Buckinghamshire society, he was able to derive a faintly malicious pleasure from watching it slowly and grudgingly bend to the rising statesman. Applied to for a cadetship by one of the county families in 1858, when he was a minister, he wrote to Stanley: 'For the Tyrwhitt Drakes to ask a service from me is the Hapsburgs soliciting something from a parvenu Napoleon. After thirty years of scorn and sullenness they have melted before time and events.'[39]

The moulding force of time and events was operating on Disraeli also, as a domesticated middle age, weighty responsibilities, constant and grinding labour, even the first beginnings of national and local acceptance made the lengthening shadow of respectability and dullness harder to evade. In the year, 1849, when he effectively assumed the leadership of the Protectionists in the Commons, the flight to Paris of Lady Blessington and of D'Orsay, his best friend and admired exemplar of the high romantic days, the pair ruined by a long course of extravagance, both recalled the rackety career of his youth and symbolised the breaking of his connection with it. So far as Protectionist misgivings about Disraeli were based on the supposed excesses of his earlier years, they were largely irrelevant by 1849: the vein of flamboyant recklessness was nearly exhausted. What remained was the vivacity of response, the excited wonder, the mocking, distancing irony, and the occasionally luxuriant fancy of the old romantic mood, even if they now sometimes seemed to be rather comfortable and familiar habits of expression than the urgent promptings of imperious genius. 'It gave me an idea of one of those great Tartar hordes of which we read –

of Genghis Khan and Attila. It was so vast, so busy, and so bovine!'
Thus Disraeli's description of the Royal Agricultural Society's 1862
show to Mrs Brydges Willyams, the elderly admirer of Jewish descent,
to whom he wrote assiduously in engagingly unbuttoned style in the
1850s and early 1860s, in consideration of the promised legacy which,
when it materialised in 1863, helped to stabilise his still precarious
finances with a ballast of some £30,000. The man who could jot down
his preference for the perfume of fruit even over that of flowers on the
ground that it was 'more mystical & thrilling; more rapturous', was in
little danger of losing his freshness of sensation or keenness of
enjoyment.[40] But there was not much employment in politics for the
romantic mode, and when its flourishes did intrude they were more
likely to bemuse than to enthuse Disraeli's backbenchers.

All the same, if, in background, ideas, temperament and style,
Disraeli was an incongruous and often isolated leader of his party, he
was not a totally inappropriate or unreliable one. It is easy to make too
much of Guizot's jibe that his becoming leader of the Tory party was
the greatest triumph that Liberalism had ever achieved, or of his own
remark to the liberally minded young Stanley in July 1850: 'we are both
on the wrong side, but there is nothing for it except to make the best of
our position'. His 'primitive' Tory argumentation of the 1830s and
1840s, and more especially his call for national regeneration in
Coningsby and *Sybil*, had a good deal in common with the line pursued
by the elder Stanley, Bentinck and their followers in the aftermath of
the repeal of the corn laws, if we follow Angus Macintyre's analysis of
the Protectionists as taking an organicist view of the state and opposing
to 'a radical free trade ideology seen as individualist and Mammon-
worshipping ... an integral nationalism under aristocratic leadership',
in which the reconciliation of classes would be achieved and the 'territorial constitution' preserved through an economic policy aimed at the
equitable balancing and safeguarding of the various interests in society,
in the tradition of 'the most liberal commercial Ministers', as Stanley
called them, including such exhibits in Disraeli's true Tory pantheon as
Pitt, Huskisson and Canning. The spirit of Young England, and in particular its most earnest embodiment in Lord John Manners's
Coningsbyesque, Sybilline, Tancredian belief in the mission of an aris-

tocracy made conscious of its social duties and of a church renewed in its spiritual vitality to unite classes sundered by a heartless and irresponsible individualism, seemed to indicate how social and national integration might be accomplished without undue increase of centralised governmental power. In so far as this was Protectionist ideology, Disraeli had been for years one of its tributary sources of inspiration and one of its ablest channels of expression. Only his distaste (shared by Bentinck) for the more bigoted flights of protestant enthusiasm and his consistent attachment to a commercial policy of mutually advantageous reciprocity, rather than to protection as such, provided any real justification for regarding him as a crypto-Liberal in the Protectionist ranks. Nor did his position give him much latitude to deviate from protectionist tenets as long as his followers believed in their applicability to the country's needs. Disraeli's status in high politics was dependent entirely on party: having risen by attacking Peel's 'betrayal' of party, he could scarcely copy it, and, unlike Peel, he had no personal following or independent stature to sustain him if he did. 'There is certainly a very prevalent impression', noted young Stanley in July 1850, 'that Disraeli has no well-defined opinions of his own: but is content to adopt, and defend, any which may be popular with the Conservative party at the time'.[41] The first clause was unfair, but the second recognised a basic constraint on Disraeli's conduct which guaranteed the party a sort of fidelity.

The security of Disraeli's job was much enhanced by its unattractiveness. 'There are', he wrote in *Lord George Bentinck*, 'few positions less inspiriting than that of the leader of a discomfited party ... Few care to share the labour which is doomed to be fruitless, and none are eager to diminish the responsibility of him whose course, however adroit, must necessarily be ineffectual.' As early as February 1851, after the elder Stanley's failure to form a government, he was talking about retiring and returning to literature, a refrain he took up at intervals in the following years, dreaming, for example, in May 1853 of going off to write another epic poem (under the astonishing delusion that the *Revolutionary Epick* was the best thing he had ever done) and his 'life of Christ from the national point of view'.[42] These were symptoms of the frustration induced by the seeming impossibility that his exertions could lead to real power. For a time, between 1847 and 1849, depressed agricultural prices and commercial uncertainty cast doubt on the validity of free trade and stimulated protectionist sentiment. Without some accession of Peelite or Whig support, however, the Protectionists could neither form a strong government nor command a majority in the constituencies: the ministry which Derby formed in February 1852 rested on a minority in the Commons and lasted only ten months. Even when, in the face of a renewal of prosperity, the Conservatives, as Derby's followers had continued to call themselves, recognised that the cause of agricultural protection which had separated them from Peel could no longer be considered practical politics, they could not greatly enlarge their political base, and Derby's second ministry, from February 1858 to June 1859, again rested upon a Commons minority.

The problem was both the Conservatives' lack of first-rate parliamentary talent and their inability, in the high tide of mid-century prosperity, to find issues on which to make a distinctive appeal that would extend their constituency base much beyond its traditional strongholds in the agricultural counties and small boroughs. The obvious remedy for the first deficiency was to bring back to the fold some of the leading politicians, Gladstone and Graham especially, who had sided with Peel in the split of 1846 and headed a Peelite group of at least forty members in the Commons. If they were not biddable, a more tenuous possibility was a junction with some of the more conservative Whigs, of whom Palmerston was the favourite. Every time Derby formed or tried to form a government, in February 1851, February 1852, January 1855 and February 1858, these avenues were explored, with much to-ing and fro-ing and penning of letters, friendly or frigid, around London; 'but', as *Punch* had it in March 1851, 'though knocking and ringing at doors continued throughout the whole day, nothing seemed to answer'. There were too many chiefs with too much unwillingness to subordinate their claims in this tight little political world, undisciplined most of the time by the urgent pressure of great national questions or aroused public opinion. 'England has been in a dreadful state for some weeks', wrote Dickens in *Bleak House* in 1853. 'Lord Coodle would go out, Sir Thomas Doodle wouldn't come in, and there being nobody in Great Britain (to speak of) except Coodle and Doodle, there has been no Government.'[43]

In the Coodling and Doodling stakes, Disraeli carried a large handicap. Some combination he was bound to seek, if his party was to get and keep office, yet since he was not a part of the aristocratic freemasonry of the inner circle of the political elite, he was likely to find himself on the outside of any arrangement to which it came. Hence he found himself constantly offering to facilitate a fusion the success of which might be fatal to his chances. There was no prospect of the leading Peelites agreeing to serve in the Commons under the man who had helped to assassinate their hero; so he offered to surrender the lead to Graham or Gladstone, or to act under young Stanley. Similarly, in 1852 and 1855, he was willing to give up the lead in order to bring in Palmerston, though he had managed to convince himself (with signal misjudgement) that, as Palmerston was now 'an old man, not capable of sustained exertion', the real authority would remain in his hands. He was protected from the submersion of his ambitions in any of these coalitions, partly by the mincing reluctance of the Peelites to surrender their political purity and the robuster determination of Palmerston to assert his own pre-eminence, partly by the desire of Lord Derby to run his own ship even at the price of exclusion from office (which, as John Vincent has pointed out, made Disraeli a useful tool for fending off mergers which would have undermined both their positions), and a good deal by the dislike of the old protectionist backbenchers for any injection of Peelite leadership, especially if it came in the overbearing and tactless form of Gladstone, whose unpopularity with the Conservative party was sometimes so marked as to expose him to the risk of physical insult in the Carlton Club, of which he was still a member. Disraeli has sometimes been seen as the only real obstacle to the return of Gladstone and the Peelites to the Conservative ranks, yet it was as much Gladstone's as his power of repulsion that ruled out what often seemed a natural, even inevitable, reunion.[44]

Failure to make friends doomed the Conservatives to near continuous opposition for twenty years after the disruption of 1846, but it kept Disraeli in his place. It is hard to say whether the frustration of denial of office was relieved or sharpened by the fact that for much of that period he led the largest single party in the Commons, its strength varying from about 230 members after the general election of 1847 to just over 300 after that of 1859, in a house of 654. The bedrock of the party was its ability to win around two-thirds of the English and Welsh and perhaps half of the Scottish and Irish county seats, which together accounted for over half its Commons strength. What prevented its progression from this formidable, overwhelmingly rural base to a national majority was its inability, even in the good year of 1859, to capture more than a third of the 395 borough seats. The Conservatives did not lack strength in the boroughs. They could always take a substantial number of those smaller boroughs which were closely attuned to the agrarian economy around them and susceptible to the influence of landed society. In the large towns, there were commercial interests of traditionally Conservative affiliation, like shipping and sugar, and even in the liberally minded and largely nonconformist bastions of manufacturing industry, A. C. Howe's study of the cotton masters has observed a steady advance of Conservatism among 'the men of growing wealth and social aspiration pushed towards the "politer faith" by the radicalism of the "Manchester School"' (and sometimes, Bright and Bagehot felt, by socially ambitious wives).[45] Yet this support was not strong enough to take the Conservatives over the threshold of national victory. In the twenty-nine towns in the leading manufacturing districts identified by Robert Stewart, they could take in the elections of 1847 to 1865 only from nine to thirteen of the forty-five seats, and never one in Birmingham or Manchester.[46] The effect of the 1846 split had been to settle the party back on its agricultural haunches just as the country was taking the decisive turn from a predominantly agrarian to a predominantly urban and industrial society. Only the drastic under-representation (in proportion to population and property) of the great centres of industry in the midlands and the north allowed this party of the shires and of the south of England the parliamentary strength which kept the possibility of power in sight.

In December 1856, Derby was 'surprised to find how mere fidelity to party ties, and some personal feeling, has for so long a time kept together so large a body of men, under most adverse circumstances and in the absence of any cry or leading question to serve as a broad line of demarcation between the two sides of the House'. Keeping the Conservatives together as a fighting force in the dispiriting circumstances of apparently permanent minority was Disraeli's ungrateful task as steward of the Stanleys' political estate. The party's central organisation, shattered in 1846, was rebuilt, Disraeli's solicitor, Philip Rose, taking over the supervision of electoral management in 1853. Disraeli tried to do something about the Conservatives' ineptitude in the cultivation of public opinion, a point totally neglected by his chief, who disliked the press and 'public curiosity'. From 1850, he was much involved in the schemes to set up a Conservative newspaper which resulted in the appearance of the weekly *Press* in 1853. 'It seems', ran his circular appeal for money, 'that the whole ability of the country is arrayed against us, and the rising generation is half ashamed of a cause which would seem to have neither wit nor reason to sustain and adorn it.' Though he supplied as much wit and reason as he could with his own pen, the *Press* was always in financial straits and was sold in 1858. In the end, the 'rising generation', that constant object of Disraeli's seductive powers, would have to be won, not by giving the party more efficient organisation and better public relations, but by finding for it a more effective political function. Malmesbury told Derby in 1856 that the Conservatives could find an inspiriting role only against 'a Minister who attacks our Institutions', a desideratum which the prime minister of that moment, Palmerston, had no intention of supplying. Until it should turn up, Derby's strategy in opposition, as analysed by Angus Hawkins, was to exacerbate the differences among Whigs, Radicals and Peelites by doing nothing and taking no distinctive line which might unite them.[47] This may have been the only realistic course, but it was no good to Disraeli, who found himself the lightning conductor for the discontent which apparent lack of direction caused among the backbenchers, and could not afford his leader's lofty indifference to short-term success. To sustain morale he had to show his hard-riding followers some sport, and to achieve power he needed to find openings which could enlarge their electoral appeal.

In the terms of parliamentary opposition, showing them an exciting line across exhilarating country meant embarrassing the government and threatening its majority whenever opportunity offered, but that too easily led Disraeli into tactical combinations which offended their prejudices and revived doubts about his soundness. For the ordinary Tory backbencher, his most disturbing tendency was to look to the Irish Roman Catholics, the union of whom with the Conservative party, he told Stanley in 1861, had been his object for twenty years. Ever since his Wycombe speech of December 1834, Disraeli had offered concessions to Irish Catholic sentiment, on the theory that Ireland, being 'agricultural, aristocratic, and religious', ought naturally to be Tory, with a little careful handling (as, electorally, half of it was in 1859).[48] He had backed Bentinck's large-visioned scheme of 1847 for Ireland, including endowment of the Catholic church, tenants' compensation for improvements, taxes on absentee landlords, and extensive railway development financed by Treasury loans. It was Russell and Palmerston who were playing the Orange cards in the 1850s, and Disraeli who might have pre-empted Gladstone's mission to pacify Ireland, but such leanings were too much for Tory protestantism to swallow, and Disraeli had to rein in, though his support of the temporal power of the Pope when it was threatened by the new Italian kingdom continued to give him a claim on Catholic sympathies, and in 1864 he refused to meet Garibaldi when the latter visited London.

Another provocative tack was to court the Radicals of the Cobden and Bright school. Disraeli respected Bright and the 'naturally well-bred' Cobden, and it was in character for him to divert himself by seeking a combination with fellow outsiders against the Whig 'official classes' who kept him and them out of office. Again, the association was not one his backbenchers could readily understand, but it consorted logically enough with his effort to solve the central conundrum of practical Conservative policy after 1846, how to give satisfaction to the claims of the agricultural interest without alienating that commercial and manufacturing interest which was already assuming economic and might one day achieve political preponderance. If Disraeli told young Stanley in 1851 that the 'real struggle of the present day was between country and town' and regarded the protection of the landed interest and the 'territorial constitution' as fundamentals of Conservative policy, he was none the less well able to see the futility of attempting to wage from the rural and Conservative side the kind of class war that some Radicals were eager to pursue from their fortresses in the great provincial towns. Whatever his strictures against the soulless, mechanical principles and narrow class ambitions of the free traders of 'the school of Manchester' (a term he seems to have invented), he understood that some composition between Manchester and the broad acres was the only way forward for the country and the Conservative party, and that the latter, as he was urging on his colleague Malmesbury in January 1853, must do something to make itself less unpalatable to urban taste.[49]

The line he initially chose, like his line on Ireland, owed a good deal to the practical ingenuity of his old commander George Bentinck, whose protectionism had embraced the idea of using a redistribution of taxation to place the agriculturalist and the manufacturer on an even footing. The primary objective of Disraeli's leadership from 1849 was to reconcile his followers to his conviction that protection (for which as an absolute principle he insisted that he had never contended) was not, in an expanding commercial and manufacturing country, a viable foundation for a party which aspired to win power. The means were to draw their attention away from protection to the removal of the unfair handicap arguably imposed on the land by the system of local taxation, which threw the whole of the charge for such communal burdens as poor relief, the administration of justice and the repair of roads on to real property. Disraeli's main proposal was to meet half the rates from national funds. But, as Avner Offer has pointed out, the relief of real property would help not only the agriculturalist but the urban houseowners and shopkeepers who formed the Radical constituency in the large boroughs. It could assist Disraeli's desire to demonstrate that in fiscal matters 'we were not always playing Country against Town, an impolitic & unpopular position'.[50] It was potentially a bridge between the landed and the urban interest, and a way either of negotiating an understanding with the urban Radicals or of undercutting their hold on their voters.

When the rivalry of Russell and Palmerston caused the former to coodle out of office in February 1852 and allowed Lord Derby to doodle in, Disraeli, feeling, as he said, 'just like a young girl going to her first ball', found himself a minister at last, without a day of official experience behind him, perhaps the least likely, probably the least solvent, chancellor of the exchequer in British history, and leader of the

Commons as well, reporting their proceedings to the Queen, she noted, 'much in the style of his books'. His creative ingenuity in that first, short taste of power flowed into the attempt to use the adjustment of taxation to compensate for the fact that protection was excluded by the 'spirit of the age', as he put it in his address for the July general election which punctuated the ministry and left it still in a minority in the Commons.[51] He did not deal with the rates, but in his second budget of the year, in December, made a different but typically audacious bid for success in that most critical and complex strategic area of Victorian politics, the balancing and reconciling of interests through the mechanism of fiscal fair play. The kernel of his plan was to give considerable help to the agricultural interest by halving the malt tax and the hop duty and assessing farmers' profits to income tax at one-third instead of one-half of rental, while at the same time appealing to a broader spectrum by reducing the tea duty and by meeting a favourite Radical, though not only Radical, proposal to distinguish for income-tax purposes between 'precarious' (earned) and 'permanent' (unearned) incomes – the former to pay 5¼d in the pound instead of the standard rate of 7d which would continue to fall on the latter.

There were two fatal flaws. One was that, pressed like most chancellors by defence spending, Disraeli had to compensate for the lost revenue by lowering the income-tax exemption limit and lowering the exemption limit and doubling the rate of the house tax, which countered the advantages offered by differentiation of the income tax, and made it easy to represent his proposals as paying for the concessions to the farmers out of the pocket of the urban property-owner. Worse, in his inexperience, he had altogether failed to grasp the intricacies of the income-tax schedules, which could not provide the neat division he wished to make between earned and unearned incomes. This left him a sitting target for the weight of financial expertise on the opposite benches, and despite his efforts to gain Radical help via Bright, his budget and the government went down to defeat on 17 December 1852. The *coup de grâce* was delivered by Gladstone, 'choked with passion',[52] in an attack which provided one of the most dramatic scenes in parliamentary history, and did much to render his return to the Conservative party impossible. His emotion perhaps derived from a recognition that

Disraeli was attempting to steal his stock-in-trade. It was significant that he invoked the name of Pitt, for it was precisely the Pittite-cum-Peelite tradition of executive competence in managing the great interests of the nation to which Disraeli was attempting to lay claim, as he must if the Conservative party was to appear capable of governing. The chancellor was trying to beat the self-righteous votaries of that tradition at their own game, which they were determined not to allow him to play. His refusal subsequently to hand over to Gladstone, who succeeded him at the exchequer, the chancellor's official robe which he believed Pitt to have worn, symbolised not a mania for mementoes but a determination to clothe himself in what he had long painted as the true mantle of Toryism.

The budget of 1852 was a setback, but Disraeli meant to go on infringing the patent of the official men opposite, and responding to the instinct of the great centres of industry and commerce, as indeed of the country as whole, for government which should be both efficient and cheap. Having already shown interest in the subject in 1852, he quickly latched on to the vogue for administrative reform stimulated by the wretched mismanagement of the Crimean War. This was a more promising line than the attempt to get up a majority against the government on a peace cry, which rested chiefly, the whip, Jolliffe, told Derby, on the argument that it was 'impossible for a party to exist without a policy, and still less possible for an opposition to be of the same policy as the Government'. Disraeli, as Lord Blake points out, was establishing the tradition that it is the business of the opposition to oppose, but Derby and the party were unsympathetic. The attack on the conduct of the war, however, was one in which Conservatives could join, at least to the extent that the charge of aristocratic incompetence in government could be directed at the great Whig official class rather than at the upper classes as a whole. Disraeli busied himself in 1855 with a large scheme for reconstruction of the government machine, and assured Stanley: 'It is the subject of the age, so far as English politics are concerned, and we, fortunately, at present may have it.'[53]

The real high road to popularity in the country, however, seemed to be economical finance, a cause jeopardised, Conservatives could argue, by Palmerston's rumbustious foreign policy and the military and naval costs it entailed. Disraeli's 1857 election address charged Palmerston with diverting attention from his lack of domestic policy through a 'turbulent and aggressive' external system which produced 'excessive expenditure, heavy taxation, and the stoppage of all social improvement'. 'A good management of the finances', Disraeli urged on Derby in October 1858, during his second term at the exchequer, 'is the only thing which really will get the country with us, and make us independent of Court and Parliament.' Sixteen months of office in another minority administration, however, gave him scant opportunity to emulate the national fisco-political reputation which Gladstone had established with his great budget of 1853, and would consolidate in 1860. 'Expenditure', as his own maxim had it, 'depends on policy', and the needs of defence policy again pressed hard on him in 1858–9. 'If we could only control the military departments in their ignorant waste', he sighed to Derby.[54]

Back in opposition a few months later, he was pressing Palmerston's government to achieve economy through a friendly understanding with Napoleon III which would remove the spectre of French invasion and permit a general reduction of armaments. This line consorted with his fixed belief that England and France working together could always ensure the peace of Europe, and with the personal diplomacy he had conducted with Napoleon behind the back of the foreign secretary, Malmesbury, in 1858–9, when he feared that England might be obliged to support Austria against a French intervention in favour of Italian independence. It might bring him at moments close to the pacifistic Radicals of the Cobdenite school, for whom free trade was the beneficial mechanism which would establish community of interest between nations and render unnecessary and absurd the military and naval establishments which supplied employment for the younger sons of the aristocracy at vast expense to the taxpayer. Disraeli had favoured in 1852 the sort of commercial treaty with France which Cobden was to negotiate in 1860. Yet that kind of alignment was not the key to strength in the great urban constituencies, where increasingly the creed of Bright and Cobden was at a discount as Palmerston displayed his ability to appeal to what E. D. Steele has characterised as a 'righteous and aggressive Protestant nationalism' powerful among both the middle classes and the unenfranchised, offering national self-satis-faction on the cheap by bullying weak states like China and Brazil, while avoiding the kind of confrontation with the strong that would have meant serious expenditure.[55]

The difficulty of wresting from the hands of Gladstone and his like the great engine of sound finance and equitable taxation which lay at the heart of mid-Victorian government limited the Conservatives' chances to emerge once again as a party able to deal with national requirements in a safe but progressive spirit. Yet that was what they had to do, if they were to snap the bonds that pinned them down to a pre-dominantly agricultural base and a permanent parliamentary minority. They could attempt it only in office, and Derby's second ministry of 1858–9 presented an opportunity that he and Disraeli tried hard to exploit. Derby's negativism in opposition, where his principal exertion of authority was often to check Disraeli's running after Radicals and Irish, on the ground that it made no sense to risk the alienation of tried supporters by the pursuit of casual liaisons, was replaced when in office by a venturesome readiness to establish the Conservatives as a realistic governmental option by following the moderately liberal line that came easily enough to one of his Canningite background, so much so that Angus Hawkins has claimed that it was really he who 'educated the mid-Victorian Conservative party'.[56] Disraeli did not need to prompt his chief in what he described in August 1858 as their endeavour 'to reconstruct the party on a wider basis, and ... to lay the foundation of a permanent system', though his vision of that reconstruction tended, perhaps to run somewhat ahead of Derby's, as when he urged that the latter's son, Stanley, who had joined his father's cabinet despite his feeling that his natural place was on the other side, should stand for a Manchester seat.

It will be [he wrote to Stanley] the inauguration of our new, and still infant, school; a public and national announcement that the *old* Whig monopoly of liberalism is *obsolete* ... our position is this: we represent progress, which is essentially practical, against mere Liberal opinions, which are fruitless. We are prepared to do all which the requirements of the State and the thought and feeling of the country will sanction: anything beyond that is mere doctrinaire gossip, which we should studiously avoid.[57]

This approach was both the natural expression of Disraeli's consistent endeavour to relieve Toryism of all that was 'obsolete, inconvenient, and … even odious', as he had put it in the *Vindication*, and, as Peter Ghosh has suggested, his indirect tribute to Peel – his resumption of the latter's bid for the support of all those who were more interested in the cause of cautiously progressive government than in the contentions of party, even though the strenuous exploitation of party which was Disraeli's only road to success made it hard for him to lend plausibility to that line. It was the Toryism of Tamworth, as prefigured in the Wycombe speech of December 1834 in which Disraeli had cleared his way to enter parliament on Peel's coat-tails. That his opponents would do everything to prevent his occupying the centre ground in this way, Disraeli well knew. 'The more Liberal our measures', he told his colleague Pakington in April 1858, 'the less inclined they will be to accept them. They will never permit us to poach on their manor, and we must postpone our Liberal battue until we have a Conservative majority.' Yet a start could be made even in a minority, and the government of 1858–9 could claim to be a reforming administration in its short life. Its main achievement was to settle the future government of India following the Mutiny and the need to replace the rule of the East India Company. Disraeli, who had criticised the repression of the Mutiny, protesting against 'meeting atrocities by atrocities', was spoken of as a possible first viceroy, but tempting though the proposal might have been, he was not to be disposed of that way.[58] On the domestic front, the principal initiatives sought to improve the representative character of parliament. A measure admitting practising Jews was at last carried, and the property qualification required of MPs in England and Ireland was abolished. More strikingly, in 1859 the Conservatives introduced a bill for parliamentary reform.

Of all Derby's and Disraeli's studied breaches of Liberal copyright, this was the most daring and the most necessary. They were not obliged to tackle reform by any weight of opinion (Bright's efforts to rouse the country for it resembled punching a feather mattress), but the question drifted in the political air and seeped into the mind of every government. The great political paradox of the 1850s and 1860s was the presentation of no fewer than six ministerial reform bills to a parliament that did not want reform and a public that was largely indifferent to it. No one could be sure what any major adjustment of the 1832 settlement would bring. Even those Radicals who spearheaded the pressure for reform were often ambivalent about it. Their chief interest lay in a redistribution of seats in closer conformity with property and population, which would give increased representation to the great urban centres of their influence in the midlands and the north. That could hardly be passed through a House of Commons the members of which disliked tampering with their own constituencies, unless it appeared as the necessary concomitant of a large extension of the franchise, reinforcing the case for giving more seats to the populous areas and helping Radicals to mobilise working-class support behind the reform cause. They could not be sure, however, that franchise extension would not loosen their grip on the places they had come to regard as their strongholds. There was little enthusiasm for reform among Whigs, but it was a useful question with which to secure Radical support, especially for Russell, manoeuvring for supremacy against Palmerston and regarding reform as his personal speciality. It was he who declared open season on further constitutional change by renouncing the 'finality' he had proclaimed in 1832, and introducing bills in 1852 and 1854.

Conservatives had no interest in clinging to representative arrangements that they felt to have been rigged against them in 1832, and that had given them only one general election victory since then; and they had every interest in not allowing their opponents to establish an exclusive right to satisfy any national need for constitutional change. Control of any measure that was to be passed was vital. Improvement of Conservative electoral prospects might seem to hang on correcting the under-representation of the county constituencies and removing from them the freehold voters dwelling in towns, who supplied an unwelcome urban challenge to the dominance of the landed interest. But that required care, for redistribution according to property and population would increase the weight in the Commons of the industrial counties and the big towns even more than of the agricultural counties. Whether franchise extension would help the Conservatives either in county or in town was an even murkier question.

In Disraeli's approach to parliamentary reform, the high national interest of sustaining the territorial constitution and the power of the landed classes exactly coincided with the tactical advantage of the Conservative party. The Liberal majority of the mid-century had to be prevented from making the representative system any more unfavourable to Conservative prospects, and the Conservatives had to take any promising opportunity to show that, in so far as a revision of the 1832 act could be held to be an essential element of national progress, they were as well able to supply it as anybody. Though Disraeli belonged in many respects to the organicist strain of conservatism, that did not involve him in any reverential attitude to constitutional details. The English constitution, he had argued in 1835, was 'a conventional arrangement', resting on a compact. As such, it could be altered, so long as the alteration conformed to the national spirit which it was the function of Toryism to express. That excluded democracy on the American pattern so profoundly admired by the Bright school. In *Lord George Bentinck*, Disraeli contended that 'ancient communities like the European must be governed either by traditionary influences or by military force', and insisted that 'the great transatlantic model' could not provide a viable third term for Britain, since the social and political conditions on which it rested found no analogy in Britain.[59]

Disraeli's notion, as he expressed it in June 1848 in the debate on Hume's motion for parliamentary reform, was of a hierarchical polity in which the gentlemen of England performed their natural function of leading the people, and the vote was not a right or a trust, but a privilege to be conferred. His conception of the national and popular character of the Conservative party made it impossible to admit that a large extension of the franchise to the working classes might be inimical to its interests. Under universal suffrage, he asserted in 1851, the artisans would prove to be for monarchy and empire. Yet there was no thought of using the franchise as a vehicle for an attempted alliance between the party and the working classes. That had never been the mechanism of Disraeli's popular politics, which in principle relied on the trading of paternalism for deference, not pledges for votes. In any case, the theme of the party and the people, as it had emerged in *Coningsby* and *Sybil*, was muted, once the novelist seeking to educate the public mind had been transformed into the party leader, necessarily pitching his voice to the narrow 1832 electorate, and the increase of prosperity had deprived the social question of much of the centrality and urgency it had possessed in the forties. The commitment to raising the moral and social condition of the working classes 'by lessening their hours of toil – by improving their means of health – and by cultivating their intelligence', affirmed in Disraeli's Buckinghamshire election address of 1847, was only fitfully pursued. The Protectionists saw the ten-hours bill through in 1847, and Manners in particular among them looked to strike up an understanding with the operatives, but Disraeli's resistance to the whittling down of the act three years later was balanced by his simultaneous opposition to an inspection of mines bill, to please his coal-owning friend, Lord Londonderry. Both the public health bill of 1848 and the General Board of Health bill of 1854 were opposed on the ground of their centralising tendency. The cultivation of intelligence came off rather better. Disraeli suggested to Derby in December 1853 that education was one of the subjects on which a Conservative opposition might be built, and took the same line in response to Pakington's educational enthusiasms thirteen months later, when an education minister, advocated by Stanley, figured in his plan of administrative reform.[60] Yet this was small beer, and the governments of 1852 and 1858–9, though willing to talk to the National Association of United Trades and friendly to attempts to give the co-operative societies legal status and to protect the legality of peaceful picketing, contemplated no initiatives of a kind designed to lay the basis of a combination between Toryism and the working classes.

Parliamentary reform would thus be a matter of partisan adjustment, rather than popular extension, of the electoral system. In October 1851, Disraeli accepted Derby's line of an open-minded attitude to reform, but resistance to any disturbance of the existing balance of interests which would give 'additional power to the congregation of large masses' and, in bringing the country franchise down to the £10 occupation level of the boroughs, would swamp the country electorate with voters dwelling in unrepresented towns. By April 1857, in the throes of electoral defeat and telling Derby that their party was 'now a corpse', he was looking to reform as a reviving cordial, urging his leader to consider 'whether a juster apportionment of MPs may not be the question on wh. a powerful & enduring party may be established', and suggesting adding fifty members to the counties at the expense of the small boroughs and taking into borough constituencies the urban householders who voted in counties, thus removing the balance of power from 'small Boro's wh. are ruled by cliques of Dissenters' (those early defeats at Wycombe never ceased to rankle).[61]

Derby did not then favour an initiative, but it was different in 1858, when his new government's address promised a reform bill, which he subsequently took a lead in formulating. The aim was to 'turn' the position of the Whigs as a reforming party, as Disraeli put it, adding: 'I fear nothing but our colleagues'. Two cabinet colleagues, in fact, Henley and Walpole, resigned over the main feature of the bill introduced in 1859, the lowering of the county occupation franchise to the £10 level obtaining in the boroughs, a step against which the Conservatives had steadily voted in the past, but which it was hard to avoid if they seriously desired to pass a measure, since the Commons had endorsed it on several occasions, the last in June 1858. It was possible to argue, in conformity with the advice that Disraeli and Philip Rose had obtained from the Conservatives' constituency agents, that the new county voters would be susceptible to Conservative influences, and that the landed interest was safeguarded from damage by the provision of the bill which met a longstanding Conservative demand by transferring urban freeholders from the county to the borough electorate. Fifteen seats were transferred from very small boroughs to the more populous counties and unrepresented towns. The creation of votes for lodgers, university graduates and professional men, and those with £10 a year from government stock or £60 in the Savings Bank or a government pension of £20, reflected Disraeli's feeling that the basis of the suffrage might usefully be varied; but he rejected a reduction of the £10 household franchise, levelling against the notion of 'democracy' the standard criticism of the day, that it would lead to a hostility to bearing public burdens combined with a great increase in public expenditure, to 'wars entered into from passion, and not from reason', to a reduction in the value of property, and to the erosion of freedom.[62]

Too extensive for the more cautious Whigs and too limited for the Radicals, the measure was not one that a minority ministry could carry.

The defeat of its second reading in March was followed by a general election which brought the Conservatives back about 306 strong, a gain of some thirty seats, but still a minority. Casting around for help to keep the government on its legs, Disraeli put aside his denunciation of democracy and sought Radical support for an enlarged reform bill, incorporating substantial redistribution and a reduction of the borough franchise to £6, more or less offering to carry any measure the Commons would accept. It was no use, and in June the government was finally turned out by that combination of Whigs, Radicals and former Peelites which provided the elements of what was increasingly known as the Liberal party.

Derby's and Disraeli's foray into Liberal territory in the ministry of 1858–9 ('everyone knows', said the latter, 'that all that we did would really have been done by our predecessors') enabled Disraeli plausibly to claim at Liverpool in October 1859 that the main result of his ten years' leadership had been to put an end to the 'monopoly of Liberalism'. It had not produced an electoral majority, however, and in so far as determination to repulse it had induced Russell and Palmerston to put aside their rivalry to form under the latter, and with Gladstone, an administration crammed with official weight and experience, it had left the Conservatives at more of a disadvantage than ever. Palmerston so commanded the crossroads where moderate liberalism and progressive conservatism intersected that the Conservative party had no vantage ground against him, and Derby assured him of its neutrality so long as his government held the more advanced tendencies of the Liberal majority firmly in check. Sounded by a newspaper editor about party policy, in March 1861, Stanley noted: 'I could tell him but little, for in truth there is no policy at this moment, except that of keeping quiet and supporting ministers.' Derby had had, as he put it himself, 'too much experience of the difference between strength enough to turn a Government out, and enough to put a Government in, to be in a hurry to repeat the experiments of 1852 and 1858'.[63]

Disraeli was in the same mood, telling Stanley in January 1862 that 'he had had enough of being a minister on sufferance, and did not wish for such a position again'. Stanley thought that this was sincere, 'for since 1859 there has been a marked change in his tactics: less apparent eagerness for office'.[64] There were at least three reasons for this uncharacteristic note of resignation, apart from Derby's instructions: weariness, lack of promising issues, and Disraeli's sense that snap combinations with Radicals or Irish to overturn a soundly conservative prime minister would be widely resented within the Conservative party. His party position was still insecure. For a decade he had had to bear the brunt of discontent both at the lack of distinctive Conservative policy and at the promiscuous parliamentary manoeuvrings with which he sought to compensate for it. His relationship with the backbenchers, even with leading colleagues, veered between the relatively close contact enforced by the parliamentary session, when he must be all the time in his place in the House, attentive and resourceful, watching through the long evening hours, often with only a handful of men behind him, sometimes walking home through the silent streets at three or four in the morning after a protracted sitting, and on the other hand the near-absolute detachment of the recess, when he could shut himself off at Hughenden to recuperate from this exhausting servitude and unnatural gregariousness. Disraeli was a wonderful House of Commons performer, not least in the interminable years of opposition, whose sinuousness and dexterity of argument, fertility of invention, vivacity of wit, force of sarcasm and power of endurance beneath the famous frozen imperturbability with which his features masked his feelings never ceased to enthral, fascinate and infuriate supporters and opponents alike. Yet he used the Commons as an arena in which he sought to dazzle and to dominate, rather than as a club in which he could be at ease among friends: this House was not a home.

Similarly, for all that he depended on party and, unlike Peel, accepted in the last resort the bonds of that dependence, he was no more intimate with it than Peel had been. The Conservatives were led by a stranger. In October 1855, the whip, Jolliffe, criticised Disraeli to Derby for keeping himself aloof from the bulk of the party, and by this time there was a distinct body of discontent with his leadership. Some of it had an anti-Semitic tinge. It was fashionable in malcontent circles to refer to 'the Jew', and Stanley noted that one of Disraeli's most prominent colleagues, Spencer Walpole, shared his wife's 'extreme jealousy of Disraeli, as a Jew, and as having counselled the admission of Jews to parliament'. The more serious misgiving, however, was that Disraeli had no attachment to Conservative principles. Even his friend, Stanley, could see little in him in the mid-fifties beyond a careerism displaying such strength of character as almost to be morally admirable.

It cannot be pretended [Stanley wrote] that he is attached to any political principles as such, or that his objects are disinterested and patriotic; yet singleness of purpose – contempt of obloquy – energy which no labour can exhaust – indifference to the ordinary pleasures and pursuits of men, which he neglects in search of power and fame – a temper usually calm, and patient under annoyances of the most trying kind – all this, joined with such intellectual powers as not one human being among a million can lay claim to, forms a combination rare in political or private life, and surely deserves some degree of respect.

Hesitating to join his father's cabinet in 1858, Stanley placed first among the disadvantages: 'Connection with Disraeli. Able as he is, this man will never command public confidence.'[65] Others shared Stanley's criticisms without his charity, notably the young Lord Robert Cecil, who first came to prominence with his acid journalistic attacks in 1859–60 on 'the Artless Dodger' who betrayed the Conservative cause to further his ambition by combining with the Radicals to beat the Whigs. In this climate of suspicion, Disraeli could not afford to seek chance alliances to ambush Palmerston and snatch at office which could be sustained only by buying Radical acquiescence.

That left few openings for political initiative in the early 1860s. In these doldrum years, Disraeli's only specifics for personal and party advancement were the impeccably Conservative ones of cultivating the crown and championing the church. 'The opinions and the prejudices of the Crown', he had declared at Wycombe in December 1834, 'must necessarily influence a rising statesman'. In the fifties he gradually wore down the mistrust that Queen Victoria had expressed on Derby's first proposing him for office, partly by hitching his star to the Prince Consort. He genuinely admired Albert's breadth of intellect, and seems to have thought that the Prince was working towards that reassertion of the power of the crown which, in *Coningsby* and *Sybil*, he had seen as the necessary mainspring of national political regeneration, 'establishing court-influence on ruins of political party ... with perseverance equal to that of George the Third, and talent infinitely greater', as he put it to Stanley. If he had hopes of playing the court Jew to a revived monarchy, Albert's death in December 1861 put paid to them, but he was able to capitalise on it by feeding the bereaved Queen's appetite for fulsome praise of the husband she idolised. 'The Prince', he told her in 1863, 'is the only person, whom Mr. Disraeli has ever known, who realized the Ideal ... There was in him an union of the manly grace and sublime simplicity, of chivalry with the intellectual splendor of the Attic Academe.' The tribute was no less toadying in its expression for being largely sincere in its content. 'He assumes vanity to be the ruling passion with all, and treats them accordingly', wrote Stanley, noting that Disraeli habitually overdid the compliments. To Victoria's vanity, personal and vicarious, Disraeli pandered with a will, even though her husband's death, he thought, meant that the monarchy would revert to 'the old thing – the Venetian constitution – a Doge'. During the Schleswig-Holstein crisis of 1864, Stanley found it hard to unravel Disraeli's attitude to the support of Denmark against the German powers, but felt sure that he would be for peace 'so long as the Queen is on that side'.[66]

Reporting on the political events of 1860 to Victoria's kinsman, the King of the Belgians, with whom he had managed to strike up a connection, Disraeli picked out the 'appearance of a Church party in the House of Commons for the first time since 1840, and the fact of the clergy throughout the country again generally acting with the Conservatives'. He told Malmesbury in February 1861 that 'in internal politics there is only one question now, the maintenance of the Church', and began to star incongruously at diocesan meetings as the defender of the Anglican establishment and its privileges against what seemed to be a swelling tide of nonconformist aggression, encouraged by the government in order to placate the Radicals. This was represented at the extreme by the Liberation Society's demand for disestablishment, and in annual parliamentary combat by bills for the abolition of church rates and the legalisation of nonconformist burial services in the church's graveyards, and by efforts to break down the church's grip on the universities, the endowed schools and the denominational system of elementary education. In 1852, Disraeli had coupled protestantism with protection in referring Henry Lennox to *Coningsby* to see how he had treated 'those exclusive and limited principles, clearly unfitted for a great and expanding country, of various elements, like this of ours', and his anxiety to attract Catholic support had for the most part kept him from encouraging the narrower religious prejudices of his party, which, like George Bentinck, he despised.[67] But by 1860 the whipping up of Anglican feeling had clear political attractions. Church defence might give the party an unimpeachably Conservative rallying-cry and Disraeli common ground with some of his sharpest critics, like Robert Cecil. It offered a means of undercutting the appeal of Gladstone to a wide spectrum of Anglican opinion, and a prospect of mobilising in the clergy an electoral auxiliary of considerable power. It was almost the only sphere in which Palmerston's conservatism did not altogether deprive the Conservative party of the conservative ground. Yet there was more to it than simple tactical convenience. If it was not possible to find the inspirational agency of national greatness in a reinvigorated monarchy, a reinvigorated church was the only alternative.

Encroaching boldly on Gladstonian territory, Disraeli stressed the national character and role of the Church of England and the need for government to be allied with the religious principle, while acknowledging, as Gladstone had had to do, the practical concessions that had to be made to the fact of religious plurality in Britain. For the church to perform the function he designed for it, it was not enough that its privileges should be protected and that its activity in national life should be made more effective through popular education, an extended episcopate, better-paid clergy, greater lay participation and other measures which he advocated at this period. The first essential was that it should maintain, unimpaired by the biblical criticism and theological innovation astir in its own ranks, its distinctive dogmatic teachings, formative of the national character on which the maintenance of the empire depended. Man's need to adore and to obey, as Sidonia had called it, could not be satisfied by confusion of doctrine. Free enquiry was not for them, Disraeli told the clergy at Aylesbury in 1861; and at Oxford in 1864, on the occasion usually remembered for the superficial jibe at the evolutionists in which he chose the side of the angels in the debate over the origins of humankind, he threw himself into the controversies engendered by the critical theology of men like Jowett and Colenso, denouncing them as purveyors of secondhand learning, derived from Germans who themselves (he typically asserted) had been anticipated by great Hebrew scholars. Freethought had helped to bring about the French Revolution, and if thrown upon his own devices for lack of institutional guidance, man would 'find altars and idols in his own heart and his own imagination'.[68]

This vision of a disciplined and disciplining national faith in union with the state did not take. Disraeli was too shallow a theologian and too implausible a lay preacher to arrest the arguments sparked off by *Essays and Reviews* or satisfy all shades of religious sentiment within the Conservative party, where not everyone relished his tactical alliance with the aggressive high churchmanship of Bishop Wilberforce or thought the danger to the church substantial as long as Palmerston held power. Church defence did not prove a successful cry in the constituencies, and in the general election of 1865 the Conservatives slipped back by about fifteen seats. 'Our game must be purely defensive', Derby told Disraeli, 'and we must be ready to support the moderate portion of the Cabinet, and watch for every opportunity of widening the breach between them and the Rads.' It was not an inspiriting prospect, and Disraeli talked of standing down to facilitate Derby's formation of a broad 'anti-revolutionary' combination. Writing 'in the decline of life', he told Derby on 6 August: 'I look upon my career in the House of Commons, so far as office is concerned, to have concluded ... The leadership of hopeless opposition is a gloomy affair, and there is little distinction when your course is not associated with the possibility of future power.' This was not the first time that he had talked of giving up. He had now reached sixty, and the toil of 'hopeless opposition' was beginning to show. 'D. seems to me either growing old or in weak health', Stanley noted in February 1864, 'he has lost his former vivacity, and sleeps much in his seat.' A year later: 'Disraeli's increasing apathy to public affairs is becoming a subject of general remark.' Stanley put this down to the state of politics, advancing age, occasional difficulty in working with Derby, 'between whom and him there is no very cordial feeling', and, possibly, the effect of the Brydges Willyams legacy in making office less of a financial object (he might have added that since

1859 Disraeli had been receiving a parliamentary pension of £2,000 a year).[69]

It was at this period that Disraeli was jotting down the fragments of recollection, anecdote, vignette and aphorism published by the Swartzes as his *Reminiscences*, which suggest that he was assembling the materials for memoirs to be written in retirement. 'I think myself', one of these notes read, 'that age, to a certain degree is a habit.' It was a habit that Disraeli seemed to be acquiring in the frustrating process of hanging at Palmerston's coat-tails, conducting an opposition the strategy of which was not to oppose. Yet through the damp chill of disappointment and despond the stimulus of events could still pierce to re-ignite the spark of eager excitement at the turns of fortune's wheel. 'It is a privilege to live in this age of rapid and brilliant events', Disraeli told Mrs Brydges Willyams in December 1862. 'What an error to consider it a utilitarian age! It is one of infinite romance. Thrones tumble down and crowns are offered, like a fairy tale, and the most powerful people in the world, male and female, a few years back, were adventurers, exiles, and demireps. *Vive la bagatelle!*'[70]

5

TOP OF THE BILL, 1865–1881

FORTUNE's wheel turned for Disraeli in October 1865, when Palmerston, whose prolonged mental and physical vigour had baffled the Conservatives for a decade, uncharacteristically died. It had long been expected that his departure would allow the more active elements of the Liberal party, with Gladstone foremost, to embark on a programme of change in which parliamentary reform was likely to figure prominently. 'The truce of parties is over. I foresee tempestuous times, and great vicissitudes in public life', wrote Disraeli, evidently relishing the idea. 'It seems', Stanley noted on 26 October, 'as if the prospect of renewed political life had excited him afresh, and that he had thrown off the lethargy which has been growing upon him for the last year or two.'[1]

The possibility that Gladstonian energy would revive the Conservatives' fortunes by frightening into their ranks those middle-of-the-roaders whom Palmerston had held in thrall was an enlivening one, but there was a tactical problem in striking a sufficiently anti-movement line to capture the Palmerstonians without abandoning the claim of the Conservative party to play its part in the solution of national questions in a liberal and progressive spirit, which it had been the endeavour of the 1858–9 ministry to establish. The issue of parliamentary reform rendered it acute. In recent years, there had been so little wind in the sails of the reformers that Disraeli had more or less repudiated the willingness he had shown in 1859 to lower the £10 borough franchise and had re-emphasised his hostility to democracy. His first thought after Palmerston's death was apparently that the Conservatives might help the new government under Earl Russell to pass a very moderate measure. On the other hand, he knew that a more substantial bill would probably be opposed by enough moderates on the Liberal benches to bring the ministry down and give the Conservatives another chance of office. In November 1865, in anticipation of Liberal dissension, he was recommending to Derby an anti-movement coalition to frustrate changes in church and state 'which neither the necessities of the country require, nor its feelings really sanction'.[2]

The Reform bill which Russell and Gladstone brought forward in March 1866 was a larger measure than either most Conservatives or most Liberals had hitherto contemplated, purporting to add some 400,000 males, about half of whom were expected to be working men, to the existing English and Welsh electorate of just over a million, by reducing the borough household franchise to £7 rental and the county occupation franchise to £14. Disraeli was planning opposition even before it was introduced, despite Derby's hesitancy. The opportunity to exploit the divisions in the Liberal party by co-operating with the Whig-Liberal anti-reformers who became known as the Adullamites was too good to miss. There was no attraction in allowing Russell to crown his career by reasserting the Liberal monopoly of constitutional change with a bill seemingly framed to damage the Conservatives' electoral base by bringing into the county electorate copyholders and leaseholders resident, and hitherto voting, in parliamentary boroughs (though Disraeli's adviser on electoral statistics, Dudley Baxter, concluded, too late to affect the issue, that the new county occupation franchise would *help* the Conservatives). Nevertheless, in the classic debates to which the measure gave rise, Disraeli was content to let Robert Lowe and other Adullamites offer the most ringing declarations against reform and the most provocative aspersions on the working men whose enfranchisement was the crucial issue. When their resistance caused the government's collapse in June 1866, and projects of Conservative-Whig combination were redoubled, he demurred to inviting Lowe into any Derby cabinet because that 'would be rather too much of a challenge to the Reform party, and would look like the decided adoption of an anti-Reform policy, "while after all, perhaps, we may be the men to settle the question"'.[3] The point of working with the Adullamites to wreck the bill had been to keep Conservative options on reform open, not to close them.

A triumphant Whig settlement of reform on a basis inimical to the Conservative party's chances was only the first of the dangers Derby and Disraeli had to avert. The second was the destruction of the party's integrity and of their own careers in the junction of Conservatives with anti-reform Whigs which the logic of events now seemed to dictate. As in 1865 Disraeli offered to surrender his own position to help Derby construct a broad-based ministry. As he perhaps expected, he was saved from extinction by the unwillingness of the Whig grandees and the Adullamites to join any government of which they did not have the lead, and the characteristic determination of Derby to take no place but the first. Coalition proved impossible, and Derby was coaxed by his lieutenant into taking office for the third time with a purely Conservative ministry, in a minority of about eighty in the House of Commons, but rendered a good deal stronger than its predecessors by the presence in cabinet of such rising men as Robert Cecil (now Viscount Cranborne), Stafford Northcote and Gathorne Hardy. The third danger, which Derby and Disraeli were resolved to avert, was that the new government would be a mere inglorious stop-gap which, as in 1859, the Liberals would overturn as soon as they had composed their differences. Parliamentary reform was likely to be a main test of the ministry's capacity to survive and even to prosper.

While no less a terrain for party manœuvre, the reform issue had assumed greater substance and urgency than when Derby and Disraeli had experimented with it in 1859. The argument had made headway that the growth in prosperity and respectability of the skilled portion of the working classes meant that it could safely be entrusted with the privileges and responsibilities of political participation. The debates of early 1866 had aroused expectation of a settlement and helped to stim-ulate the emergence of a sizeable agitation orchestrated by the Reform League among the working classes of the great towns, against the dis-turbing background of trade depression and a serious outbreak of the cholera. The Hyde Park riots of 22–3 July, when the Reform League's supporters forcefully asserted against the government's ban their right to meet in the Park, and the ability of Bright to attract huge crowds to reform demonstrations in the midlands and north in the latter half of the year, reminded politicians that they were now dealing with a real national question of potentially explosive force. They were not unnerved, but they could not be indifferent, and, if popular pressure did not force the Conservatives into reform, the need to quiet 'agitation' became an additional argument in favour of taking action. Disraeli used it in July (though apparently before the Hyde Park riots) when suggesting to Derby that they might get the issue out of the way quickly by passing a modified version of the bill they had just helped to defeat, and was to use it again in May 1867, a few days after another trial of strength between the government and the League over Hyde Park, as a handy justification for his acquiescence in the radical extension of the Conservatives' own measure. It was clearly in Derby's mind when he acknowledged in September 1866 that there was a 'genuine demand *now*, however it may have been excited' for 'a moderate and Conservative measure', and reluctantly concluded that the government would have to respond. It was an element in the Queen's anxiety to have her ministers settle the question, which bore powerfully on them from September onwards. If the Conservatives were going to renew the strategy of the 1858–9 ministry and poach on the Whigs' preserves, they might as well appropriate the classical constitutional function on which the Whigs prided themselves and, as Sir Francis Baring had put it, 'when the people are roused, stand between the constitution and revolution, and go with the people, but not to extremities'.[4]

Perhaps Derby's Whig antecedents helped him to recognise the merits of this concessionary argument. Disraeli, however, picked it up and put it down according to the fluctuations of a mood determined by his sense of what would keep the government from running on the rocks at Westminster, rather than by any attention to what itinerant spouters might be threatening at Birmingham or Manchester. After his initial idea of whisking the problem out of the way in the fag-end of the 1866 session, his inclination seems to have been to evade it if at all possible. In August, he suggested to Derby that a vigorous assault on Admiralty maladministration would divert opinion from reform,[5] and he fell only reluctantly into line with his chief's growing conviction that government initiative was unavoidable. His thinking at this moment is hard to unravel, but there is no overt sign of that intention to 'educate' his party on the subject of reform with which he would credit himself after the event. He was reconciled to Derby's decision to move only by the device which the latter suggested of proceeding by a series of generally phrased resolutions on reform, which would seek out in advance of a bill what might be acceptable to a House of Commons which had rejected five ministerial reform measures in fourteen years, and might revive and prolong the Liberals' disagreements.

To feel for what could be piloted through the Commons was a natural tactic for a minority government, but one vulnerable to the impatience of opponents and even of supporters that the ministry should show its hand. From the moment Disraeli introduced the government's resolutions on 11 February 1867, it was clear that only a bill would satisfy the House, and the cabinet had to make up its mind what constituted a safe conservative settlement. In December, as a subject to occupy the royal commission which the resolutions proposed, Derby had cheerfully put forward, as the best of 'all possible hares to start', household suffrage in the boroughs, coupled with additional votes to reinforce the influence of property (without plural voting, he told Disraeli in February, household suffrage would give the working classes a majority of nearly two to one in the boroughs, and 'our friends would not, and I think ought not, to listen to it for a moment').[6] This was the idea on which the success of the Conservative bill was to hinge. A Radical demand which Conservatives had conventionally opposed, the granting of votes on the basis of household occupancy could be made 'safe' in the terms of the day, not only by counterbalancing it with plural voting, but by limiting it by the test of personal payment of rates, which would exclude the large mass of householders, known as 'compounders', who paid through their landlords. In the cabinet discussions of early 1867, however, it proved too much for three ministers, Cranborne, the earl of Carnarvon and General Peel, who felt that the counterpoises and checks could not be guaranteed by a government without a majority, and that, in any case, the proposal would swamp the small borough constituencies which were vital to the Conservatives. To accommodate their fears and preserve its unity, the cabinet of 25 February dropped household suffrage from the measure which was to be presented that very afternoon to the party and then to the Commons, and cobbled together the so-called 'ten minute bill' on the basis of a £6 rating franchise. It was immediately obvious that this botch would pass muster neither with the House nor with the party. Disraeli was able to encourage, then exploit, feeling among the Conservative backbenchers in favour of household suffrage as the most likely route to a settlement, and on 2 March the cabinet reverted to that scheme, whereupon its three dissidents resigned. The bill introduced on 18 March made household suffrage conditional on two years' residence and on personal payment of rates, and counterbalanced it with the 'fancy franchises' – votes for educational qualifications, the possession of £50 in the funds or the Savings Bank, and payment of £1 a year in direct taxation – and with the dual vote, that is, a second vote for householders meeting the £1 direct taxation qualification. The county occupation franchise was reduced from £50 to £15.

This was the kind of measure, superficially radical in its leading provision, moderate in its overall effect, which Derby and Disraeli needed to play on Liberal divisions and give themselves a viable election platform if they were turned out, but the desire to achieve the first great parliamentary success which their party could claim for a generation bound them from the start to accept almost any modifications necessary to fight it through a House which they did not control. His son found Derby on 10 March 'bent on remaining in power at whatever cost, and ready to make the largest concessions with that object'.[7] In the course of a few weeks, the fancy franchises and the dual vote were struck out, the residence requirement was reduced to one year, a lodger franchise was introduced, and the county occupation franchise came down to £12, with £5 copyhold and leasehold franchises. These were matters of small moment, but on 17 May, without consulting a single colleague, Disraeli accepted the tenor of an amendment from the Liberal Hodgkinson, which, by abolishing the practice of compounding in parliamentary boroughs, opened the franchise to between 400,000 and 500,000 compound householders hitherto potentially excluded and ensured a working-class majority in the borough electorate.

For conspiracy theorists like Cranborne, this was proof that Disraeli had designed all along to inveigle his party into entrusting its fortunes to 'democracy'. In fact, the government had been trapped by its reliance on household suffrage as the 'principle' of its bill. Attractive in seeming to provide a logical and permanent resting point for the borough franchise (as indeed it was to do for fifty years), household suffrage became indefensible when combined with personal payment of rates, because the very uneven incidence of compounding would have produced vast anomalies between constituencies. Disraeli took the only course open to him to remove the problem while preserving the 'principle' and saving the bill. To his first lieutenant in the Commons, Gathorne Hardy, he emphasised that he had taken a chance to 'destroy the present agitation and extinguish Gladstone and Co.'.[8]

He had put the same two objectives to Derby in suggesting a coup on reform in July 1866, and the second was not the less important. Once the Reform bill was in the Commons, passing it became a matter of disrupting Gladstone's hold on the Liberal majority. The adoption of the rated household suffrage cry brilliantly achieved this, by attracting away from Gladstone the support of those Liberals who saw it as the basis of a comprehensive settlement and the means of avoiding a dissolution, or simply feared to oppose it, and thus preventing him from mobilising his party around the £5 rating line which he favoured as the foundation of a sound constituency. Working sometimes with the old friend of his rakish youth, James Clay, Radical MP for Hull, Disraeli was able to frustrate Gladstone's opposition to the bill and enjoy an outstanding parliamentary triumph, which not only enhanced his hold on the Conservative party at Westminster but established his reputation in the country. His new private secretary, Monty Corry, reported his aunt's carpenter in Shropshire as having 'heard say that Mr. Disraeli had laid Mr. Gladstone on his back'. It was near enough the truth. Gladstone was hampered by the fact that he understood a good deal of the intricate technicalities of reform in a House where few did: in the end his disquisitions became boring. His desire to stultify a government measure based on an apparently conclusive principle alienated men on all sides who wanted to get rid of the question and were afraid of a dissolution only two years after meeting the expenses of the last election. His imperious temper and his irritability played into the hands of a Disraeli who was, as Stanley would note later, 'quite aware of the advantage which he possesses in his natural calmness', and mockingly reflected how fortunate it was that 'a good broad piece of furniture' separated him from his furious opponent across the floor of the House.[9]

Disraeli's performance was an outstanding exhibition not only of parliamentary skill but of mental and physical endurance for a man in his sixty-third year. He thought at first that the task was impossible, and before his great speech closing the second reading debate on 26 March Stanley found him 'in a state of nervousness and depression almost painful to witness'. The whole conduct of the bill rested on his shoulders: there was often no time to consult colleagues on vital points. The unwearying assiduity, infinite tact with the House, fertility of resource and agility of mind with which he navigated his ship through innumerable shoals brought him to the summit of his parliamentary career. But, however ingenious, he could discomfit Gladstone and carry the bill only by turning household suffrage into a reality that would enlist the Liberal left and all those anxious for an apparently final settlement, and that meant abandoning the exclusion of the compounder that had initially recommended it as safe to his own backbenchers and to him. Perhaps in an effort to reassure the party, he promptly agreed to provisions that would have reduced the impact of Hodgkinson's amendment by allowing compounding to continue on an optional basis, but they had no chance of passing. His inviting his followers to embrace the compounder was hardly less of a facer than Peel's inviting his to relinquish the corn laws. Yet there was no revolt – Cranborne was more interested in winning arguments than in organising resistance, and the bulk of the backbenchers were swept on by the novel exhilaration of the only great party victory they could remember. The fillip to their sporting instincts was manifest in the words with which Disraeli was toasted in the Carlton Club after the first great division in which he had demonstrated his ability to foil Gladstone's attacks: 'Here's the man who rode the race, who took the time, who kept the time, and who did the trick!'[10]

It needs no more than the inspiration of party conflict and the ambition at all costs to succeed and stay in office to explain Disraeli's conduct of the 1867 reform bill and his acceptance of Hodgkinson's amendment. For both him and Derby, the essential objectives were those which they had pursued with less success in 1858–9 – in many ways a dry run for 1866–7. As he put it in his Mansion House speech towards the close of the session, echoing his Liverpool speech of

October 1859, they were 'the termination of the monopoly of Liberalism' over constitutional change, and the resumption of 'its natural functions in the government of the country' by a Tory party representative of 'national feeling'. The hopes of 'realising the dream of my life and re-establishing Toryism on a national foundation', of which Disraeli wrote to his friend Lord Beauchamp in April, a few days after the triumph which made him the toast of the Carlton Club, were of a piece with the aspirations he had expressed since he had first sought to turn the Tory party into the appropriate vehicle of his career. His vision of national and popular Toryism was social as well as – or more than – political. It rested on the notion of a nexus of reciprocal obligation uniting all orders in a mutually advantageous social hierarchy, which it was the function of the Tory party to represent and to preserve. Nothing in it dictated commitment to a very restricted franchise or precluded consideration of a very extensive one. Political representation was a function of the underlying social structure and an expression of the national character, both in the form it assumed and in the way it worked. Disraeli's reply to Radicals like Bright who preached the virtue of American democracy was simply that American institutions had no relevance to a traditionary society like England. The proper purpose of reform, he insisted in 1867, was not to recognise democratic rights but to extend popular privileges. He explained to the Commons:

Popular privileges are consistent with a state of society in which there is great inequality of condition. Democratic rights, on the contrary, demand that there should be equality of condition as the fundamental basis of the society which they regulate ... We do not, however, live – and I trust it will never be the fate of this country to live – under a democracy.

He was saying no more and no less than he had caused Egremont to say in *Sybil* more than twenty years earlier: 'The future principle of English politics will not be a levelling principle; not a principle adverse to privileges, but favourable to their extension. It will seek to ensure equality, not by levelling the Few, but by elevating the Many.'[11]

How far popular political privileges should be extended depended on the requirements of society, as interpreted in 1867 in the light of the inescapable dictates of party advantage and parliamentary manœuvre.

When, at the end of February and the beginning of March, Disraeli encouraged the growing feeling of his backbenchers in favour of household suffrage with personal payment of rates as the basis of a settlement, and used it to bring the cabinet back to its original intention, it seems that both he and they found the attraction of the proposal as much in its limitations as in its superficial generosity: the exclusion of the compounder was the essential barrier to a working-class predominance that no one desired. Yet when the compounder had to be hastily enrolled into the ranks of the respectable on whom political power could safely be conferred, Disraeli's conception of national and popular Toryism had no ideological difficulty in coping with him. To the extent that it was determinedly inclusive and integrationist, its logic and its rhetoric could assimilate almost any degree of enfranchisement, so long as its confidence in the capacity of social ties and influences to shape and bind the political sphere could be sustained. Gertrude Himmelfarb has suggested that it was easier for the Conservatives than for the Liberals to contemplate a large measure of reform, because where the latter tended to see an uncohesive, competitive society in which accretions of political power would naturally be employed as weapons in a social struggle, the former more easily assumed a social stability and order by which new political forces would be canalised and constrained – an argument that chimes with John Vincent's point that Disraeli was 'a Conservative social optimist, too sceptical to feel threatened or fearful as Liberal reactionaries genuinely did'.[12]

If Disraeli was guided by no concealed purpose to launch his party into 'Tory Democracy', he was certainly operating with a conception of Toryism which made it easy and in a sense obligatory to trust the political reliability of the people to any extent necessary to pass a Conservative reform bill.

What impact the electorate he was calling into being would have on Conservative fortunes, Disraeli could know no better than anyone else. Reassuring Derby on 28 February, he wrote: 'What are called the "working classes" in the small boroughs are those who are under the patronage of the Upper Classes and depend on them for employment and existence. In great towns the "working classes" are powerful trades formed into Unions and the employers are dependent on them.' The comment tends to substantiate the view of F. B. Smith and Lord Blake that, when Disraeli weighed the electoral implications of various reform proposals, he thought in terms of the politics he had known all his life, in which Toryism was based on the management by traditional methods of the counties and small towns, and had largely resigned itself to the predominance of the Liberals in the great centres of industry and commerce.[13] Social influences could be relied on to control the new electors in the small boroughs, where the Conservatives had many seats; in the large towns, where they had few, the influx of working-class votes would intensify the difficulties bourgeois Liberalism was experiencing in retaining its hold. Stanley had for some time been noting the social tensions in the Lancashire towns and their stimulus to Conservativism. Bright, he was told by an informant in 1863, was 'more feared by the leading mill-owners than by the aristocracy – the trade unions have caused the change'. A year later, he thought that there was no longer any 'quarrel between Ld. D and Manchester – meaning by Manchester not the Bright-Cobden section, but the leading merchants and manufacturers'.[14]

The trend of moderate middle-class opinion towards the Conservative party was marked by the mid-sixties. Up to the moment when the exigencies of the political situation demanded a reform bill from the Conservatives, cultivation of that opinion had encouraged a cautious attitude to reform. Once driven into a large measure, however, the Conservatives could hope that the advent of a working-class majority in the electorate of the great towns would in the long run hasten the movement of the middle classes. There was nothing here of confidence that the working-class voters might themselves prove positively Tory. But the suggestion that going down to a household suffrage line would discover, beneath the skilled artisans with their trade union and Radical propensities, a stratum open to Conservative influences, was a familiar one. Among cabinet ministers, Malmesbury had argued the advantage to the party of 'universal' suffrage as long ago as 1853; Carnarvon had heard Bagehot speak in a similar sense in November 1866; and Hardy agreed in 1867 with the bishop of Rochester that 'our security is in going lower than the combining class'. Disraeli is not known to have speculated along these lines, but there was little reason for him to shrink from a gamble on the new electorate's proving better than the old, which had refused him a majority at four successive general elections. The Liberal MP Sir William Gregory claimed later to recall having 'heard him a hundred times in private proclaim his preference for the working-man over the sleek, narrow-minded, dissenting rulers of the boroughs', and when Disraeli told the Queen in August 1876 that the 'Nonconformist party in the country has been weakened by the last Reform Bill', he was describing an effect for which, in 1867, he may have found reason to hope.[15]

In any case, it was not as big a gamble as it has often been made to appear. Disraeli was not prone to the exaggerated estimate of the significance of household suffrage that disturbed the sleep of some of his contemporaries and has distorted the vision of some historians. Whatever the extent of the borough franchise, its impact on the balance of political power was as always largely dependent on the distribution of parliamentary seats. Though here as elsewhere the government was pushed beyond its original intentions, the Reform act redistributed only 45 seats. Of those, 25 went to the counties and one to the University of London; only 15 went to new boroughs, and only 4 to large towns already represented. The huge increase in the borough electorate of the United Kingdom (reform bills for Scotland and Ireland were passed in 1868) from about 600,000 to about 1,400,000 was concentrated in great towns which remained drastically under-represented in proportion to population and wealth. Even in the mid-1880s, the 111,000 inhabitants of 15 small boroughs in Cornwall, Devon and Wiltshire would return 18 members, while the 2,100,000 inhabitants of Birmingham, Leeds, Liverpool, Manchester, Sheffield and Wolverhampton returned only 16. Thus household suffrage, already tempered by the residential requirement, was a giant bound in chains. Of course the chains would sooner or later be burst: in the sense that it created an anomaly between enfranchisement and effective political representation, too gross to be sustainable, the second Reform act led towards a more democratic political system. But that was not what ministers had designed it to do, and not what it immediately did. The Conservative party was able to exploit the fear of 'democracy' which its measure exacerbated, without having to face the reality. The counties and small towns which constituted its electoral base retained their weight in the political system. The efforts of the boundary commission set up by the government to take suburban districts into parliamentary boroughs were likely to improve its hold on the counties, where the electorate increased by little more than a third, and, as Disraeli had intimated to his chief, traditional influences would curtail the impact of the new franchise in the small boroughs; while in the great towns the battalions of new voters would at least cast into flux the politics of constituencies hitherto largely set in a Liberal mould.

Disraeli was at pains throughout to make it explicit that he envisaged not the inauguration of a new political system but the broadening and strengthening of the old. There was no possibility that franchise extension would lead to democracy in a highly stratified traditionary society. 'Believe me', he assured the Merchant Taylors in June 1867, 'that the elements of democracy do not exist in England. England is a country of classes, and the change that is impending in this country will only make those classes more united, more complete, and more cordial.' If the proclamation of the age of cordiality was necessary to conciliate the nervous, it none the less genuinely represented Disraeli's recipe for dealing with the extended working-class franchise, so far as he had one. Working men were not different for him because many more of them were becoming voters: they occupied the same place in his Tory universe as before, a class among others, which must recognise its community of interest with the rest in upholding the national institutions which secured to all their liberties and their privileges. None were so interested in maintaining the institutions of the country as the working classes, he told the Westminster Working Men's Constitutional Association: 'The rich and the powerful will not find much difficulty under any circumstances in maintaining their rights, but the privileges of the people can only be defended and secured by popular institutions.'[16]

In October at Edinburgh, in one of his rare addresses to a working-class audience, he dismissed the 'assumed and affected antagonism between the interests of what are called the Conservative classes and the labouring classes', and declared:

I have always looked on the interests of the labouring classes as essentially the most conservative interests of the country ... I have always thought that those who were most interested in the stability and even in the glory of a State are the great mass of the population, happy to enjoy the privileges of freemen under good laws, and proud at the same time of the country which confers on its inhabitants a name of honour and of glorious reputation in every quarter of the globe ... do not listen to those who pretend to you that society is to be revolutionised because the people are trusted. Do not listen to those who tell you that you have been invested with democratic rights and that, therefore, you must effect great changes in the fortunes and form of one of the most considerable nations and Governments that ever existed. Be proud of the confidence which the constituted authorities of the country have reposed in you, by investing you with popular privileges; prove that you know the value of such privileges; and that you will exercise them to maintain the institutions of your country, and to increase its power, its glory, and its fame.[17]

Patriotism, pride and privilege were to associate the working-class voter with the party that claimed to guarantee the security of the institutions and the prestige of the nation on which all three depended. Only in one particular did Disraeli address the Edinburgh working men in terms which seemed to recognise that they might have an interest distinct from that of other classes. Emphasising the support he had given to measures of social improvement over thirty years, he stressed that the 'rights of labour have been to me always as sacred as the rights of property', and made play with the work of the session just closed, which had shown that ministers had not forgotten 'that which is one of the first and principal duties of any Minister, which is to consider whether, by legislation, the condition of the great body of the people can be improved'. Social reform was, indeed, a significant theme in the Conservative ministry of 1866–8, which extended the factory acts, legislated for the health of London's paupers and of merchant seamen, supported measures for working-class housing and for the amendment of the law of master and servant in a sense favourable to employees, and introduced an abortive bill which would have established a minister for education – a step which Stanley and Disraeli had advocated in 1855, and with which the former now coupled the idea of a minister of health. In all this, the aim of 'putting us right with the Working Classes', as

Manners expressed it to Disraeli in October 1866, was manifest, but the government was drawing on the stock repertoire of social paternalism as circumstances dictated rather than pursuing a concerted policy of appealing to a distinct working-class interest.[18]

That Disraeli, if he had called into being a working-class majority in the borough electorate, had done so with no notion of making it the target of an appeal in the name of some 'democratic' Toryism was made sufficiently obvious when the next election arrived. By that time, his long service, and sometimes servitude, as second-in-command had come to an end. Derby's increasing ill-health forced his resignation in February 1868, and the Queen sent for Disraeli, as she had already told him she would. The triumph of the Reform bill had raised his stature both in the party and in the country, and though critics like Cranborne were reluctant to accept his succession as inevitable, they were in the same position as their predecessors twenty years before: they had no one else. Disraeli had become prime minister as he had become leader in the Commons, by talent and by default, sheltering a little still under the mantle of Derby, whose policy he claimed in his 1868 election address to have followed 'without deviation', and whose advice he continued to solicit until the latter's death in October 1869 removed the presence which had both protected and constricted the whole of his front-bench career.[19]

Gladstone moved at once to challenge the new premier's tenure and revenge the humiliation of the previous year by taking up Ireland as the issue with which he could restore his control of the Liberal party and eject the minority government. Disraeli had habitually spoken for conciliation of Irish grievances, and his cabinet was contemplating concessions on religious, educational and tenurial questions, but they were outbid by Gladstone's introduction of resolutions calling for the disestablishment of the Church of Ireland, an institution serving so small a minority of the Irish people as to make its privileges hard to defend, even when Disraeli subsumed the particular case under the defence of establishments in general and the connection of secular authority with religion ('If government is not divine' he declared, 'it is nothing. It is a mere affair of the police office, of the tax-gatherer, of the guardroom').[20] Defeated on the resolutions in April, Disraeli determined to carry the issue to the electors rather than resign. His decision not to dissolve until an election could take place on the new register created by the Reform act gave the Conservatives several months in which to organise their appeal to the people and take their first step into the era of mass politics in the boroughs.

Mass politics, however, were not Disraeli's forte. The supreme paradox of his performance in 1867 was that he almost casually fashioned an electorate with which he had little desire to communicate and an arena in which he had little aptitude to perform. He had never cared for electors much. For thirty years, his stage had been the House of Commons, not the platform. His skills had been honed in the intimate politics of the debating chamber and the closed, clubby elite, not in the reaching out to and communing with mass audiences which Gladstone added to his repertoire in the 1860s. Disraeli and Gladstone, arriving at the head of their respective parties at the same moment and with only five years difference of age, found themselves quite suddenly the only major survivors of a political world the dominant figures of which, Palmerston, Russell and Derby, all disappeared from public life between 1865 and 1868, and the shape of which the second Reform act had commenced to alter. Both were increasingly old-fashioned figures, formed by the conventions and the contests of an earlier age. It was Gladstone who showed the greater capacity to adapt, in the nature of his political technique, if not in the content of his fundamental beliefs, to the more extensive popular participation in politics heralded by reform. Disraeli, in part no doubt because he lacked the violent physical and mental energy of his opponent, had little ability to transpose from the politics of the salon and the senate to those of the mass meeting and starring on the stump. In any case he disdained the politics of vulgar arousal, and was happy to leave them to Gladstone. His address to the Edinburgh working men was a rare approach to a popular audience. More characteristic was his response to the 'great mob' which cheered him on Carlisle station while he was on his way to Balmoral in 1868: 'It was an ordeal of ten minutes; I bowed to them and went on reading; but was glad when the train moved.'[21] Cranborne, who thought Disraeli had tricked the Tories into a democratic franchise, would later as third marquess of Salisbury exhibit precisely the same reaction to being lionised at train stops: they disliked 'democracy' about equally, as a social intrusion as much as a political danger.

In the 1865 election, Gladstone had defined Liberalism as trust in the people, Toryism as 'mistrust ... only relieved by fear'.[22] Disraeli's reform coup had the enduring virtue of enabling his party to rebut that imputation, but little advantage was taken of it in the contest of 1868. A number of younger Conservatives had established in the National Union of Conservative and Constitutional Associations a body to co-ordinate the organisation of working-class Conservativism across the country, but Disraeli and the party managers kept it at arm's length, afraid of embarrassment from its activities and disliking the segregation of working men into separate bodies, which clashed with the integrationism of popularist Tory doctrine. There was no willingness to employ it in 1868 as the vehicle of a general electoral appeal to the working-class voters, and only in a few large urban constituencies with progressively minded Conservative candidates did the supposed interest of the new voters figure largely. Paradoxically, the immediate effect of the new borough franchise was to discourage rather than to stimulate pandering to the working man: both parties feared to encourage the emergence of a politics of class in which the old depositaries of political power would be overwhelmed by the new. Anxious to raise a large fighting fund, and telling the Queen that 'victory will probably be to the party wh. is wealthiest & best organised', Disraeli was thinking in terms of tackling the enlarged electorate by the traditional means of management rather than by the arts of the demagogue. The leading issue was the one his opponent had selected, and it proved very unfavourable to him. With little understanding of the complexities of religious politics, he vastly over-estimated the possibility of raising a great protestant tide in defence of the Irish Church, and in his election address descended into the ludicrous exaggeration which usually marked his presentation of a weak case, when he conjured up the bogey of the advancing power of Rome. Only Hardy's prompting secured a reference to 'those legal and social improvements which are so much required'.[23]

At the polls in November 1868 the Conservatives secured only 25 of the 114 seats in towns with a population of over 50,000. Altogether,

TOP OF THE BILL, 1865–1881

according to a contemporary estimate, the boroughs (excluding Ireland) returned 91 Conservatives representing a population of two million and 235 Liberals representing a population of eight million. Only a strong showing in Manchester, Liverpool and the lesser south Lancashire towns (where protestant and anti-Irish feeling was powerful among the working men) gave some colour to Disraeli's claim to the Queen that the Conservatives' 'moral influence appeared to be increased from the remarkably popular elements of which the Conservative party was now formed under the influence of the new Reform act'. Even more than before, the party was dependent on the counties, which supplied nearly 60 per cent of its seats, and on the small boroughs. Its total of about 274 seats represented a net loss of 15–20 and left it in a minority of approximately 110.[24] The ministry's second constitutional innovation of the year (the first being the virtual assertion of the doctrine of the mandate by demanding that Gladstone's Irish Church proposals be submitted to the electorate), was to resign before the assembling of the new House of Commons, in which it was certain to be defeated.

To the extent that reform had been a Conservative gamble on the favours of the new electorate, it seemed clearly to have failed. The party had lost its sixth general election in a row and Disraeli's position was correspondingly weakened. It was a natural moment for retirement. Yet instead of accepting the peerage conventionally at the disposal of ex-prime ministers and removing himself gracefully from the leadership, Disraeli induced the Queen to make his wife Viscountess Beaconsfield in her own right, and carried on. He knew no other life, but a further spell of hopeless opposition, facing, in Gladstone's first ministry, one of the most energetic governments of the century, was bound to be a wearisome business. In December 1869 he admitted to Derby (Stanley had become the fifteenth earl on his father's death in October) that

though still willing to exert himself for the benefit of the party if necessary, his interest in it was diminished, he had obtained his object, and if he never held office again, he should not feel that his life had been a failure. He had often doubted whether he should go on with the leadership in the Commons: the fatigue was considerable: but he saw no one in whose hands he could leave it, and that circumstance had decided him.[25]

Disraeli's conviction of indispensability was not shared by all his followers, and in the two years after the general election he was seriously threatened by a movement to make the bitterest of his critics, Salisbury (Cranborne had succeeded to the marquisate in April 1868), the leader of the Conservative peers, which would have rendered his position intolerable. Through 1869 and 1870 he followed a policy of 'the utmost reserve and quietness', offering no serious resistance as Gladstone employed his huge majority to disestablish the Irish Church, legislate for Irish tenant right as the Conservatives had been contemplating doing two years earlier, and pass a great education measure. Derby noted in May 1870 that 'from want of health he has virtually abdicated during the present session'.[26] It was back to the unheroic strategy of the Palmerston era: waiting for the divisions in the heterogeneous Liberal body to appear.

Meanwhile, Disraeli talked 'literature, philosophy, history – everything rather than politics' on Derby's December 1869 visit to Hughenden, and in secret employed his unusual leisure to write his first novel for twenty-five years. *Lothair*, which appeared in May 1870, went immediately through eight editions, sold spectacularly in the United States of America, was used to promote a new collected edition of the novels, and did something to buttress Disraeli's never quite secure finances. Yet it reinforces the impression of diminished power conveyed by Disraeli's political life at this epoch. The formula was the one he had adopted in the 1840s. The Odyssey of a young aristocrat beginning the world enabled him to pursue his characteristic fascinations, with youth, the glitter of society, the influence of woman, and the movement of profound forces – in this case the clash of the revolutionary and religious principles in Europe, with the evolutionary controversy thrown in – beneath the exciting rush of events. Disraeli's style had gained in polish, and his knowledge of society in precision since his early novels. The social satire is more adept, the contemporary debates are more skilfully assimilated into the narrative, without the authorial lectures of the past, and the eager delight in the world's parade is as taking as ever ('town was beginning to blaze. Broughams whirled and bright barouches glanced …').[27] But some of the old sparkle and spontaneity had gone. The tone is too serious for Disraeli's depth, the pace too slow, the wit too studiously chiselled. Lothair, like Tancred, is too much of a booby in search of a belief to supply a strong central interest and Disraeli's intellectual energy was no longer up to the task of compensating for thin characterisation by force of idea. As usual, he had no notion how to end the book: plucked by fate from the grasp successively of a ravishing heroine of the movement for Italian freedom and a nubile postulant nun, Lothair subsides tamely into the arms of an English rose of Anglican principles, his spiritual questionings apparently unresolved and his message for humanity undisclosed.

This kind of excursion was hardly what the Conservative party looked for in its leader. By 1871 Gladstone's government was losing its air of impregnability as its reforming activities ran it into a thicket of problems and raised powerful interests against it. As by-elections began to run conspicuously in their favour, some Conservatives started to look for a more positive lead than Disraeli seemed willing or able to supply, and feeling in favour of the fifteenth earl of Derby ran strongly enough for an important group of the party's frontbenchers to discuss the possibility of his taking over the leadership at a meeting at Lord Exeter's house, Burghley, at the end of January 1872.

Yet it was hard to imagine deposing Disraeli, and it was not in his nature to allow himself to be put aside. He had been anxious to avoid any premature movement, preferring to let time ripen the government's embarrassments, but as the ministry stumbled over Ireland, taxation, licensing, army reform and the ballot in the overcrowded session of 1871 he intervened more actively, and in January 1872, even before the Burghley discussion, was reasserting himself in the party's affairs briskly enough for Cairns to remark: 'after two years apathy he is beginning to wake up & fancies all beside are asleep'. For well over a year, he had been fending off invitations to lend himself to a great popular Conservative demonstration in Lancashire. Now the moment was opportune for a gesture, and it must have seemed even more so when his enthusiastic reception by the London crowd at the thanksgiving ceremony for the Prince of Wales's recovery from typhoid fever, on 27 February, signalled a popularity that he had never hitherto enjoyed. He had reached the age at which politicians sometimes become sympathetic by the familiarity of long usage and the reassurance that their ambitions are sufficiently sated and their faculties sufficiently dimmed to prevent their attempting much further harm; but there was more to it than that. His appeal as an original and a card, the most piquant joker in the pack, his indomitable nerve, as a faintly raffish outsider, in scaling the highest peaks of public life, added spice to his status as the leader of the opposition to an increasingly unpopular government. Perhaps, too, the depth of the attachment between him and the odd figure at his side touched a chord. Sometime in 1872, according to André Maurois, the French chargé d'affaires beheld in a London drawing-room 'a strange being trapped out like a kind of pagoda, whom he took for some aged rajah. It was Mary Anne, and behind her was Dizzy, painted and sepulchral, his last ringlet dyed jet-black and fixed on his bald brow. On her heart Mary Anne wore as one wears the badge of an order, a huge medallion which framed a portrait of her husband.'[28]

She was eighty, and dying of stomach cancer, but she went with Disraeli to Manchester in April to receive the homage of the Lancashire Conservatives. Shaking hands, as they presented their addresses, with over a hundred representatives of the county's Conservative associations which paraded before them, her husband had his first and only experience of what Englishmen regarded as the 'American' practice of pressing the flesh. Next day, to a great audience in the Free Trade Hall, he began the definition of the Conservative position which he completed when he addressed the National Union at the Crystal Palace on 24 June. Only in the October 1867 foray to Edinburgh had he previously chosen to set his exposition of Conservative principles in the frame of personal communion with the working-class Conservativism which reform had made it desirable to cultivate, and the Manchester expedition and the Crystal Palace speech were to be his major and almost his last direct essays in mass politics. In keeping, however, with both the doctrine of Toryism and the realities of the political situation, their tone had to be that of national and not class appeal. It was sufficiently obvious that the electoral drift towards the Conservatives was in large part a middle-class phenomenon; Disraeli could gauge as well as anyone the implications of the capture of the East Surrey seat in August 1871 by a brewer, Watney, trading, so Robert Lowe sneered, on the desire of the *nouveaux riches* to appear genteel when they moved from the metropolis into the suburbs.[29] His mass politics would have to be pitched as much to upwardly mobile villadom as to the teeming and toiling inner city.

His colleagues were nervous about what he might say, and so was he, getting Derby to vet the Manchester speech before delivery. Necessarily, the bulk of both addresses recognised that the attraction of the Conservatives lay in their Conservatism, and consisted in a routine defence of the established institutions of crown, lords and church, which guaranteed the liberties and the rights of the people against a Liberalism bent on menacing not only them but 'every interest, every class, and every calling in the country'.[30] Beyond, and to some degree through, these banalities, however, Disraeli pursued a delicate strategy of validating the established order in the eyes of the enlarged electorate and integrating the various classes of society for the safeguard of national unity and power against pressing internal and external threats.

The wider horizons of his thinking were what they had always been, with the extension required by the tendencies of the age. In 1870 in the 'General Preface' to the collected edition of his novels, he had congratulated himself on the success of *Coningsby*, *Sybil* and *Tancred* in realising his design of instructing the English people on its political, social and spiritual situation, and reasserted the fundamental ideas of those works without a hint of revision.

They recognised imagination in the government of nations as a quality not less important than reason. They trusted much to a popular sentiment, which rested on an heroic tradition and was sustained by the high spirit of a free aristocracy ... they looked upon the health and knowledge of the multitude as not the least precious part of the wealth of nations. In asserting the doctrine of race they were entirely opposed to the equality of man, and similar abstract dogmas, which have destroyed ancient society without creating a satisfactory substitute. Resting on popular sympathies and popular privileges, they held that no society could be durable unless it was built upon the principles of loyalty and religious reverence.[31]

To the analysis of the state of England which he had given in the 1840s, Disraeli had sought to add in *Lothair* a dramatic panorama of the state of Europe in 1870 and of England's role within it. He returned to the theme he had adumbrated in *Lord George Bentinck* nearly twenty years earlier, in the aftermath of the revolutions of 1848, when he had portrayed the fate of European civilisation as dependent on the outcome of the mortal combat between the revolutionary secret societies, 'which now cover Europe like networks', and the principles of religion ('the Semitic revelation'), property and order.[32] The struggle as Lothair rather bemusedly experiences it is symbolised by the contest between Italian nationalism and the papacy for possession of Rome. Neither side, of course, is suitable for a young English aristocrat of immense property. After nearly being killed fighting for the Italian cause under the influence of the superb Theodora, and nearly being converted to Catholicism under the guidance of the ethereal Clare Arundel, Lothair opts for sensible, gardening Lady Corisande and the *via media Anglicana*. Cosmopolitanism's claims, whether in the form of the atheistical secret societies which back the Italian cause or of the absolutist pretensions of the Roman Catholic church, are symbolically rebuffed in favour of the English national solution to the problems of political order and spiritual consolation.

There is a good deal of *opéra bouffe* in *Lothair*, with its descriptions of the 'Standing Committee of the Holy Alliance of Peoples', plotting Fenian insurrection and toasting the 'Mary-Anne' societies of France in a London coffee house, and the 'Madre Natura' conspirators resolved to 'expel from the Aryan settlement of Romulus the creeds and sovereignty of what they styled the Semitic invasion'. Yet not only was the International at work in London and Fenian activity a recent memory, within weeks of the publication of *Lothair*, Catholic claims were spectacularly displayed in the proclamation of the doctrine of papal infallibility; within a few months Italian forces had assumed control of Rome; and within a year the barricades of the insurrectionary Commune had gone up in Paris. The perils of ultramontanism on the one hand, godless revolution on the other did not seem unreal or distant to a part of the national audience that it was Disraeli's business to address in 1872, nor did it find ridiculous the notion that, as he was to put it in his inimitable way to the Glasgow Conservatives in November 1873, England might feel her destiny to lie in guarding civilisation 'alike from the withering blast of atheism and from the simoon of sacerdotal usurpation'.[33]

It was, however, difficult to be confident that England could guard either civilisation or herself. Not the least of the Gladstone government's vulnerabilities was the impression it gave of presiding over a sharp descent from the apparent power and prestige of the Palmerstonian era. Britain's inability in 1871 to prevent Russia from denouncing the Crimean settlement which had kept her warships out of the Black Sea, and to deter the American government from pressing massive claims for the indirect as well as the direct consequences of the commerce raiding carried out during the Civil War by Confederate vessels built in British ports, created feelings of impotence and humiliation. The revolution in the European balance of power brought about by Prussia's defeat of France in 1870 and the creation of the German Empire inspired nervousness about national security: the appearance in *Blackwood's* in 1871 of Colonel Chesney's tale of German invasion, 'The Battle of Dorking', was the beginning of a new genre of invasion literature. Disraeli's task at Manchester and the Crystal Palace was not only to vindicate the virtues of England's national course against the excesses of the Continent and the corrosion of doctrinaire Liberalism but to reassure his countrywide audience that under Conservative guidance the nation and its institutions could still muster the vitality to sustain it in the face of the old world or the new.

In England, 'the type of deferential countries', Walter Bagehot had written in *The English Constitution* in 1867, 'the few rule by their hold, not over the reason of the multitude, but over their imaginations, and their habits'. Disraeli had never doubted it. In the 'General Preface' he had reaffirmed his belief in the appeal to imagination as an essential technique of government. Arguably, it was even more true of the new electors than of the old that they needed, in the words of Sidonia, 'to adore and to obey'. Disraeli had noted in his description of a great trades union demonstration in *Sybil* the receptiveness of working people to the claims of ceremony and form.[34] It was not a simple matter, however, to organise the instincts of reverence around the national institutions the continuing effectiveness and relevance of which it was the prime business of the 1872 speeches to assert. Disraeli knew that the force of tradition alone could not sustain them. They had to be seen to work, but in the early 1870s their usefulness was fiercely challenged.

Disraeli himself, as he avowed in the 'General Preface', had long since lost confidence in the Church of England as a promising vehicle for national regeneration through faith. As for the House of Lords, he shared with Gladstone, an equally stout believer in aristocracy, natural and hereditary, a taste for putting peers in the cabinet and a plaintive hope that their order would vindicate its claim to lead by buckling to the performance of public duty, but it was a losing cause, and his impatience with his patrons flickered in Phoebus's characterisation of the English aristocracy in *Lothair*, 'excelling in athletic sports, speaking no other language than their own, and never reading'. Both Anglican establishment and the constitutional vitality of the Lords were conscientiously defended at Manchester and the Crystal Palace, but neither could supply a cynosure to focus the national imagination. There remained the monarchy. For a decade, the Queen's withdrawal from public engagements to indulge a mawkish cult of her dead husband had cut her off from her people, while her penchant for her Highland servant, John Brown, spattered the dignity of the crown with ridicule. Disraeli, Stanley noted in March 1869, 'says he thinks the monarchy in danger, which he never did before ... from gradual loss of prestige: the Queen has thrown away her chances, people find out that they can do as well without a court, etc.'.[35] By 1871 there was a vocal republican movement, and a widespread scepticism as to whether the royal family justified its cost to the taxpayer. The Prince of Wales's illness, however, seemed to encourage a swing of popular sentiment, which, manifested in the thanksgiving of February 1872, gave Disraeli his cue. If his defence of the crown at Manchester rested partly on the unromantic plea that it gave value for money, it nevertheless reasserted the role of monarchy as the necessary condition and symbol of the stability, order and justice which guaranteed the rights and privileges of society. Dull, dowdy and, in a civic sense, disobliging as Victoria might be, she would have to do, and she had the advantage from Disraeli's point of view of being by this time a thorough Conservative.

This was maintenance work, propping and gilding a creaking social structure. Something more was required to offer assurance that the country's traditional elites were capable of preserving its cohesion in the face of domestic controversy and its power in the face of external threat. Discussing in August 1871 the sort of policy declaration that was needed for the grand Conservative demonstration which they were planning, the leading Lancashire Conservatives Viscount Sandon and R. A. Cross had come down in favour of 'Social administrative & economical reform' and 'colonial matters so as to unite our Empire'.[36] There is no evidence that Disraeli's antennae picked up these distant murmurs, but social reform and empire both decked his discourse a few months later.

He began at Manchester with social reform. 'Social problems are the fashion at present', says Hugo Bohun in *Lothair*. The subject was both topical and likely to be tactically advantageous. Social questions figured prominently in the government's programme for the 1872 session. Disraeli had suggested in conversation the previous summer that when they came to the fore they would provoke division in the Liberal party, and he seems to have countenanced the involvement of some of his principal colleagues in what came to public attention as the New Social Movement – an indirect and tentative negotiation with a group of prominent working-class leaders as to possible future legislation to benefit the working classes. When the New Social Movement leaked into the press in October 1871, the main Conservative daily, the *Standard* – its editor having consulted Disraeli as to the line to take – welcomed the aim of diverting legislation from 'factious contests and artificial attempts at needless political and constitutional change to greatly-needed social reform'. Shortly before he spoke at Manchester, Disraeli had himself briefed on the two public health bills then before parliament by the promoter of one of them and Conservative spokesman on the subject, Charles Adderley, and it was sanitary reform that he picked out on the platform as the area in which the legislature might properly intervene to help the working classes. At the Crystal Palace, a few days after an interview with a veteran of the factory reform movement, Philip Grant, he widened the prospectus to include improvement of working hours and conditions, so long as 'those principles of economic truth upon which the prosperity of all States depends' were not transgressed.[37]

Social reform in this somewhat limited formulation was a bid for working-class votes. Yet particular inducements to the working men were hardly necessary or justified if Disraeli believed his own declaration that the second Reform act had been 'founded on a confidence that the great body of the people of this country were "Conservative"'. In its broader application, social reform had to be a bid for the votes of all who believed that the country could not meet the challenges of class conflict and international competition, each undermining its ability to subdue the other, without a policy designed to integrate the working classes fully into the body of the nation. Disraeli was anticipating, as Peter Ghosh has remarked, the turn-of-the-century politics of 'national efficiency': social reform was to strengthen at once the fitness and the unity of the nation. Social Darwinism, with its sense of inevitable struggle between peoples, was already pervasive. Disraeli had represented the importance of public health in 1864 in terms of the certain loss of national greatness 'if the race becomes inferior', the importance of education at Edinburgh in 1867 and Aylesbury in 1868 in terms of its contribution to enabling Britain's limited population to sustain her imperial position and industrial competitiveness ('if we want to maintain our power, we ought to make one Englishman equal really in the business of life to three other men that any other nation can furnish'). At Manchester, the maxim that 'the first consideration of a minister should be the health of the people' was supported on the observation that, however great a country's civilisation, 'if the population every ten years decreases, and the stature of the race every ten years diminishes, the history of that country will soon be the history of the past'.[38] An imperial destiny required an imperial breed, and the breeder must to some extent be the state.

Empire was the second of Disraeli's specifics in 1872, and the one on which he most relied to create an image and an object of common national interest and mission. In taking up the imperial theme, he was, as with social reform, both drawing on past professions and asserting a tactically advantageous Conservative position in a lively current debate. Despite the celebrated remarks about the colonies as a 'millstone round our necks' and as 'deadweights', wrung in 1852 and 1866 respectively from an exasperated chancellor of the exchequer struggling with the costs of imperial defence, Disraeli had always been susceptible to the majesty, and conscious of the moral and material advantages, of an empire combining, as he had put it in the *Vindication*, 'the durability of Rome with the adventure of Carthage'. The problem was how to achieve an organisation of the empire which would make the colonies a source of strength rather than a drain on the mother country's energy and resources. In the framework of a protectionist prescription for national development, between 1847 and 1851, Disraeli had canvassed the ideas of an imperial free-trade area and colonial representation in the House of Commons, and asserted that political power and commercial wealth could be maintained only by 'the consolidation of our Colonial Empire'. His attack at the Crystal Palace on successive Liberal governments for attempting to dismember the empire by the progressive grant of colonial self-government, was part of a long-running controversy over the costs and benefits of imperial rule, in which Disraeli had been steadily in favour of empire as a factor of British power. He was not hostile to colonial self-government, he explained, but it ought to have been conceded as part of a policy of consolidation incorporating an imperial tariff, imperial defence agreements, and a 'representative council' in London. The opportunity had been thrown away, but 'no minister in this country will do his duty who neglects any opportunity of reconstructing as much as possible our Colonial Empire'.[39]

The subject must have seemed especially topical in the summer of 1872 as the newspapers reported H. M. Stanley's search for Livingstone, and Disraeli was showing his customary facility for catching at what was in the wind. His attack on the Liberals' alleged policy of 'disintegration' paralleled J. A. Froude's in *Fraser's Magazine* in 1870, while his suggestion that the grant of colonial self-government should have been accompanied by 'securities for the people of England for the enjoyment of unappropriated lands which belonged to the Sovereign as their trustee' not only picked up, as Froude had done, the familiar theme of emigration to the colonies as a means of relieving working-class poverty, but seemed almost to endorse the argument of the working-class paper, the *Bee-Hive*, in its advocacy in 1869 of state-assisted emigration, that colonial lands were not the Queen's personal property but belonged to all her subjects.[40] Schemes for imperial consolidation and development were a commonplace of the day, endlessly canvassed at the Royal Colonial Institute and elsewhere, and in 1870 pressed on Disraeli by the colonialist Sir George Grey and taken up by his erstwhile colleague Carnarvon in parliament.

There was nothing original in what Disraeli said about empire in 1872. What was novel was his promoting empire to the centre of the Conservative platform which he was constructing, not only as an issue on which the Liberals seemed vulnerable, but as one which could perform a vital integrating function in providing for all classes a common symbol of national stature, a common source of national prosperity, and a common object of national pride and endeavour. This was image-making, not policy-making. Disraeli offered nothing in the way of practical propositions for 'reconstructing as much as possible our Colonial Empire'. In simultaneously advocating 'consolidation' and repeating what he had said in response to Grey's pleas, that the moment had been let slip, he neatly charged the Liberals with missing the imperial omnibus without committing the Conservatives to belatedly running after it. Empire as an integrating cause was not necessarily a matter of forward movement, or of any movement at all. The thesis that the Abyssinian expedition of 1867 had represented the attempt of Disraeli and his colleagues to pursue national unity and self-reassurance through a military and expansionist exploitation of the imperial idea does not seem to consort with the watchwords of 'consolidation' and 'maintenance' adopted in 1872.[41]

Disraeli's imperialism was defensive rather than aggressive. It was bound to be, given the anxiety he had expressed at Oxford in November 1864 and reiterated in the Commons in May 1865 about England's capacity to sustain her imperial and commercial greatness when 'the base – the material base – of that empire is by no means equal to the colonial superstructure'. It was not ships and regiments that had created and must maintain the empire but 'the character of the people'. The task was not to extend imperial over-stretch to breaking-point but to preserve the empire as a buttress to British power amidst a changing balance of world forces, and to use its symbolic attractions to foster the cohesion between classes, the attachment to established institutions and the sense of national purpose which alone could ensure that the efforts needed to preserve it were forthcoming. Behind these mundanities lay the deeper function of empire in supplying the national teleology which protestant patriotism and Disraeli desired for their different reasons. Imperialism defined what Disraeli had spoken of in March 1865 as 'the duty that Providence has called upon us to fulfil'; it offered the justificatory purpose which the sense of God's special dispensation for the English required, and the universal, world-historical role through which Disraeli's sense of his country as the destined inheritor of the civilising mission of his race could be expressed. 'England', Sir John Skelton had noted on meeting him at Edinburgh in 1867, 'is the Israel of his imagination.'[42] The British empire was its divinely ordained diaspora.

Disraeli's proclamation at the Crystal Palace of the 'three great objects' of 'the national party', to maintain the monarchy, the House of Lords and the church, to 'uphold the Empire of England', and to elevate 'the condition of the people' summed up the Tory doctrines he had been preaching for nearly forty years. He was reasserting the indispensability of his leadership by defining Toryism in the terms he had patented, summoning his followers to march to the music only he knew how to play. The strategy of protecting the institutional and social order by seeking national integration both through the focusing of popular sentiment on the symbols of crown and empire and through attention to the material bases of popular well-being in the frame of national efficiency would supply the Conservative party with the major elements of its appeal to the mass electorate for almost a century, until empire was no longer sustainable and social welfare no longer seen as efficient. Though the Manchester and Crystal Palace speeches were as close to the direct practice of mass political appeal as Disraeli ever came, they were addressed to the nation and the party rather than to the new urban electors whom the second Reform act had created. Disraeli was at pains to stress that the act had simply corrected the balance of representation distorted by the virtual exclusion of the working class from the franchise in 1832, in the confidence that the great body of the people was

'Conservative' in the 'purest and loftiest sense'. 'My hope in them hourly increases!' he had written of the working men in October 1870, but he hoped in them less as a new force which demanded a new approach than as a reinforcement of reliable recruits to an army the traditional values of which they were assumed to share and the hereditary officer-class of which they were expected to obey.[43]

Disraeli was introducing his party to the politics of mass mobilisation, but hardly to those of mass participation, and certainly not to those of mass arousal. For mass arousal, he had not only no taste but no technique. His Manchester speech opened with a lengthy and not lively constitutional lecture: the sanitary section for which it is best remembered 'was delivered to an audience already exhausted, and in a weaker voice, not heard throughout the entire room', noted Derby, who thought the address on the whole 'fell flat'.[44] Disraeli was not a rabble-rouser, in part because he saw no rabble to rouse. He regarded the working men not as a segregated and inferior species but as a body 'in possession of personal privileges – of personal rights and liberties – which are not enjoyed by the aristocracies of other countries'. He thought in terms not of classes assumed to possess separate and antagonistic interests but of orders and estates, defined by their functions in a system of mutual interdependence, the interest of each coinciding with that of all, in the healthy functioning of the organism. It was not a scheme which gave the working man an independent or initiatory role. The 1872 speeches were designed, not to invite him to assert his claims from below, but to assure him of the satisfaction of his needs by beneficial agency from above. They were also designed to keep him and others out of mischief, to turn attention from the restless pursuit of institutional change into less damaging channels. The people knew, Disraeli asserted, that 'the time has arrived when social, and not political improvement is the object which they ought to pursue'. Empire and social reform could be neatly combined in this diversionary tactic: colonisation overseas was a substitute for the 'home colonisation' and land nationalisation advocated by the Radicals of the Land and Labour League, the 'policy of sewage' derided by the Liberals was a model of practical utility to set against the 'ineffable mysteries' of the ballot. Manchester and the Crystal Palace, rather than welcome the working man into the political arena, sought to persuade him of the merits of staying out of it – except to vote Conservative. There was more there of the politics of mass sedation than of those of mass arousal.[45]

'No programme, as how could there be?' was Hardy's comment on the Manchester speech, which Disraeli had introduced explicitly as an answer to the taunt that the Conservatives had no programme. Even if he had had any, the Conservative leader was too fly to tie himself to specific policies that might give second thoughts to those who were being pushed over to his side by the government's combination of interference with powerful interests at home – church, land and liquor prominent among them – and apparent impotence abroad. That possible sanitary and factory measures could be featured so prominently reflected their relatively uncontroversial character and had no immediate practical impact – the public health bills praised at Manchester ran into some obstruction in the Commons from Conservative champions of local autonomy and economy in the rates, though Disraeli tried to smooth their passage. The need was above all to capitalise on the increasing weakness of the government, that 'range of exhausted volcanoes' on the treasury bench, as Disraeli called them, in perhaps the most deadly of the attacking metaphors in which he specialised.[46] The technique which Disraeli handed to the Conservatives of his own and future generations was to exploit as a tool of partisan politics the desire for national consensus, or simply for peace and quiet, which the contentions raised by their opponents' initiatives helped to inspire.

'I am a party man', he declared at Manchester. As in his rise, so in his maturity, he depended on the exaggeration of party difference to bring him place and power. At the Crystal Palace, he managed to allow that England might learn from the experience of 'Continental nations of not inferior civilisation' and that many of the Liberal measures of the past forty years had been improvements, while almost in the same breath denouncing the Liberal party for attempting to foist 'cosmopolitan ideas' on the English people, in the course of attacking the country's institutions 'under the name of Reform' and making war on its manners and customs 'under the pretext of Progress'. In first announcing in *Lord George Bentinck* the great battle of the age between 'the patriotic and the cosmopolitan principle', he had identified with the machinations of the secret societies, 'striking at property and Christ', what was held up to admiration in England as the progress of Liberalism on the Continent. The Crystal Palace speech, like *Lothair*, embodied a subdued reprise of this theme, designed to trade on the unease created by the Paris Commune and the International and by the flaring of domestic republicanism, to cast the party contest into a pseudo-Manichean mould, with the Liberal dupes of cosmopolitan notions playing the satanic and un-English role against the efforts ('unconscious efforts, sometimes', Disraeli had to admit) of the Conservatives to restore true national principles.[47] The picture was not the less effective for being wildly overdrawn. The device of appropriating English nationality and thrusting their opponents to the fringes (often the Celtic fringes) of the *pays réel* was to serve the Conservatives well. The cause of national unity became the possession of a party and the definition of national consensus was made to exclude half the nation.

The 1872 speeches thus signalled the definitive ending of the Palmerstonian truce of parties and the revival by Disraeli of the politics of confrontation under the banner of consensus, on which his career depended. The atmosphere seems to have been favourable to the multiplication of ritual dramatic combat between opposing teams before gawping spectators: the FA cup competition, the England–Scotland soccer internationals and the county cricket championship all began in 1871–3. Party politics played as national drama or even national music-hall would rest as much on style of presentation as on force of reason, but Disraeli's strongpoint was style and too much ratiocination in political matters smacked of the 'cosmopolitan' delusions he deprecated. The question was how far his vitality was now equal to the task of leading his troops to battle. In December 1872 Mary Anne died. 'I am very sorry for poor Dizzy', wrote the earl of Harrowby. 'He is a solitary, self-contained Being, & has lost in his wife every thing, that took him out of himself.' Disraeli moved into Edwards's Hotel and was kept on his legs by the devoted attention of his debonair yet very efficient private secretary, Monty Corry, but it was a sad business: 'hotel life in an evening', he said, 'is a cave of despair'. In February 1873, he told Derby that he wanted to retire, but (of course) 'did not see who was to do the work'.[48]

The further weakening of the government no doubt helped to sustain him. In March 1873, Gladstone's attempt to settle the impossible question of Irish university education led to his defeat in the Commons, but Disraeli refused to take office in a minority, preferring to let the government stew in its unpopularity as long as possible. Explaining himself to the Commons, he set the tone of his party's approach to the election which must come soon. He was able to exploit the very achievements of Liberalism to sweep out of the way as settled the great fiscal and commercial questions on which it had established its supremacy, and to proclaim the position of the monarchy, the church and landed property as the issues of the future, on which he believed that the supremacy of 'a great Constitutional Party' could be built. He seems also to have believed that the way to spice the cause of constitutional, religious and social defence for consumption by the great urban electorates among which the Conservatives must make progress in order to win a majority was (as in 1849) to sympathise with the grievances of the lower middle-class ratepayer, as the party conspicuously did in the budget debates of 1873, with perplexing implications for the social measures that caused the rates to swell. The working men, he argued, had less need of fiscal relief. As he had done at Manchester, he contended that they had had their full share of the advance of national prosperity: they believed themselves to have realised 'the dream of their youth, "A fair day's wage for a fair day's work"', and to have secured at last 'that share of profits, which, in the partnership between labour and capital, labour ought to secure'. At Glasgow in November, while he reiterated the now conventional line of pursuing useful social improvement in place of meddling with established institutions and interests, he was concerned to impress on the operatives the limitations imposed on legislative intervention in their relations with their employers by 'those inexorable rules of political economy to which we must all bow', as well as to indicate his disapproval of the segregation of Conservative working men in separate organisations.[49]

When Gladstone precipitated the general election, on the cry of repealing the income tax, in January 1874, the address which Disraeli hurriedly put together followed entirely defensive and negative lines, except in so far as it offered to substitute measures to improve the condition of the people for the 'incessant and harassing legislation' charged against the Liberal government. While Conservative candidates in the industrial north were obliged to promise support for the trade unionists' demands for amendment of the labour laws and a nine-hour day, the overriding issue was the record of the government and the direction it might take under Radical impulsion if re-elected, the overriding attraction of the Conservatives lay in their not being Liberals, and the overriding reason for Liberal defeat was less large-scale conversion to Conservatism than large-scale apathy and abstention on the part of disillusioned former supporters. With a net gain of sixty seats, the Conservatives came back 351 strong, against 301 Liberals and Irish Home Rulers. In achieving their first majority since 1841, they made nineteen net gains in the towns of over 50,000 population, with conspicuous advances in London, Lancashire and Yorkshire, drawing increased support from both middle and working classes, and their greater urban strength enlarged the proportion of businessmen on their benches. Yet the balance of the party was shifted only slightly: it gained in counties and small towns too, and the English and Welsh counties and the English boroughs of under 20,000 inhabitants still provided 60 per cent of its seats, and the landed interest still dominated its ranks.[50] The second Reform act, given fuller effect now than in 1868 by adjustment of the borough ratepaying conditions, had produced at the second time of asking a Conservative victory, but one that in its preparation and its result moved the party only a fraction towards a 'Tory democracy'.

'It came at last', Disraeli had written in *Sybil*, 'as everything does if men are firm and calm.'[51] He had waited most of his life for office with power. It is conventional to say that it came too late, and that in any case he had no idea what to do with it. There is something in both propositions – Disraeli himself voiced the first – yet it did not come too late to be relished and he was not without a sense of direction for its use.

He had just turned sixty-nine when he became prime minister for the second time. Never robust even in youth, he was now a fugitive from the east wind, much attacked by asthma, bronchitis and the gout, which once obliged him to sit on the front bench in 'a black velvet shoe of Venetian fashion' intended for a masked ball. 'Both at this and the last Cabinet', Derby noted in May 1875, 'D. has appeared much exhausted: and today he fell asleep and remained so some minutes: which I never saw him do before. The work is too heavy for a man of 70.'[52] The worst, however, was not physical decrepitude but emotional deprivation. His wife's death had rent the carefully constructed cocoon of domestic content which supported his career. Public life without private was almost unsupportable, and private did not mean the freemasonry of the Commons and the clubs. Disraeli had hardly any close friends in his political circle, though he sentimentally found a cabinet place for Lord John Manners, who had long survived his youthful promise, and a lesser post for Henry Lennox, whose shady business connections rendered it shortlived. Men, in any case, were not what he needed.

'I owe everything to woman', he wrote in 1874, 'and if, in the sunset of life, I have still a young heart, it is due to that influence.' He sidestepped the dowager Lady Cardigan, who proposed marriage with a dash hardly less precipitate than her late husband's at Balaclava, and, from the spring of 1873, directed the still powerful emotional charge of his nature towards two sisters, grandmothers both, whom he had known for many years, the widowed countess of Chesterfield, a couple of years older than he, and Selina, countess of Bradford, who was in her mid-fifties. Though he proposed to the former, she was largely an avenue to the latter, who was the target of more than two-thirds of the 1,600 letters with which he bombarded them over eight years, sometimes at the rate of two or three a day, if need be by special messenger from Downing Street or the treasury bench. When you have the government of a country on your shoulders, he told Lady Bradford in November 1874,

to *love* a person and to be *in love* with a person makes all the difference. In the first case, everything that distracts your mind from yr. great purpose, weakens and wearies you. In the second instance, the difficulty of seeing your beloved, or communicating with her, only animates and excites you. I have devised schemes of seeing, or writing to, you in the midst of stately councils, and the thought and memory of you, instead of being an obstacle, has been to me an inspiration.[53]

This was more, in Disraeli's eyes, than the gentle *amitié amoureuse* that his age and station might have suggested as appropriate. 'Threescore and ten, at the present day', he had written in *Lothair*, 'is the period of romantic passions.' He was as egoistical, exigent, jealous, unbearable and self-pitying as in his twenties. 'I am certain', he confided to Selina, 'there is no greater misfortune, than to have a heart that will not grow old.' Lady Bradford did her duty by queen and country, and kept him supplied with the mittens – 'a ceaseless charm ... never off my hands' (Hughenden was cold in October) – and pencil cases which went as far in the way of requital as she was able to go, but, *noblesse oblige* or not, having to add to the responsibilities of a wife and *châtelaine* the management of a spoony, septuagenarian prime minister was a trial, and, if she was not ruthless enough to get rid of him, she could not help making it plain sometimes that she found him embarrassing, difficult and spoiled. Historians can only be grateful for her forbearance, for Disraeli's letters to her and her sister restore the angle of vision into his intimate thoughts cut off by the death of Mrs Brydges Willyams ten years earlier. 'I live for Power and the Affections', he told her in April 1874, and her consent, if not to return, at least to endure the one was a vital element in enabling him to support the other.[54]

Power and the affections were conjoined in Disraeli's relationship with his other woman friend of these years. As a minister between 1866 and 1868, he had completed his conquest of Queen Victoria's favour by indulging her in her cult of her late husband and by expressing a dutiful desire to conduct public affairs in every possible way according to her wishes. He used his literary talents to the full on her. 'She declares', reported Lady Augusta Stanley, 'that she has never had such letters in her life, which is probably true, and that she never before knew *everything*!' The Queen for her part embarked on the primrose path by beginning a regular practice of sending Disraeli spring flowers. They slipped comfortably back into the same system in 1874, the more eagerly on Victoria's part for having had five years of Gladstone's stern awkwardness. 'He repeatedly said whatever I wished shd. be done whatever his difficulties might be!', she noted on commissioning Disraeli to form a government.[55]

The impression is easily formed that he cynically practised on the vanity and loneliness of a woman in intellect and guile much his inferior. The reality was more complex. Manipulation was not necessarily limited to one side. The Queen's private secretary, Ponsonby, rather suspected that each humbugged the other, Disraeli with his ornate deference which verged on satire, Victoria with her carefully tended widow's woes which excused her from doing what she disliked. If Disraeli saw through the Queen's act, she probably saw through his, but it mattered little, since it was in the interest of each to play the other's game, Victoria to fend off a Gladstonian Liberalism she had come to mistrust, Disraeli because the crown was the symbol he required to lay hold of to form the finial of his Conservative political – and social – order. Nor were mutual esteem and even a species of affection absent. The Queen appreciated her prime minister's consideration as well as his capacity to entertain with wonderful vignettes, like that of Gladstone (who had abdicated the Liberal leadership after his electoral defeat) thundering back into debate on his 'return from Elba' in 1875: 'The new members trembled and fluttered like small birds when a hawk is in the air.' He knew that, if rigid in her ideas and inclined to behave, he told Derby, 'like a spoilt child', she was not without shrewdness: she opened her mind to him at Balmoral in September 1874 and, he noted, 'rose immensely in my intellectual estimation'. He meant what he had said at Manchester in 1872, that it was unthinkable for a wise minister to ignore the accumulated political knowledge and wisdom of an experienced sovereign. Victoria's friendly advice was worth listening to. She reminded him in 1874 that when he had left office in 1868, she had urged on him the importance of keeping the Conservative party to conservatism, and not trying to be '*more liberal* than the Liberal party, which the passing of the Reform bill (which was forced no doubt upon the late Lord Derby) rather led them to appear to be' (perhaps she had forgotten her own pressure on Derby to deal with reform). Now she counselled, with her characteristic emphases, against any '*retrograde* policy', which would be '*very* dangerous'.[56]

Both pieces of advice were tactically sound. Yet there were dangers for both sides in this partisan partnership of minister and crown.

Liberals could hardly help feeling that the balance of the constitution was endangered when they saw their sovereign two-stepping with their principal opponent. Derby warned Disraeli in the form of a question in May 1874: 'Nobody can have managed the lady better than you have, but is there not just a risk of encouraging her in too large ideas of her personal power, and too great indifference to what the public expects?'[57] Disraeli's habit of circumventing the usual official channels of communication with the monarchy, getting Corry to write to one of the ladies of the bedchamber on his behalf, gave colour to the notion that he was developing a novel constitutional relationship. No doubt he and the Queen knew well enough the practical limits of the latter's freedom of action, and no doubt Disraeli could usually manage his vigorously opinionated constitutional spouse, but the appeasement of the Queen's prejudices that was an essential part of Disraeli's system could lead occasionally to serious embarrassments.

One such was the affair of the Public Worship Regulation bill, which provided most of the parliamentary fireworks of the 1874 session. The Queen had told Archbishop Tait that 'Something *must be done*' to suppress the ritualistic practices of those high-church clergy who seemed to be leading their flocks, at best into error, at worst towards Rome, and the government found itself struggling to put Tait's bill into workable form. The issue was well adapted to demonstrate how unsuitable a leader Disraeli was in relation to some of his party's most deep-seated beliefs and prejudices. He was seen by many Conservatives as unsound on church matters, which was true in the sense that he neither grasped their intricacies nor sympathised with the passions they provoked, and he had secured the high-church Salisbury for his cabinet largely by assuring him that he was a high churchman too, and that the government would not support measures against ritualists. Amidst much acrimony and under pressure from the Queen, Disraeli eventually came out in favour of putting down the 'Mass in masquerade' and managed to hold in line Salisbury and other powerful high-church voices in his cabinet, but the enforcement of the act made a number of clerical martyrs, and his ill-conceived protestant gesture incurred the lasting enmity of a socially and politically influential group. Matters were not improved by his insouciance in approving the appointment, as the first judge to hear ritualism cases, of a lawyer who had made his reputation in the divorce court.[58]

Had it not been for the royal wrath against altar lights and incense, the new government could perfectly well have boarded parliament up for the session of 1874. It had come in, Disraeli reminded the home secretary, 'on the principle of not harassing the country'. The cabinet was one of the strongest of the nineteenth century, eleven of its twelve members blooded by experience in that of 1866–8, six of them in the same posts. Despite his still lively detestation of Disraeli, Salisbury decided not to stall his political career by staying out, and Carnarvon came with him, both determined to restrain any repetition of the adventures of 1867, but reassured by Lady Derby that the prime minister was a changed man, cautious and averse from innovation. If the cabinet's membership largely reflected the traditional landed and southern English base of the party, the industrial north, or at least Lancashire, was represented in the persons of Derby at the Foreign Office and the provincial lawyer and banker, R. A. Cross, at the Home Office. With the metropolitan member W. H. Smith, 'the bookstall man', who became secretary to the Treasury, Cross betokened the government's awareness of the rising force of urban middle-class Conservatism, though not Disraeli's reconciliation to middle-class manners – the latter exploded to Lady Bradford on one occasion that Cross had 'talked, I see, of the Prime Minister's absence [from the Commons] on account of the *state of his health!!!* What language!'[59] The question was what this experience and talent, old and new, were to do, carried as they had been on a current of mild reaction into an apparently tranquil ocean of domestic and international calm.

The suddenly promoted Cross was naively surprised to find that the cabinet had some difficulty in putting a Queen's speech together: from Disraeli's pronouncements, he had 'quite expected that his mind was full of legislative schemes, but such did not prove to be the case'. The prime minister had never troubled much about the translation of his ideas into the prosaic detail of bills, which in any case, in thirty years of near-continuous opposition, he had had little chance to pass. He enjoyed himself in attaining and savouring power quite irrespective of any consideration of what might be done with it. The deference it brought him from those to whom he had had to defer for a lifetime was a sweet social revenge. It was gratifying to be the Queen's first minister, to distribute government appointments, to make Selina's husband master of the horse, telling Victoria how important it was that 'the high nobility should be encouraged to cluster round the throne'. It was like the realisation of one of his own novels. Musing, in September 1874, over the 'wondrous' year that had just elapsed, he told Lady Bradford: 'I have had at last my dream.'[60]

The elegiac note, however, owed much to a bad attack of gout. The dream was not finished, and it was not confined entirely to the narcissistic enjoyment of a great position. To a correspondent in January 1874, Disraeli had written: 'I have, for forty years, been labouring to replace the Tory party in their natural and historical position in this country. I am in the sunset of life, but I do not despair of seeing my purpose effected.'[61] Like the 'General Preface', this mission statement might be read as the claim to lifelong consistency of a man vain of his intellectual coherence and integrity, rather than as the expression of a living and breathing resolve. Yet the romantic transformation of the Conservative party was not a dead ideal, and power was to be employed as well as enjoyed. If Disraeli had no pre-formed legislative programme, he had a conceptual compass to guide him. Set in the 1830s, it had been re-adjusted only slightly in the 1872 speeches, which had defined, not what a Conservative ministry would do, but by what stars it would steer. After Manchester and the Crystal Palace, Disraeli said nothing more about the conduct of Conservative politics in a general sense, for he had nothing more to say. The years from 1874 saw the application to opportunity of the idea of conserving British institutions and the British empire by the action of a national party, integrative in its composition, its conduct and its creed, which he had been preaching all his life.

The Conservatives' election victory itself had relieved the immediate pressure on the institutions, and there was no urgent threat to the empire. The moment was right in 1874 for that pursuit of uncontentious social improvement which it had suited the party to represent as being blocked by Gladstone's disruptive 'violence'. The equation, indeed, was neatly reversed, and social improvement used as a block to the threat of further constitutional upheaval, when Disraeli, in May

1874, resisted the 'fever for organic change' expressed in the demand for household suffrage in the county constituencies with the argument that 'the disposition of the country is favourable, beyond any preceding time that I can recall, to a successful consideration of the social wants of the great body of the people'.[62] The rhetoric of popular Toryism precluded his opposing in principle the assimilation of the county to the borough franchise, but the disruption threatened to the Conservatives' electoral strongholds could be fended off on the plea that the agricultural labourer wanted the improvement of his social condition rather than political change.

Yet if the direction to be taken was plain, no precise route had been mapped out. Precipitated into office as it had been, the government composed its programme for 1874 from whatever ministers found to hand. From his intervention in the formulation of the budget, it seems that Disraeli's initial strategy was to consolidate the Conservative victory by rewarding those on whose votes it had mainly rested, the party's traditional supporters among the landed and agricultural classes and the lower middle-class ratepayers to whom its appeal had been conspicuously directed. A penny reduction brought the income tax to twopence, while the great local taxation grievance, which Disraeli himself had promoted to the forefront of Conservative politics in the 1850s, was in his eyes 'virtually settled' by substantial government relief to the rates in respect of lunatics, police and prisons (the exchequer grant to local authorities almost doubling between 1873 and 1876). If, however, the priority was to lessen the weight of direct taxation on the middle classes, the working classes were not ignored. The repeal of the sugar duties offered a sop to 'the free traders and the democracy', as Disraeli put it, and the chancellor, Northcote, pointed out that redress of the local taxation grievance was an essential preliminary to legislation for improvements in health, housing and education which could only be effected by local agency. Avner Offer has argued that, in 'offering to transfer the fiscal obligations of social welfare from tenurial proprietors to the State', Disraeli 'gave an impetus to the emergence of a centralised welfare state'.[63] The impetus was unwitting, but Disraeli understood well enough the delicate balance of fiscal interests and burdens which underlay Victorian social policy, and attacking the local taxation problem was a necessary step on the road of Conservative social reform.

The ministry passed in 1874 a clumsily handled licensing measure which, in extending drinking hours, looked very like a concession to the trade alleged by its opponents to have helped place it in office. More important, Cross forestalled Liberal pressure by a factory act which came close to giving textile workers the nine-hour day that many northern Conservative candidates had been obliged to support on their election platforms. This, however, was mere skirmishing ahead of the general advance of 1875, when the ministry, for perhaps the first time in parliamentary history, devoted the session mainly to social reform, introducing nine important bills and passing seven. Social questions, Lord Shaftesbury noted, had become 'Imperial' subjects.[64]

Three of the measures, on health, housing and the adulteration of food, dealt with matters to which Disraeli had pointed directly at Manchester and the Crystal Palace. The Public Health act carried out the much needed consolidation of the sanitary laws for which Adderley had procured Disraeli's support in 1872, while the Sale of Food and Drugs act sought to safeguard what the prime minister had called the purity of the people's provisions. 'Our chief measure'[65] in Disraeli's eyes was, however, Cross's Artizans' Dwellings act, which empowered municipal authorities in London and the larger towns to take over slum areas, using compulsory purchase and cheap state loans if necessary, and to provide for the building of new housing by private enterprise. These measures touched working people (and others) as individuals, as did the Employers and Workmen act, which met a long-standing labour grievance about discriminatory treatment by removing (with a few exceptions) breaches of contract by employees from the purview of the criminal law. The government also defined the attitude of the state to the great organisations of the working class. A Friendly Societies act was designed to further the sound management of the main agencies of working-class self-help, but much more important was the decision to give the trade unions, in the Conspiracy and Protection of Property act, the freedom from the threat of prosecution for conspiracy and from restrictions on peaceful picketing which they had pressed for during the election, with considerable impact on Conservative candidates in the north of England. Much of this legislation looked to the urban and industrial part of the country, but there was an Agricultural Holdings act, too, to give outgoing tenants compensation for the value of the improvements they had carried out (unexhausted improvements). The pace of 1875 could hardly be sustained, but the two failures of that session were converted into successful measures in the next, when a Merchant Shipping act tightened provisions against unseaworthy ships, though much less than the Plimsoll agitation wanted, and an act against the pollution of rivers was passed. At the same time, a Commons act sought to preserve open spaces for public enjoyment, and an important education act took a long stride towards compulsory school attendance, in part to improve the finances of the church voluntary schools which were a bulwark of Conservative influence in the countryside.

This impressive burst of activity represented not a coherent Conservative social policy but the government's intention to give colour to past rhetoric and do something serious about social reform, by taking up piecemeal the problems which it found ripe for attention. Precisely what was done depended on pressure, preparation and prejudice – the pressure of public need and concern, the preparation of issues for action by public and private enquiry and civil service expertise, and the prejudice which most Conservatives and most Liberals entertained against too much extension of central control, too much diminution of individuals' responsibility for their own welfare, too heavy burdens on taxation, too much encouragement of 'class' politics, and, as Salisbury put it, 'laying down new principles of legislation which ... under a political system where power resided with the greatest numbers, would some day be used most disadvantageously against them'. Inevitably, the real bite of the measures was less than the parade of their titles might suggest. Their application of the force of the state was reluctant and mild, especially where they embodied the permissive principle of granting powers instead of imposing duties, as with the Artizans' Dwellings act, which few local authorities proved willing to utilise. All the same they represented a corpus of social legislation unparalleled until the ministries of 1905 and 1945, and they were advanced in their day. Cross later alleged that the parliamentary draughtsman, Thring, refused to execute his instructions for the Artizans' Dwellings bill on the ground that it amounted to 'Communism and Confiscation'. The two labour measures of 1875 went a long way in the direction of relieving working people of the legal stigma of inferior status, and as Ross McKibbin has pointed out, the treatment of the trade unions, which extended to them what seemed (at least until the legal decisions of the nineties) 'an almost archaic corporate immunity', was a remarkable exercise in fostering a fair balance of force in the relations between capital and labour.[66]

In his Mansion House speech of August 1875, Disraeli preened himself on the government's having redeemed its 'pledges' to elevate the condition of the people. The legislation of that year flowed naturally from the policy guidelines he had laid down for the Conservative party in 1872, but, if it depended on his sanction, it seldom bore his impress. Cross, Carnarvon and, from the sidelines, Walter Bagehot all received the impression that Derby recorded in November 1875: 'he dislikes detail, is easily wearied by it, and cares little about the preparation of bills while the session is still distant'. His role as prime minister was to set the course and leave the departmental ministers to settle details, and his health would hardly have supported the burden of a close super-vision of his colleagues. Yet when it seemed desirable to give a matter the accolade of his personal interest or the benefit of his personal inter-vention, he did so. He was much concerned with the passage of the Agricultural Holdings bill, when the very limited nature of his support for state intervention, at least where the landed interest was concerned, came out in a celebration of permissive legislation as 'the characteristic of a free people', designed in this case to give landlords an escape route from the burden of compensation for tenants' improvements.[67] The most dramatic episode was perhaps when he had to struggle with the consequences of the mishandling of the 1875 Merchant Shipping bill in the face of Plimsoll's tempestuous agitation, rather enjoying the atmo-sphere of crisis and the display of his considerable skills in extricating his ministry from embarrassment.

Housing and the labour laws, however, were the prime objects of his concern, the Queen's interest perhaps acting as a spur in the former case. Visiting the Shaftesbury Park housing scheme in July 1874, he saw, he told Lady Bradford, 'an astonishing spectacle, which may change England more than all the Reform Bills – and change it always for the better'. The Artizans' Dwellings and Friendly Societies bills, the same correspondent was informed, 'indicate a policy round wh. the country can rally'. With the labour laws he was particularly keen to identify himself. He had picked the subject up in mid-1873 as one likely to be prominent, no doubt sensing the growing tension between capital and labour, which was signalled in July by the formation of the National Federation of Associated Employers of Labour to counter the recently founded Trades Union Congress, and was tending to drive a wedge into a political alliance on which urban Liberalism heavily depended. In 1875 he complacently assured Lady Bradford that it was his influence which enabled Cross to override the report of a royal commission and pursue a more concessionary line than some of his colleagues and many employers liked: 'when Secy. X explained his plan to the Cabinet, many were agst. it, and none for it but myself; and it was only in deference to the P. Min[iste]r that a decision was postponed to another day. In the interval the thing was better understood and managed.' He conveyed his excitement at the passage of the bill's second reading to all three of his women, Ladies Bradford and Chesterfield and the Queen, on the following day. As he put it to the first: 'I cannot express to you the importance of last night. It is one of those measures that root and consolidate a party. We have settled the long and vexatious contest bet[wee]n capital and labor.'[68] Of course they had not settled it, and, even allowing for a habit of hyperbole, the remark raises a question as to how well Disraeli understood what was happening in this sphere. What the labour laws, much approved of by Liberals, really did was to wash government's and politicians' hands of the contest between capital and labour by placing it carefully outside politics in what was now assumed to be a fair field for both parties.

It is a question, too, how far he was justified in his supposition that measures like the labour laws would damp down social discontents and 'gain and retain for the Tories the lasting affection of the working classes'. In the sense that they removed a prime cause of friction in the political connection between the leaders of organised labour and the Liberal party, the labour laws, however highly appreciated by labour leaders, were hardly an unmixed Conservative gain. In general, it is doubtful how much the government's social legislation counted to the political credit of the Conservative party, even when it was welcomed by those it was supposed to benefit (and working people were not necessarily eager to see their rookeries demolished, or their children's earnings taken away by enforced school attendance). Many of the reforms were so bi-partisan as hardly to seem linked to party. Liberal speakers, like Samuel Plimsoll addressing his Derby constituents in November 1877, could applaud the measures of these years as though they had nothing in particular to do with the Conservatives. Disraelian social reform was possibly more satisfactory to middle-class opinion looking for a turn away from political upheaval to moderate social improvement than it was immediately appealing to working men and women. It was, however, an essential element in Disraeli's baptising of the Conservatives into the national party faith, and it was to serve its party purpose in a thousand propaganda fights in the future. On 29 June 1885, in a debate at the Higham Hill Liberal Club, Walthamstow, John Cropley, a Conservative working man, laid £5 that he could produce as many measures passed in the interest of the working classes by the Conservatives in 1874–80 as his opponents could for the Liberal government of 1880–5. He triumphed by seventeen acts to eight, and one hopes he spent part of his winnings on a bunch of primroses in memory of Disraeli, who had gone to school hard by.[69]

As the government pushed its education bill through the fag end of the 1876 session, Disraeli was much annoyed by its falling, as he put it to the Queen, 'into one of those messes of ecclesiastical weakness which seem inevitable, every now and then, for the Conservative party'. A body of his backbenchers imperilled the progress of the measure by forcing upon ministers a clause which provided for the dissolution of school boards surplus to requirements, thus delivering what he termed 'a petty assault on the Nonconformists', by reducing their ability to secure the undenominational board school education they preferred in areas dominated by Church of England schools. This sort of issue was well calculated to emphasise the gulf of sympathy and temperament which still existed between Disraeli and the party he led. 'The Chief', wrote Northcote, who thought the issue capable of breaking the party up, 'really does not know the feeling of our friends on the subject.' He did not want to know anything at once so earnest and so vulgar, and they were his friends only in the parliamentary sense. If he could take pleasure still in encouraging the youthful talent of the party, he was weary of the incessant labour of managing its graceless bulk in the House of Commons, which deteriorating health was beginning to render insupportable. When Lady Bradford's absence from town broke the link with 'the domestic principle' on which he relied, he told her:

Now life seems quite inhuman – nothing to soften or distract it; nothing but Parliaments, and Councils, and despatches, without a gentle thought or graceful deed! Alas! there was the daily letter always, and the little visit, to charm away cares and sometimes to solve difficulties; for in talking to those in whom we can confide, the knot often falls to pieces.[70]

Through the dying session of 1876, he moved towards the exit, talking of retirement as his preferred course, but happy enough to let Queen and colleagues protest his indispensability and usher him into the House of Lords in August as earl of Beaconsfield. The earls of Derby and Bradford introduced him into the House, the son of his old master and the husband of his new, though platonic and reluctant, mistress. In February 1877, he bore the sword of state by the Queen's side when she opened parliament. The Lords could never compensate for the loss of the kaleidoscopic drama of the Commons, but it was lighter work, and under his new, homeopathic doctor, Kidd, who put him on claret instead of port, Disraeli regained enough strength to carry him through, so long as he husbanded his resources and avoided too many impositions like the Lord Mayor's banquet, 'where', he told Lady Bradford, 'I eat nothing; and where, after three or four hours of gas, inane conversation, and every other species of exhaustion, I have to get up, with a confused brain and exhausted body, to make a speech, every word of which will be criticised for a month'. He still went much into society, all the same, relishing the grand position which it now accorded him, as he gave away the bride at the earl of Rosebery's wedding to Hannah Rothschild or gravely mediated in the Prince of Wales's quarrel with Lord Randolph Churchill. As always with him, society was not a relaxation from politics but a concomitant of them, the careful cultivation of the one a precondition of the successful management of the other. Commenting to Lady Bradford in 1876 on the lack of Tory hostesses, he wrote: 'I never knew a party so deserted by all social influences as ours. I wonder how they are kept together.'[71]

The Lords formed an appropriate setting for the high imperial business which dominated the later years of the government. The social reform session of 1875 had not quite reached its close when an outbreak of revolt against Turkish government in Herzegovina pitted the claims of Orthodox Christianity and Balkan nationality against Muslim rule in south-eastern Europe and began to revive a central issue of European politics which had been apparently dormant since the Crimean War. By November 1875, Disraeli had realised that the Eastern question, that major preoccupation of the statesmen of the previous generation, 'will fall to my lot to encounter – dare I say to settle?'[72] As his remarks indicate, the problem chose him, not he it. Entering office at an epoch when Britain's security was under no immediate threat and her empire not in an expansionist phase, he had no external policy and needed none, beyond a general intention to make British power influential and respected as the Liberals were accused of having failed to do. What he did have, from his earliest days, was a fascination with foreign politics as the supreme arena for the exhibition of the statesman's genius, and for the conclusive demonstration of that fusion of his own identity and interest with the higher identity and interest of the nation which constituted the ultimate form of his settlement on English soil.

It is true, as Lord Blake points out, that there were strict limits to the familiarity with the wider world that he liked to profess. He had been little abroad – not at all since 1856 – and was no linguist (unlike Gladstone).[73] Yet he did not need to leave London to meet most of the leading European statesmen of the age, from Metternich onwards, and the European intelligence network of his Rothschild friends helped to sustain his armchair sense of acquaintance with the courts, chanceries and coulisses of continental politics, even if he never saw them. His picture of European events combined shrewdness with a taste for romance and a childlike thrill in knowing secrets and penetrating mysteries which led him to ascribe ludicrously much to backstairs intrigue and the secret societies. Yet, highly coloured though his map of abroad might be, his views on what to do about it were sober enough. The common idea that he donned Palmerston's mantle in foreign policy is accurate only if the cut of that cloth is properly recognised and his reservations about some of its gaudier trimmings noted.

Palmerston in his later career combined a sometimes truculent demonstrativeness in foreign policy with considerable practical caution in dealing with major powers. Disraeli was inclined to be less demonstrative, certainly less truculent, and not a whit less cautious. He understood that Britain's relations with the great European land powers were conditioned by the fact that her power was mainly commercial, not primarily on land, and largely extra-European. Heralding, in 1859, the coming replacement of a European by a global balance of power, he declared that, if continental Europe reduced itself to exhaustion and inferiority by internal strife, England, connected by her geographical position, laws, language and religion 'as much with the New World as with the Old', would still have an illustrious future alongside 'those great States which our own planting and colonising energies have created'. The testing of that vision to destruction would be left to a later age, but its immediate implication was that England should avoid provocative and unproductive interference in continental affairs. In 1848, Disraeli had denounced Palmerston's alleged policy of trying to force English forms of government on to other countries, and in 1850 the latter's bullying of Greece in the Don Pacifico affair had drawn a warning lest meddlesome policies cause other powers to combine as formerly against Venice, 'to terminate the intolerable career of the great commercial aristocracy which had offended them by its wealth and insulted them by its arrogance'. Provocativeness was not only dangerous but bad business for great commercial aristocracies. Disraeli, as Peter Ghosh has emphasised, believed quite as much as Gladstone, if for partisan rather than for moral reasons, in the political virtue of low taxation, and grasped that the nationalism of the middle classes and the artisans, the tone of which Palmerston caught, if it wanted assertiveness in foreign policy, wanted it at the keenest price, not pushed so far as to involve expensive collisions with substantial enemies or good customers.[74]

The difficulty about the conservatism which the Conservative party was inclined to pursue in foreign affairs was that it risked appearing as no more than a pale, pragmatic echo of a Cobdenite creed and a Peelite tradition which its opponents could propound more convincingly. As Disraeli's factotum, Ralph Earle, put it in September 1866, non-interventionism might have been a useful line against Palmerston, but the Tories were in danger of seeming 'colourless, neither Cobdenite nor Imperial ... a little more expensive than Gladstone and not a whit more glorious and national'. By December, Disraeli was telling the foreign secretary, Stanley: 'Reaction is the law of all human affairs; and the reaction from non-intervention must sooner or later set in.' As usual, he caught the breeze from the court, responding in August 1867 to the Queen's appeal for a more assertive policy over the Luxembourg question than Derby and Stanley were minded to follow with a reference to 'the decaying theory and system of non-interference'.[75] Though he encouraged Victoria to believe that Stanley might be brought to abandon that system, this was perhaps the moment when a fundamental divergence of approach manifested itself between Disraeli and the man he was to make foreign secretary in 1874.

As yet, however, it was a mere matter of shading and tone. The Conservatives made easy political capital in the early seventies out of the Gladstone government's supposed failure to uphold British prestige, when Russia breached the Crimean settlement with impunity by denouncing the provisions excluding her warships from the Black Sea, and when the *Alabama* claims were taken to arbitration. However, when Disraeli censured the Liberals' 'negligence and blundering' at Manchester in 1872, it was not clear how differently he would have behaved had he been in office: he was careful to point out that he had resisted 'a turbulent and aggressive diplomacy' for much of his life, and to acknowledge that 'the policy of England with respect to Europe should be a policy of reserve, but proud reserve'.[76] There seemed little alternative to reserve, proud or otherwise. After his youthful anti-French fling in the *Gallomania*, Disraeli had come consistently to maintain that Britain's right policy in the interest of European stability was to work closely with France — a country where he was well received and which spoke the only continental tongue he (more or less) understood — but that system was wrecked in 1870, when defeat by Prussia virtually destroyed France as a factor in the European balance.

Possessed of neither a great conscript army nor a powerful ally, Britain had no means of exercising decisive influence in continental politics, now dominated by the Three Emperors' League of Russia, Prussia and Austria. Disraeli came into office seeking, as Richard Millman puts it, 'that respect for Britain which he long attempted to win for himself', but with no idea how to obtain it.[77] His first essay in European politics, in May 1875, amounted to no more than throwing a pennyweight into Russia's scale by joining her in warning Germany off a further excursion against France. 'There is no balance', he explained to Lady Bradford in September, 'and unless we go out of our way to act with the Northern Powers, they can act without us, wh. is not agreeable for a State like England.'[78]

In this frustrating condition of continental affairs, the revival of the Eastern question opened up a different arena, where Britain appeared to have clear-cut interests, a well understood policy, and the ability to execute it. If Balkan insurrection under Russian patronage brought about the disintegration of the Ottoman empire, a barrier would be removed to Russia's southward expansion, and the security be menaced both of Britain's route to India via the recently opened Suez canal, and of India itself, already seriously threatened by the gravitation of the Amir of Afghanistan towards Russia after the arrival of her forces at Khiva in 1873. Coming into office in 1866, Disraeli had excused the Derby government's prospective impotence in European affairs by reminding his countrymen that Britain's responsibilities were global: she was 'really more an Asiatic power than a European'.[79] The Near East could be taken as her imperial centre of gravity, where the naval force that sustained her global role could be brought to bear. Since the time of Pitt, her statesmen had sought to protect her interest by bolstering Turkey against Russian pressure, urging on the sultan the reforms which would remove the excuse for external intervention to protect his Christian subjects and would reassure his empire's European creditors – a pressing consideration in 1875 when Turkey defaulted on the interest payments on its foreign debt. The treaties of 1841 and 1856, designed to prevent Russian access to the Mediterranean via the Bosphorus and the Dardanelles, gave a standing ground in international law for resistance to any Russian move on Constantinople, even if it had not been possible to prevent the unilateral denunciation of the Black Sea clauses by Russia in 1870.

The threat of the crumbling of Turkey in Europe introduced severe tensions into the Three Emperors' League by holding out the prospect of collision between Russian and Austrian interests in the Balkans. Meanwhile Bismarck's anxiety to avoid Germany's being drawn into such complications offered the possibility that Britain would be able to work with the strongest continental power – a nation of similar race and religion Disraeli had already pointed out, in February 1875 – in the interest of stabilisation, thus allowing Disraeli to indulge the Queen's family feeling for a German connection. Britain and Germany together, no doubt seconded by Austria–Hungary, would have little difficulty in checking Russia, whose merits as an opponent were enhanced by the fact that, while she presented an impressively menacing exterior, her real capacity to threaten British interests in the Near East or in India was doubtful: a brave Benjamin had little to lose in squaring up to this somewhat disjointed Goliath. It was not, however, Disraeli's intention to invite a conflict, but rather to make sure that in that resolution of Balkan and Near Eastern issues which seemed about to be precipitated, Britain would play a leading role in the consultations of the powers. 'To escape isolation by consenting to play a secondary part does not become Your Majesty', he told the Queen in June 1876.[80] The Eastern question seemed to offer the ideal means for an 'Asiatic power' to make itself felt in European affairs, and bring in the Orient to redress the balance of the Occident: had it not existed, Disraeli might almost have been tempted to invent it.

It was precisely in June 1876, however, that reports began to emerge of atrocities against the Bulgarian Christian population by Turkish irregular troops, which both greatly increased the likelihood of Russia's intervention as the protector of Orthodox Christianity, and so outraged a powerful section of British opinion as to render bitterly controversial any degree of support on the government's part for Ottoman territorial integrity. In September, Gladstone's vehement pamphlet on *The Bulgarian Horrors and the Question of the East* stoked an agitation which for some months placed the government on the defensive against a tide of sentiment combining emotional sympathy for the Balkan Christians with a virulent suspicion, not least among high churchmen seeking retribution for the Public Worship Regulation act, that Disraeli's apparent lack of concern for them demonstrated a fundamental Jewish preference for the Ottomans. In telling his wife that Disraeli 'may be willing to risk his government for his Judaic feeling, – the deepest and truest, now that his wife has gone, in his whole mind', Gladstone voiced in private an interpretation that some of his allies were ready to assert in public: Turk and Jew were 'leagued against the Christian' claimed the historian E. A. Freeman in 1877, and Disraeli was sacrificing the 'policy of England' to 'Hebrew sentiment'.[81]

It is true that Jewish feeling was largely pro-Turk, on the rational calculation that the Jews, recognised by Islam as a people of scripture, were likely to get a better deal from Turkish suzerainty than from that of Christian Slav nationalists. Disraeli had maintained his interest in the biblical history of his race with the materials supplied to him by the chief rabbi's secretary and Rothschild family tutor, Marcus M. Kalisch, and it may be that he still dreamed the dream revealed to Stanley in 1851 of restoring the Jews to Palestine by negotiation with the Ottoman government – his later interest in Lawrence Oliphant's investigations of the possibility of Jewish colonisation under a British protectorate lends some credence to that view. It may be also that there lingered with him some of that fascination with the rich colour and voluptuous ease of Ottoman life engendered by his tour to the East in 1830–1, though the expression of his Turkish sympathies in the intervening years does not seem to have gone beyond such trivia as trying to get the Turkish ambassador into Crockford's or encouraging Mary Anne, in 1843, to christen the first Turkish steam frigate built in England. Yet the evidence is not strong enough to support an interpretation of his policy as fundamentally inspired, rather than marginally reinforced, either by Semitic exaltation or by Turkish delight. He was prime minister of England. The 'race' with which he had identified himself in politics as the destined carrier of the Semitic inheritance was the English. English, or British, interests were more immediately important than Hebraic or Ottoman sentiment: Disraeli was not sentimental. Salisbury recollected that he had doubts about the traditional policy of buttressing Turkey, 'but he always said that the policy of Lord Palmerston must be upheld', because consistency of policy was essential.[82] Richard Millman concludes, in the most detailed modern study of the Eastern question, that he was ready for any sacrifice of Turkish interests that British needs might require. The protection of the Balkan Jews does not seem to have been in the forefront of his mind, though, canvassed by Lionel de Rothschild, the Board of Deputies, and Bismarck's Jewish financier, Bleichröder, he may, as was widely supposed, have had a hand in the insertion of minority rights provisions in the decisions of the Congress of Berlin.[83]

Disraeli fell foul of the atrocities agitation not because his policy was pro-Turkish or crypto-Jewish but because some of his enemies were ready to use any slur against him, because his view of the right conduct of government ruled out anything that looked like bowing to a sentimental popular cry got up by people he mostly despised, and above all because the rebellious Balkan Christians, manipulated, he felt sure, by Russia, in threatening the survival of European Turkey were threatening the foundations of British policy in the Near East. He was incautious and provocative in dismissing the early reports of massacres on insufficient information, and he inflamed matters by his off-hand cynicism about Turkish methods of dealing with rebels. He was too much of a moral relativist to judge eastern practice by western conventions. His desire for a jaunt with the Turkish army suppressing the Albanian revolt in 1830 had not been at all restrained by the consideration that its commander was, as he cheerfully put it, 'daily decapitating half the province'. His criteria for judging the Balkan situation were political, not religious or humanitarian, and it was on political as much as moral grounds that he clashed with Gladstone.

Already over the Romanian question in 1858, as Richard Shannon points out, the two had differed as to whether Russian advance was better checked by bolstering the Ottoman empire or, as Gladstone thought, by encouraging the emergence of independent national states in the Balkans.[84] Like many nineteenth-century European conservatives, Disraeli did not believe in what he called in 1848 'this modern, new-fangled sentimental principle of nationality', threatening to wreck the stability of the European state system for the benefit of nations half-invented by the exertions of philologists, antiquarians and adventurers.

Whatever radical flourishes had marked his youthful attitude to domestic politics, his attitude to foreign affairs had been thoroughly conservative, from the moment when, visiting Greece in 1830, he had characterised the British naval intervention which had assisted Greek independence by shattering the Turkish fleet at Navarino as a 'bloody blunder'. The Polish insurrectionaries of 1863 he had compared to Neapolitan brigands, and he saw the Bosnian rebels of 1875 in no more favourable a light. 'Fancy autonomy for Bosnia, with a mixed population', he sniffed to Lady Bradford: 'autonomy for Ireland wd. be less absurd, for there are more Turks in proportion to Xtians in Bosnia than Ulster *v.* the three other provinces.' In the sense that he thought European stability and peace much more important than the claims of peoples struggling to be free, he merited Gladstone's verdict that one of his most striking characteristics was 'the utter absence in him of a love of liberty'. The atrocities agitation represented for him the subordination of political realism, patriotic interest and European order to neurotic sensibility and partisan manoeuvre. Foreign policy could not be conducted by deference to ignorant and over-excited public opinion outside Westminster: it required, he had declared long ago in the *Gallomania*, 'a really philosophic mind, – a mind above prejudice or passion'.[85]

This Olympian and ruthlessly pragmatic stance troubled even some of Disraeli's colleagues – Cairns wished that he could show 'a touch, even the slightest, of sentiment' for the Balkan Christians – but it was sustainable. The agitation gradually blew itself out. It alienated more than it intimidated the Conservative party, and the Liberals were by no means unanimously behind it: Hartington in the Commons and Granville in the Lords, who had taken over the formal leadership when Gladstone threw it up in 1875, were little more inclined than Disraeli to have their line dictated by enthusiasts. Disraeli's problem became less to keep a majority in parliament and support in the country than to control his own cabinet, where the degree of assistance to be afforded the Turks and the risks to be run in warning off the Russians were matters of much disquiet. The high churchmen, Carnarvon and Salisbury, and the presbyterian Cairns found it hard to envisage a settlement which did not grant autonomy or independence to Turkey's European Christian subjects: Disraeli told the Queen in 1877 that the first was influenced by a 'strange sacerdotal crew' and the second 'thinking more of raising the Cross on the cupola of St Sophia, than the power of England'. The biggest problem was the reluctance of Derby, as foreign secretary, to pursue any decided course of action which might seem to imperil peace. This was the end of Disraeli's long partnership with the house of Stanley. Only the deferential habits of years and a determination to avoid a disruption – Salisbury judged that his only fixed political principle was 'that the party must on no account be broken up' – can account for his continuing as long as he did with a colleague who was suspected of undermining the government's position by feeding information about its uncertainties through his wife to the Russian ambassador (furious though this made Disraeli, his novelist's imagination and his fascination with the influence of women can hardly have failed to be tickled at the end of 1876, when Count Shuvalov worked on Lady Derby and Olga Novikov on Gladstone in London, and Madame Ignatieff practised her pan-Slav charms on the unpromising person of Salisbury during the conference convened on British initiative in Constantinople).[86]

Derby acted in the interests of peace as he saw them. He did not believe Russia planned to march to Constantinople; he did believe that Disraeli, while not wanting a conflict, was all too likely to precipitate one by striking provocative postures for the ends solely of prestige, which Derby thought he believed in inordinately 'as all foreigners do'. For the prime minister, Derby wrote in October 1876, 'the main thing is to please and surprise the public by bold strokes and unexpected moves: he would rather run serious national risks than hear his policy called feeble or commonplace'. Like Salisbury, Derby found his chief a short-sighted, improvisatory statesman, combining 'great acuteness to see what is most convenient for the moment' with 'apparent indifference to what is to come of it in the long run'. Historians have tended to agree: for Richard Shannon, Disraeli's approach to foreign policy is summed up by his words to Corry in April 1876: 'Turkish & Egyptian affairs get worse every day ... we have plenty of troubles ahead, but perhaps they will vanish when encountered.'[87]

Criticisms of this kind are not unfair, but they ignore the possibility that Disraeli's politics of gesture, improvisation and waiting on events were peculiarly appropriate to the situation he found in 1875–8. Britain had little power to influence Balkan events, until the point when the Russians advanced far enough to suggest that they were genuinely threatening the occupation of Constantinople and the destruction of the Ottoman empire, and thereby enabled the British government to take advantage of Austrian and German displeasure as well as of the reaction of its own public. At the beginning of the internationalisation of the crisis, in the first half of 1876, as Austria, Germany and Russia put concerted pressure on Turkey in the interest of her European Christian peoples, there was not much the cabinet could do to assert a British role but tag along, as in the case of the Andrassy note, or adopt an attitude of faintly petulant independence, as with the rejection of the Berlin memorandum, when Disraeli angrily complained to the Russian ambassador that Britain was being treated like Bosnia or Montenegro. Meanwhile, the fleet could be moved up and down to Besika Bay, near the Dardanelles, as an earnest of British readiness to intervene, but it could have little immediate influence until Constantinople and the Dardanelles were seriously menaced, and there was a good deal of rust beneath the warpaint of its ironclads. Admiral Hornby, its commander, was keenly aware that lack of planning for war meant that 'the out-break of one will go far to ruin our naval reputation', and matters had not been helped by the cheeseparing of successive chancellors of the exchequer, Disraeli among them (he had been hot in January 1868 against 'the wild suggestions of these ignorant and narrow-minded Admirals'). Disraeli's policy could only be to hope that the Turks would crush their rebels fast enough to preclude outside interference and would implement enough of the reforms which Britain and other powers enjoined on them to remove the justification for it. When the Turks proved unmalleable, his problem was to strike a tone which did not encourage their intransigence by reassuring them that Britain would in the last resort fight to preserve Ottoman territorial integrity, yet deterred the Russians by persuading *them* that Britain might do just that. In the circumstances, there necessarily arose an apparent tension between the principles for the conduct of foreign policy which Disraeli expounded to the Commons in February 1876, which stressed the paramountcy of conciliation and compromise, and the loud voice which he sometimes had to employ to conceal the fact that, in European terms, Britain was carrying a very small stick.[88]

Policies of deterrence and policies of prestige cannot succeed unless war is accepted as in the last resort not only a conceivable but an acceptable outcome. Disraeli's strength in 1876–8 was his recognition of the fact; his weakness was his inability – perhaps also, especially in his dealings with Derby, his reluctance – to make his colleagues face it at the price of possible cabinet disruption. His conviction was that an unflinchingly firm line, while entailing the possibility of war, would avoid the necessity for it, as, he told Hardy, it would have averted the 'vile' Crimean War. The risks, however, were too daunting for his colleagues readily to accept. 'There is among the leading members [of the government]', he told the Queen in May 1877, 'too great a fear of responsibility! This is not the way ... to maintain empires.' It was perhaps his salvation that the Queen took the same view. Contemptuous of the 'mawkish sentimentality' of the atrocities agitation, convinced that Gladstone was crazy ('Is there no friend', she asked her prime minister, 'who could get him away for his own sake?'), and bitterly opposed to 'a miserable cotton-spinning, milk & water, peace-at-all-price policy', Victoria was ready, indeed eager, to lean heavily on Disraeli's critics in the cabinet and to supply him ('Only say if the Queen can do anything ... ') with fulminating messages to reprove that body's hesitations: her letter to be read in cabinet on 21 April 1877 urged 'the absolute necessity of showing a bold and united front to the enemy in the country as well as outside it', and asserted that the question was not one of upholding Turkey but of 'Russian or British supremacy in the world!'[89] Russia was declaring war on Turkey at that moment, so precipitating the final stage of the crisis, in which Queen and prime minister collaborated to conduct foreign relations behind the back of their foot-dragging foreign secretary, through the ambassador, Layard, at Constantinople, Colonel Wellesley at Russian headquarters, and special emissaries in Vienna, where, as Disraeli explained to his impatient sovereign, it was essential to secure co-operation if Russia was to be halted.

When the long-sustained Turkish resistance crumbled at Plevna in December 1877 and the Russians moved towards Constantinople,

British policy seemed faced by a choice between war and a humiliating failure to achieve its aims. Yet it was the Russian advance that threw the game into Disraeli's hands. It breathed some life into his airy declaration that Constantinople was 'the key of India', based on the imaginative notion that a Russia established on the Bosphorus would be in a position to threaten Suez via Syria. It brought bubbling up the patriotic froth of the London crowd, whose music-hall refrain,

> We don't want to fight, but, by Jingo, if we do,
> We've got the ships, we've got the men, we've got the money, too,

was a not unfaithful rendition of the front Disraeli had exhibited to Europe in his Guildhall speech of November 1876. It hardened the resolve of the government's supporters – the whip, Hart Dyke, reported in January 1878: 'one thing only can injure the Tory Party of the Future – namely if ever it can be hinted either in Public or Private that in a great national emergency, of two courses open – its Leaders forsook the brave one & preferred the timid'.[90] More important than any of these domestic benefits, it created the prospect of a European concert to limit Russian expansion in which Britain could play a prominent part, especially when at San Stefano in March 1878 the Russians attempted to carve out of European Turkey a large Bulgarian state which would be a tool of their influence. Disraeli was at last able to carry the cabinet with him, and to proclaim the seriousness of British intentions by sending the fleet through the Dardanelles to the Sea of Marmora to warn the Russians off Constantinople, calling up the reserves, and sending Indian troops to the Mediterranean. The resignations of Carnarvon and then Derby were nullified by the support of Salisbury, who took over the Foreign Office and promptly gave a crisper tone to British diplomacy. It was now possible to trade support of Austria's ambition to annex Bosnia for her assistance in forcing the Russians to limit the size of the new Bulgaria, the *quid pro quo* for Russian concessions being the acceptance of the independence of Serbia and acquiescence in Russian gains in Bessarabia and Armenia. Having helped to save the Turkish position in Eastern Roumelia (the southern part of the Bulgarian state proposed at San Stefano), Britain claimed Cyprus from the Turks as a Mediterranean base, in return for a guarantee of Asiatic

Turkey against further Russian attack. The essential decisions had all been taken by the time the Congress of Berlin met in June 1878 to set Europe's seal on the settlement of the Eastern question.

'This is a wondrous scene; life in its highest form', Disraeli told Lady Bradford. His appearance at Berlin among the foremost European statesmen, settling the destiny of nations amid a blaze of high society, was indeed the summit not only of his life but of his conception of life. It was the concrete, public and personal manifestation of the power for which alone, Vivian Grey had concluded, 'men, real men should strive'. It was that for which all the striving, all the patience, all the tenacity had been worthwhile – not just the glittering show of it, but the ultimate materialisation and demonstration of superior genius. Not that Disraeli's genius lay in the finer details of diplomatic negotiation and territorial adjustments. He left the tedious work to Salisbury, who in return dilated on his shortcomings in letters home: 'What with deafness, ignorance of French, and Bismarck's extraordinary mode of speech, Beaconsfield has the dimmest idea of what is going on – understands everything crossways – and imagines a perpetual conspiracy.' Yet on the ground of high policy and personal dealing with the great, Disraeli had his own skills and displayed his own form of dedication to duty. In convincing Bismarck that England meant business about Eastern Roumelia, he even smoked with the German chancellor: 'I believe I gave the last blow to my shattered constitution, but I felt it absolutely necessary.' Lord Odo Russell, the British ambassador in Berlin, would tell Eddy Hamilton that 'the impression which Lord Beaconsfield made … was extraordinarily great, and that it was impossible to overrate the extreme ability with which he conducted much of the Congress business. The other representatives were evidently afraid of him, and of all the marked men assembled there, no one was regarded with so much curiosity or treated with so much deference.'[91]

There were limits to the success registered at Berlin. Russophobes feared that Turkey in Europe had been too much undermined and disliked the acquisition by the Russians of Kars and Batoum in the east, while friends of Balkan nationalism and Christianity thought that too little had been done to recognise their claims. Yet, from a starting point of external weakness and internal uncertainty, Disraeli, by persisting in the belief that firmness would deter and that the brink was the most productive vantage point to occupy, had achieved his policy objectives. By holding on until the Russians played into his hands, he had been able to rally Conservative sentiment, secure a leading role in a European settlement which preserved what he had defined as essential British interests and provided Cyprus as a further bastion for their defence, and, above all, assist in the dislocation of the Three Emperors' League. He had made Britain count.

He had also, however, made her count the cost of the military and naval preparations required to sustain an active foreign policy. The income tax went up a penny in 1877, and a further penny, to fivepence, in 1878. When Disraeli and Salisbury returned bearing 'peace with honour' from Berlin, to receive a gift of garters from the royal haberdashery, the whip, Hart Dyke, discouraged exploiting the popular enthusiasm by a dissolution on the ground that it was better to wait for the reduced expenditure on the armed forces and the improved budgets that could now be expected. It was the Palmerstonian lesson once more: the electorate might relish a great role for Britain among the powers, but it must not be bought too dear. Unfortunately, the taxpayers' patience was now to undergo a further test, as to the costs of European prestige were added those of imperial ambition.

It was not Disraeli's ambition that caused the problem. He had raised the banner of empire in 1872 on a consolidatory, not an expansionist, basis. He used empire as an inspirational vision and a device of incantatory rhetoric, and he had a firm if occasionally naive confidence in its ability to weigh in the European balance of power, but, as prime minister, he showed little inclination to do anything about it. His one striking personal initiative was to purchase in November 1875 the Khedive of Egypt's near half-interest in the shares of the company running the Suez Canal, in order to keep them out of French hands. There was no real danger to British use of the canal but Disraeli and the public relished the theatrical coup, even if the Treasury pulled a face at the commission charged by his Rothschild friends, who put up the money.

The forward movements of empire were the result, not of Disraeli's imperialism, but of his excessively loose control of the cabinet and of government policy evident in the Eastern crisis. Though suspicious of his precipitancy and subjection to the influence of the imperial enthusiast J. A. Froude, Disraeli allowed the colonial secretary, Carnarvon, to attempt to reproduce in South Africa the scheme of confederation which he had successfully implemented in 1867 in Canada. The Boer republic of the Transvaal was annexed in 1877, but the determination of Sir Bartle Frere, chosen by Carnarvon as high commissioner, to subdue the military power of the Zulus hurried on a conflict which began with the destruction of a British force at Isandhlwana in January 1879. Disraeli had been dissuaded by the Queen and Hicks Beach, Carnarvon's successor at the Colonial Office, from recalling Frere after his ultimatum to the Zulus had flouted the government's wishes. Now the high commissioner was both censured and retained.

The lack of firm control (even allowing for the difficulties imposed by distance) was simultaneously evident on the north-west frontier of India. Here the man on the spot was the viceroy, Lord Lytton, son of Disraeli's old comrade Bulwer Lytton. Perhaps projecting on to another the qualities he admired in himself, Disraeli chose to regard him as a man of 'ambition, imagination, some vanity, and much will', ideally suited to the task of repelling Russian and advancing British influence in Afghanistan.[92] Living up to this billing, Lytton was as truculently venturesome as Frere. His attempt to force a British mission on the Afghans in supersession of a Russian, without waiting for the issue of Anglo-Russian negotiations then in progress, incurred a rebuff to which a reluctant government felt it had to respond by the invasion of Afghanistan in November 1878. The Amir was obliged to receive a British resident at Kabul in May 1879; his mutinous troops slaughtered the envoy, Cavagnari, with his staff, in September, and a British force took the city the following month.

Though the superiority of British power was quickly reasserted, both Isandhlwana and the Kabul massacre fuelled criticism of the government's imperial policy and contributed to the comprehensive indictment of 'Beaconsfieldism' which Gladstone was to perfect in his Midlothian campaign at the end of 1879. Imperial affairs were rolled up with the Eastern question to portray 'Beaconsfieldism' as a sinister system of policy, which not merely involved the country in immoral, vainglorious and expensive external adventures, inimical to peace and to the rights of small peoples, but aimed at nothing less than the subversion of parliamentary government in favour of some simulacrum of the oriental despotism its creator was alleged to admire. Most of this was partisan extravaganza, worthy of its target's own excursions against the Whigs. A system of policy was exactly what Disraeli's government had never possessed or its leader sought to devise. Yet some colour could be given to it by reference to Disraeli's flights of fancy and to the partnership which he had struck up with the crown.

It was necessary to go back thirty years to find Fakredeen, in *Tancred*, looking on England as doomed to destruction by the Irish problem, the drying up of demand for cotton textiles and the loss of island security through the coming of steamships, and recommending the transfer of the court to Delhi, where the Queen might rule over a great eastern empire without 'the embarrassment of her Chambers'. Yet in the light of that flourish and Disraeli's phrases about a revivified monarchy as a focal point of national resurgence, it was possible to contrive a sufficiently lurid interpretation of the direction of his premiership since he had caused parliament, in 1876, to confer upon Victoria the title of Empress of India. The Royal Titles act was the result of the Queen's anxiety to stand on a titular par with the three leading continental sovereigns, and was rather embarrassedly presented by her minister, but it could be made to look like the construction of an imperial centre of gravity divorced from Westminster, and the movement of Indian troops to Malta in May 1878, executed, like the Cyprus convention the next month, without consultation of parliament, and evoking from Gladstone a reference to the epoch of Charles I, reinforced the impression that India was to be at the heart of a system in which minister and monarch bypassed the ordinary restraints of constitutional government. Disraeli was certainly fascinated by India, as by Turkey, and at least from the time of the Mutiny had urged its closer connection with the crown, but that was more a matter of using the sovereign to consolidate British rule by acting on 'the imagination of the Indian populations' (his characteristic recipe for effective government) than of making Delhi into a seat of power alternative to London, or constructing a model of despotic authority which might reflect back on to the home country – though it seems that Lytton's Imperial Assemblage of January 1877 (it had to be, said Salisbury, 'gaudy enough to impress the orientals, yet not enough to give hold for ridicule here') was meant to lift the prestige of the government in Britain as well as in India.[93]

Greater plausibility resided in the charge that Disraeli's exploitation of the Queen's influence in the handling of the Eastern crisis challenged constitutional propriety, and fuller knowledge would have reinforced it. In 1877 he more than once encouraged Victoria's assertion of her authority by holding up the Public Worship Regulation and the Royal Titles acts as demonstrating 'how great is the power of the Sovereign in this country, if firm and faithfully served' (both measures, he asserted, having been passed 'without the support of the Cabinet'). He reported to her the views expressed by individual ministers in cabinet and had no reluctance about her putting pressure on recalcitrants or on the cabinet as a whole. As the Eastern crisis reached its height, he spoke to her, in November 1877, of enforcing *her* policy on the cabinet, and, a few weeks later, described his success in getting his way with his colleagues as 'another proof of what may be done when the Sovereign and the Minister act together'. The partnership was close enough by this time for the ordinary conventions of relationship between sovereign and subject to be relaxed. The Queen's visit to Hughenden in December was a deliberate demonstration both of her support for her prime minister's policy and of the particular friendship which she shared with him. 'All his own thoughts and feelings and duties and affections are now concentrated in your Majesty', wrote Disraeli in January 1878, following this up with a communication in the first person which produced a reply signed 'Yours aff'ly, V.R.&I.'.[94]

Much of this represented more the mingling of political sympathy with a mutually consolatory fantasy of devotion between two elderly people than it did an attempt to shift the balance of the constitution. The Queen was effectively a Conservative, and she strongly believed in her prime minister's line towards Russia. It was inevitable that Disraeli should capitalise on her support for what it was worth, and in foreign affairs her long experience and network of family contacts gave her a degree of knowledge and grasp which no government could easily ignore. At moments the vehemence of her views was too strong even for her prime minister, and his powers of management were severely taxed. Occasionally he withstood her, as when in 1879 he refused to show favour to Lord Chelmsford, the commander responsible for the initial military reverse in South Africa. But he certainly used her influence and her friendship as a political resource, if not to subvert parliamentary government – neither of them was foolish enough to think that possible, even if either had wished it – then at least to infuse into it a little of the animating force of that revived royal authority, supported by 'national opinion', for which Coningsby had once called. The trouble was that the crown's future as a unifying national symbol – something which Gladstone, who had frequently attempted as prime minister to bring the Queen out of seclusion and into the performance of public duty, wished to promote just as much as Disraeli – depended on its abstinence from open partisanship. In making the Queen supreme governor of the Conservative party, Disraeli risked undermining rather than enlarging her constitutional utility.

For E. A. Freeman, the Queen's lunching at Hughenden was 'going ostentatiously to eat with Disraeli in his ghetto'. Perhaps it was appropriate that a distinguished historian of Anglo-Saxon England should thus voice the exclusiveness of the Anglo-Saxon protestant brand of nationalism that felt itself so sorely provoked by Disraeli's actions. Underlying, sometimes overlaying, the charge that 'Beaconsfieldism' was aimed at subverting English liberties was the suggestion that it must naturally be so, because Beaconsfield himself was not English. Disraeli's racialism rebounded on him as the conventional legal and constitutional view of nationality was increasingly challenged by one based on antecedents. He had himself contributed to the shift of emphasis by devising an essentially cultural interpretation of the English nation in which Jews, as the indispensable carriers of the values and beliefs which informed Christian civilisation and pointed out the historic mission of the English race, had an integral place and might play an eminent role. That interpretation all too easily struck his enemies as no more than the local facade for a Jewish universalist chauvinism of which he proposed to make England a subsidiary. His imperial policy, wrote the nonconformist preacher William Crosbie in 1879, was only 'a vulgar parody of the ancient Jewish dream' of temporal power following the appearance of the Messiah. The racial thinking he had adopted could be turned to the extrusion of Jews, baptised and unbaptised, from the core of a nation choosing to find its roots in Saxondom rather than in Sinai and the expression of its religious genius in the English reformation rather than in the Hebrew canticles. The abuse that descended on Disraeli at this time formed part of the appearance of so-called modern political anti-Semitism across Europe at the end of the 1870s.[95] Goldwin Smith's question in the *Nineteenth Century* in 1878, 'Can Jews be Patriots?' anticipated by sixteen years Edouard Drumont's sneering exoneration of Dreyfus from the charge of betraying his country on the argument that a Jew could not have a country. Disraeli's hits at the Liberals' 'cosmopolitanism' were being returned on him with interest. At the moment when he attained to the apogee of his power in the nation onto which he had taken such pains to graft himself, a large part of it rejected him as an alien sprig.

The Lancashire operatives had long been saying, 'We shall never have good luck under a Jew', Salisbury was told in May 1880.[96] In the end, it was perhaps as much economic recession as imperial imbroglio that gave anti-Semitic superstition its bite. It was the misfortune of Disraeli's government neatly to coincide with the arrival of the long-term depression which followed the collapse of the world railway boom in 1873. By the winter of 1878–9, the fall in prices, profits and employment, accompanied by pressure for the downward adjustment of wages, was creating widespread unease in the centres of trade and industry and much hardship among the industrial working classes. The foreign competition which, producers complained, was being unleashed upon a defenceless, free-trade Britain from behind tariff walls was felt even more acutely in agriculture, where a flood of cheap wheat from North America exacerbated the effects of a run of exceptionally bad summers, culminating in the worst harvest of the century in 1879. The ministry was not responsible for these shocks, nor did current economic thinking suggest that it could, or should attempt to, do much about them. It got the blame none the less, and the effect of bad trade on the revenue, at a time when the costs of the Eastern crisis, Afghanistan and South Africa had to be met, contributed to a series of large budget deficits, rising to £3.35 million in 1879–80. For political reasons, ministers were inhibited from responding by new taxation. In 1879 Disraeli forbade Northcote to increase the tea duties to pay for the Zulu war, and forced him to resort not only to fresh borrowing but to raiding the sinking fund, thus laying the government open to the charge of financial imprudence so damaging with the mid-Victorian middle classes, and supplying the finishing touch to the blazing condemnation of 'Beaconsfieldism' as an immoral, extravagant and incompetent system of government with which Gladstone opened his candidature for the Midlothian constituency in November and December 1879.

Disraeli's disdaining to notice the passionate rhetoric of the first Midlothian campaign was perhaps an error, but it was a forced error: he possessed neither the manner nor the matter for an effective counter to the new style of popular politics which Gladstone was inaugurating. However much he believed in politics as an appeal to the imagination, he was incapable of projecting them in dramatised form to the nascent democracy. It was Gladstone, descending on the Scots by special train and torchlight procession, who, as John Vincent has put it, 'created a national theatre for England [read 'Britain'] as Verdi did for nine-teenth-century Italy',[97] and used it to denounce the theatricality of his rival's government by grand gesture. Disraeli's theatre of politics lay in parliament and in society, not on the platform. Going on the stump to mass audiences was alien to his idea of responsible statesmanship and beyond his physical resources. In a climate of depressed trade, it was in any case difficult to produce a vindication of the government's record which would convince the electors.

It was hard to resist the impression that the ministry, after nearly six years in office, was dying on its feet. The great press of foreign and imperial business, combined with the brake imposed on legislation by the obstructionist tactics of Irish members in the Commons and by the need for economy, had much curtailed its domestic programme. The impetus of social reform had almost run out. Cross consolidated the factory acts in 1878, but the ministry fumbled ineffectively with the complicated question of employers' liability for injuries to workmen, and by 1879 Northcote was struggling to reduce expenditure on edu-cation and to restrict government loans to local authorities, which were mostly for sanitary or educational purposes. Revitalisation of the government's energies in face of its difficulties was beyond the prime minister. '"The stars in their courses have fought against" me' was his fatalistic response to bad times. Like everybody else, he saw no choice but to await the inevitable turn of the economic cycle. Once an advocate of reciprocity in Britain's commercial relations, and of imperial preference, he refused now to respond to a flicker of feeling in his party in favour of retaliatory duties against those countries whose tariff barriers hindered British trade. It was too late, and, if the spectre of food taxes were raised, politically too risky, to reverse the commitment to free trade. Very dependent by this time on others' prompting, Disraeli picked up from the journalist Frederick Greenwood the idea of a national fund to relieve distress and then dropped it at Northcote's instigation, telling Lady Bradford in December 1878: 'There are so many plans, so many schemes and so many reasons why there shd. be neither plans nor schemes' adding 'the property of the nation to support the numbers of unemployed labor? Worse than socialism.' There was nothing to be done.[98]

The most alarming feature of the recession from Disraeli's point of view was the crisis in arable farming, because it threatened to shatter that landed society in the service of which he had made his career, and on the cohesion and prosperity of which he believed the stability of the nation and the strength of the Conservative party to depend. The world he knew was literally menaced by collapse: in October 1879, he was retailing to Lady Bradford the current gossip that 'as the consequence of the landed break-up' there was to be 'no more turf, and no more London seasons'.[99] The most serious danger was that economic crisis would splinter the rural community of landlords, farmers and labourers into antagonistic interests. Disraeli counselled patience, rent reductions, and the use of the government's Agricultural Holdings act to compensate tenants for their unexhausted improvements, and a royal commission on agricultural depression was set up, but these means of holding the landed interest together were insufficient to prevent the emergence of organised discontent in the shape of a Farmers' Alliance. It was as much as anything the instinct to summon up the Conservatives' traditional county strength before the farmers' movement and its exploitation by the opposition could undermine it that inclined Disraeli to appeal to the country while the parliament still had a year of its term to run. The ministry faced a variety of problems if it continued for another session, prominent among them Irish difficulties and the fiasco of Cross's attempt to buy out the London water companies on what were widely denounced as excessively generous terms. Encouraged by an apparently favourable trend in by-elections, the cabinet decided on 6 March 1880 to dissolve.

As it had come in on no particular policy, so the government went out on none. Disraeli's strategy in the election was that of 1874, to consolidate the defenders of established interests and the opponents of fundamental change, this time by proclaiming the need to resist the home rule movement in Ireland, which he insinuated his opponents might not, just as he hinted that they would be unable to maintain the power of England, and the peace of Europe which he alleged to depend on it. The Irish issue was not a happy choice. The Conservatives had never recovered from Gladstone's snatching the Irish question from their hands in 1868, and Disraeli had largely put it out of his sight, complacently telling the Queen after an Irish debate in 1876 that he did not believe that the banner of home rule would ever again be unfurled in the House of Commons.[100] Though the outgoing cabinet had been considering measures to counter the agrarian agitation in Ireland, including an extension of provision for land purchase, they scarcely had an Irish policy, and the issue had little appeal for British electors, with small immediate interest in Irish problems but a lively consciousness of their own.

It was inevitable that the election would be fought mainly on the government's record, and under the shadow of the recession to which, its opponents agreed, the tendency of its showy and expensive foreign and imperial policies to disturb commercial confidence had greatly contributed. While Gladstone rampaged in a second Midlothian campaign, Disraeli, debarred, as a peer, from direct engagement in the electoral battle, awaited the outcome at Hatfield, which Salisbury had placed at his disposal, sipping the 1870 Margaux which his host had, embarrassingly, ordered to be served to him alone. He needed its consolation, though he had been warned by Corry to be sceptical of the party managers' confident forecasts. The expenditure of a good deal of money from sources such as the Church Defence Institution, the Orange Order and the Licensed Victuallers' Association could not save the Conservatives from a loss of over 100 seats, leaving them only 237 strong in face of 353 Liberals and 62 Home Rulers. Their advances of 1874 in the bigger towns were reversed: they now held only 24 of the 114 seats in boroughs with over 50,000 inhabitants at the 1871 census. They were routed with a net loss of 36 in Ireland, Scotland and Wales (where they were reduced to two seats). Disraeli's party was being forced back on the English rural haunches on which it had squatted in the frustrating fifties and sixties, and even that posture was insecure, as the disturbing loss of 29 English county seats with only one gain made clear.[101]

It was hardly an advertisement for the appeal of the Toryism of imperial destiny, European power and domestic reform which Disraeli had conjured up. He chose to ascribe the *débâcle* first, and probably correctly, to 'Hard Times' and 'that sympathy for change which is inherent in man' (in other words, the swing of the pendulum, which was now coming into vogue as an explanation, or description, of the behaviour of the mass electorate). Next he picked on the 'new foreign political organisation' of the Liberals (that is, the Brummagem 'caucus' system), though he was more reluctant than many of his colleagues to blame correspondingly the defects widely alleged to exist in Conservative organisation after six years of office. What he would not do was admit that the results cast any doubt on the attraction of his brand of Toryism for the voters he had brought into being in 1867. He combined the two Conservative gains in large urban constituencies, at Greenwich and Sheffield, with the successes in the City and Westminster to demonstrate that 'the enlightened masses are with us'; and, 'sympathy for change' or no, he argued to a party meeting on 19 May 1880 that 'the great and sudden change was not due, as some would have it, to the fickleness of the newly enfranchised classes ... he analysed our losses, so as to show that they had been most marked in the counties, where the suffrage is more restricted'. Writing to Manners about the Irish question in December, he would declare: 'The only portion of the Constituencies, in my opinion, who may be depended on when affairs are riper, are the English working-classes.'[102] But for the present no ringing popular appeal could be made, even had Disraeli been able to think of one. The strategy he enjoined on the party was its conventional one in face of large, hostile majorities, as practised by Peel in the thirties and by Disraeli himself in the sixties, propping the Whigs against the Radicals and Irish to defend property and the constitution and waiting to reap the benefit of the inevitable dissensions amongst them.

The government had resigned without meeting parliament and the Queen had relinquished her favourite minister with anguished reluctance, looking forward to a speedy return of the Conservatives, pending which Disraeli was to see to it that the Liberals did not do too much damage. The confidential correspondence she subsequently maintained with him in the first person might have challenged constitutional propriety had it done anything more than pander to prejudices already long established. Desire to answer his sovereign's call for support was perhaps one element in persuading Disraeli not to take immediately the retirement from the Conservative leadership that a severe electoral rebuff might seem to make natural and inevitable for a man in his seventy-seventh year. Another was his customary inability to conceive how the party could do without him, at a moment, as he saw it, of grave peril for the interests it existed to defend and the nation it existed to unite.

His principal message to the meeting of 19 May was to watch out for attempts to revolutionise the tenure of land and pull down the aristocracy. The designs of Radicals to undermine landlord power seemed manifest in 1880 and 1881; in minor key in the Hares and Rabbits bill, which, in appealing to the anxiety of farmers to control ground game, emphasised the opposition between their interests and the landlords' which had damaged the Conservatives' county showing at the election; and in major key in a measure responding to the agrarian problem in Ireland by restraining the eviction of tenants for non-payment of rent, which Disraeli characterised as 'the opening of a great attack on the land'. The issues were too complicated to make simple politics. Disraeli could not lead the landlords in the Upper House to reject the Hares and Rabbits bill for fear of losing 'the only classes on wh. we once thought we cd. rely – the landed interest in all its divisions', but, as Shannon points out, all the Liberals achieved with the measure, and with the abolition of the malt tax in Gladstone's 1880 budget, was to make it easier for that interest to cohere again behind its Conservative champions.[103] As it emerged that the government would offer to the Irish tenantry the 'three Fs' of fair rent, fixity of tenure and free sale, Disraeli veered between Salisbury's pressure to strike an attitude of intransigent resistance to the curtailment of landlords' rights and the warnings of Cairns that it would be difficult for the Conservatives to resist the extension to the whole of Ireland of that tenant right which was customary among their only reliable Irish supporters, in Ulster. The Irish landlords, he was forced to conclude, would accept, and hence the Lords swallow, the 'three Fs'. Yet all the same he meant to resist.

Given Disraeli's lifelong conviction that, as he now put it to Salisbury, 'the greatness and character of this country depended on our landed tenure', his stance was inevitable. By now, however, the conduct of the Conservative party as predominantly a vehicle for defence of the landed interest was coming to look anachronistic to some of its keenest supporters. Its middle-class provincial activists were beginning to stir against the domination of the 'old identity' which ran the party, with its over-concentration on the land and its ineptitude in appealing to the big urban electorates. Voiced through the National Union, and ripe for exploitation by a cavalier careerist like the young Lord Randolph Churchill, their discontent foreshadowed a contest for the rebalancing and reorientation of the party that Disraeli would hardly be equipped to control. The ebullience of Churchill and his Fourth Party frondeurs, who harried the government and their own, too uncombative, front bench in the Commons in 1880, he could appreciate and enjoy as a kind of latter-day Young England, though at the risk of undermining the authority of his lieutenant in the Commons, Northcote. It was impossible for him to sympathise or cope with a shift in the balance of the party's management, away from the landed circles to which he had attached himself in order to rise, and towards the middle-class urban Conservativism which he hardly knew or cared to know. He appreciated the uses of men like Cross, and had placed W. H. Smith at the Admiralty in 1877, despite the Queen's misgivings, in part to respond to the complaint that the Conservative borough members were not represented in the cabinet. Derby, however, had noted in that year his 'odd dislike of middle-class men, though they are the strength of our party'; and Derby's departure in 1878 had given him an opportunity of demonstrating his attachment both to the principle of parity of representation of the Lords in the cabinet and to the old aristocratic houses, by replacing a Stanley with a Percy, in the shape of the duke of Northumberland.[104]

At a moment when the party was being seriously challenged in its traditional rural base and would have to look increasingly for its prospects of revival to the cultivation of its urban middle-class sympathisers, Disraeli was in danger of losing touch with its needs. His loneliness in his party was more marked than ever. Salisbury was told by his nephew, Arthur Balfour, in January 1881, that Disraeli was anxious to have confidential communication with him, in part because of 'the contempt with which he regards a large number of his late colleagues'. It was symptomatic that almost the one man with whom Disraeli could contemplate intimate political relations, and whom he could readily envisage as a successor, was the most impeccably aristocratic and doggedly anti-democratic figure the upper echelons of the party possessed. The two of them confronted the parliamentary session of 1881, gloomily surveying the prospect of the despairing defence of a decaying world against the tide of tenurial revolution and imperial disintegration. 'We can but die', Disraeli told Balfour, 'like gentlemen.'[105]

At least there were some compensations for the political despondency of these months. Defeat in April 1880 had enabled Disraeli to look forward, as he told Earl Barrington, to passing spring and summer in the woods of Hughenden, 'which he had never been able to do, and longed for'. Northcote visited him at Hughenden in July and talked books with him, noting: 'the Chief is always at his best in his library'. In fact, he was not only talking books, but writing one. *Endymion*, a novel probably largely composed in the early seventies, was now finished in time for publication in November by Longman, who had paid £10,000 for it. Much of the habitual verve and wit and all the old enchantment with the scenes of life were there, as they continued to be in Disraeli's social correspondence (the Prince of Wales, on a continental trip, he told Lady Bradford, 'has seen a great deal in his fortnight's absence: all the great men and, I suppose, some of the famous women').[106] The creative drive was sufficient to carry him into beginning a new novel, *Falconet*, of which he completed nine chapters. Where *Endymion* had been in some ways a nostalgic retrospect over the social and political world of his younger days, *Falconet* reflected his never wearied fascination with the events and ideas of the moment. Apart from setting out to lampoon Gladstone (as Joseph Toplady Falconet, whom 'all the prigs' spoke of as the coming man), it promised to be a panorama of the revolutionary philosophical and social doctrines and movements of the day, not least the nihilists, who in March 1881 provided spectacular advance publicity by assassinating Tsar Alexander II.

Disraeli's appearance in the Lords on 15 March to support the vote of condolence to the Queen on the death of her relative was his last in parliament. He had been struggling as usual with asthma and gout through an unusually bitter winter and chill spring, and the only foe he ever dreaded, the east wind, caught him at last. He had no capacity of physical resistance left. By the end of March his condition was serious. He lingered for three weeks, and died peacefully in the early morning of 19 April, at his new house in Curzon Street, with his secretaries, Rowton and Barrington, his man of business, Rose, and his doctors by his side. It was the anniversary of Byron's death. Disraeli was a great contriver, but perhaps it was an indulgent fate that contrived that. In his will, he had left instructions for a quiet burial, beside his wife in the churchyard at Hughenden. It was not the false affectation of simplicity that Gladstone, who had offered a public funeral, exasperatedly supposed. It was the desire that had run through all his striving in the country of his sojourn, to rest at last at home.

ENVOI: THE PRIMROSE SPHINX

A MONG a sample of nearly a quarter of the parliamentary Conservative party, responding in 1994 to the question which books or authors had most influenced their political beliefs, sixteen per cent cited Disraeli, who came top of the list, ahead of Edmund Burke. Why Disraeli's name and ideas should have continued to ring inspirationally down decades of Conservative history has sometimes puzzled those who have noted that, in electoral terms, he was a far less successful leader than Salisbury, who followed him, and that the practice of the party after him might seem to bear the marks more of sober Peelite pragmatism, incorporating the middle classes into the defence of property and the social order, than of Disraelian rhetoric and romance. John Vincent in particular has sketched with verve the case for regarding Disraeli's career as a 'failure'.[1]

For most of its course it was less a failure than a sideshow, albeit a sparkling and dramatic sideshow. Disraeli made little immediate difference to the Conservative party or to British politics. His political importance in mid-century is greatly exaggerated by the interpretation that sees him as the man who, by toppling Peel and making it impossible subsequently for the Peelites to rejoin the Conservative ranks, might almost have claimed to be, in Lord Blake's words, 'the unconscious founder of the Liberal party',[2] and condemned his own side to nearly thirty years of parliamentary minority and almost continuous opposition. Peel rode for a fall, and was unhorsed by his wilful incomprehension of the conditions of party politics, not by Disraeli's dexterity in pointing it out. The failure of the Peelites to reunite with the main body of the Conservatives owed as much to the latter's resentment of Gladstone's overbearing arrogance as to the former's distaste for Disraeli. The long years out of power, and the six successive electoral defeats from 1847 to 1868, were the consequence of the failure of Peel and his acolytes to find the means of reconciling executive and party government and uniting property and respectability under the Conservative banner; not of the distrust inspired by Disraeli's parti-coloured past. In any case, if Disraeli lowered the tone of the party, so did Derby, who was without question its real leader. Not just his taste for the odds and the tricks, but, as Jonathan Parry has pointed out,[3] the immoderation of his opposition to his former Whig colleagues after his resignation from Grey's cabinet in 1834, rendered his reliability suspect. The Conservative party was handicapped in mid-century not because it had one leader whose brilliance in debate failed to compensate in the public mind for a certain lack of gravitas, but because it had two.

The junior of them had no natural root in the party and no natural affinity with his followers, amongst whom he had scarcely a real friend. He had also, in parliamentary talent, scarcely a rival, but he held on at the top not only because he was, in Lord Blake's phrase, 'an indis-pensable liability'[4] to the party but because it was an indispensable lia-bility to him. Unconnected with the governing elite, unassisted by the public school and the 'crack college' which helped to slide newcomers like Gladstone gracefully into it, he could rise only on the surf of party antagonism. If the Conservative party was condemned to put up with him, he was condemned to put up with it, over long, ungrateful years of virtual estrangement. Even had the party been able to replace him, however, little would have been gained. No Conservative leader in the middle of the nineteenth century could have overcome the disad-vantage imposed by Peel's failure, in the pivotal phase of transition from a predominantly agrarian to a predominantly industrial economy, to graft urban appeal on to an agricultural base. All that Disraeli could do in the Commons was to maintain a brave face and a ready wit, and make himself, in the full flush of his mature ambition for power, the outstanding opposition leader of the century. Even the Reform act of 1867 was a brilliant opposition manoeuvre, executed in office. Designed to disrupt a seemingly permanent Liberal majority by infringing the Liberals' monopoly of constructive legislation on national issues, as Derby and Disraeli had tried to do in 1859, it was followed by the election of a much larger Liberal majority. It strengthened the

Conservatives only by strengthening the force of urban radical Liberalism to the point at which, after the cascade of institutional reform in Gladstone's first government, the middle-class vote which had followed Palmerston as the soundest conservative in the country began to wonder where the Liberal party might go next. Disraeli was saved, as he had been in the days of expected Peelite return to the Conservative fold, not by his own power of attraction but by others' of repulsion. The Conservative party did not so much mount to victory as find itself suddenly exposed by the ebbing of the Liberal tide which had submerged it for nearly thirty years. If any leader would have lost the elections of 1847 to 1865, it is arguable that almost any would have won that of 1874.

Perhaps any Conservative prime minister, too, could have accomplished the mandate of the 1874 government, which was to do nothing in particular, and accomplished it better than Disraeli, whose instinct was to do something, without knowing what it was. The social reform by which the first years of Disraeli's administration were distinguished, in large measure uncontroversial and almost bi-partisan, was a means for ministers to make themselves useful in the vast spaces of parliamentary time freed by the disappearance of the institutional innovations and Irish preoccupations of the previous ministry. When Disraeli's desire to leave a mark led him into an assertive foreign policy and (more reluctantly) into acquiescence in imperial expansion, the result was to destroy the newly won Conservative majority. The costs of global prestige, coinciding with recession, wrecked the attempt to take over from Gladstone and the Liberals the Pittite and Peelite tradition of prudent financial administration which had been the kernel of Derby's and Disraeli's strategy in mid-century. Disraeli may have wagered correctly in 1872 that the electorate wanted a stronger British profile in the world, but it was no longer possible to perform Palmerston's trick of securing it on the cheap. Defeat in the general election of 1880 seemed to signify the inevitable end of a Conservative parenthesis in a Liberal polity.

Yet if, in 1880, the primrose path of Disraeli's leadership might seem to have led straight to the electoral bonfire, it was soon beginning to be erected into a potent political myth. 'Last week on the 19th', noted Eddy Hamilton, Gladstone's private secretary, in his diary for 23 April

1883, 'the Beaconsfield statue was unveiled, and on that day a sentimental hobby has been started of wearing Primroses – henceforth to
be called Primrose Day – in honour of Lord B. whose favourite flower
was supposed to be primroses. Marvellously inappropriate and un-
English!' Lord Randolph Churchill's invocation of 'the great Tory
Democracy, which Lord Beaconsfield partly constructed' seized hold of
Disraeli as an inspirational mentor of those Conservatives who thought
the future of the party in the age of 'mass' politics depended on a radical
broadening of its basis and approach. The establishment of the
Primrose League, with its 'knights' and 'dames' and 'habitations', paid
tribute to Disraeli in neatly combining with the medieval flummery of
Young England an institutionalised bringing together of upper-class
leadership and lower-class deference in an important development of
the mass electoral organisation needed to cope with the consequences of
the 1867 Reform act (appropriately, it was the first party auxiliary sys-
tematically to harness the political energies of women).[5]

Down the decades, a carefully cultivated Disraelian tradition covered
the actions of Tory 'democrats', social reformers and class conciliators,
and to a lesser degree imperialists and patriots, achieving its fullest
flowering, perhaps, in the One Nation group of the post-1945 years;
until in the 1970s it became less a banner of advance than a shield under
which the so-called 'wets' huddled together for protection against a
new Conservative ideology, which seemed to eliminate the Disraelian
problem of how to achieve social integration by denying the existence
of society. Even those who appeared to be its assailants, however, were
unwilling entirely to dispense with the incantatory value of the name.
Two years after securing the leadership of the Conservative party,
Margaret Thatcher was still referring to Disraeli as 'the architect of
modern Toryism', albeit on the basis of a rather vague formulation of
his views – though not so vague, perhaps, as that which a little earlier
had led President Richard Nixon to describe his policy as 'probably that
of a Disraeli Conservative'. Delivering to the St Stephen's
Constitutional Club in 1985 the first Disraeli Lecture, the then
chairman of the Conservative party, Norman Tebbitt, press-ganged
Disraeli unceremoniously into the ranks of posthumous patrons of the
Thatcherite revolution. Five years later, it was the turn of a historian,

John Vincent, to claim Disraeli as an exponent of 'capitalist modernism', anti-statism and the free-market economy, though even on Vincent's analysis, and even if Adam Smith did finally appear in the Tory canon as enumerated by the George Smythe figure in *Endymion*, it is hard to swallow as a plausible proto-Thatcherite a politician who specialised in irony, believed in 'society' in both senses of the word, castigated the 'triple worship' of Mammon, despised economic pedants and ideological prigs, and, in saying of Joseph Chamberlain that he 'looked, and spoke, like a cheesemonger', was hardly ringing a till for the moral values, intellectual sophistications and social style of the corner shop.[6]

Disraeli's vigorous after-life in politics witnesses to the need of Conservatives, especially on the left of the party, to operate under the aegis of a colourable tradition, as he did with Bolingbroke, but also to the vivacity and suggestiveness of his ideas and their relevance to the problems of modern social and political organisation. His contribution to Conservative history was not to lead the party to victory or to change its nature in his own day, but to bequeath a fund of insights and watchwords on which it could draw productively in the future. Disraeli's ideas were designed for personal rather than party ends, but, in situating his genius against the background of world trends in which he sought to play a heroic part, and in seeking to integrate it in a leading role into the society in which an arbitrary fate had placed it, he was led to develop both a view of modern politics and a version of England's mission that were bound to influence, if they could not transform, the party which he chose as the vehicle of his career. The bedrock of his Conservatism was a routine enough reaction against the French Revolution, 'which has not yet ended, and which is certainly the greatest event that has happened in the history of man', as he put it in 1864.[7] Give or take a few ringing phrases, the defence of authority, hierarchy, property and faith against anarchy, atheism, egalitarianism and the military tyranny to which they naturally led was no more original in his hands than in those of other European conservatives, and told his party nothing that it did not already know. But, in his trilogy of novels especially, he set the Conservative task in England in the context of two world-historical forces which, by the 1840s, were beginning to dominate debate on society and politics: the alleged influence of race, and the explosive effect of the immense acceleration of the pace of economic and social change brought about by the application of steam power and capitalist industrial organisation. It was the supreme spiritual and civilising genius of the Semitic races, as he proclaimed it, that supplied Disraeli with his title to lay down the law to the English, and, transmitted through the Christianity that he held to be its ultimate expression, supplied the English, another valiant little nation and people of the book, with their title to pursue across the world the mission imparted by the lays of ancient Israel. The stimulation of an English sense of imperial destiny was the means of trying to infuse a common pride and purpose into a society threatened with disintegration and decay by the second of the two great dramas which pulsed through the trilogy, the shattering of old forms of community and old principles of authority by the advance of industrialisation and the emergence of antagonistic classes of rich and poor without organic social relationship or uniting faith.

If much of this bypassed the squires who 'did not read, and did not understand the ideas of their own time', it did keep the Conservative party in touch with the common market of European political ideas and offer it a view of what politics in the post-agrarian phase of western European history might be about, and of how a party of tradition might react to them. Disraeli's critics then and since have been right to point out that he did not supply any precise answers to the questions he threw, sometimes brilliantly, into relief. The revival of the power of the crown as an independent arbiter amid competing factions and interests, the revivification of the church as a source of spiritual energy and social ministry, the recognition by the upper classes of their paternal responsibilities to the lower, the frustration of the assertion of democratic rights by the protection of popular liberties and the timely extension of 'popular privileges', were vague enough formulas for the restoration of community out of the crowd into which liberal individualism was alleged to have dissolved the nation. Not much was done with them in practice, though the 1867 Reform act, at least in its rhetorical presentation, could be seen as implementing the last of them, and the social reform with which Disraeli identified himself as giving content to the paternalist posture. The assertion of national mission and the pampering of the appetite for national prestige in an era when the balance of economic and military power was beginning to tilt against Britain, not least after 1870 and what Disraeli called 'the German revolution',[8] led to some precarious paradoxes in the 1870s, with Disraeli starring as the impresario of English national identity, though he was more 'cosmopolitan' than most of the Liberals whom he lampooned for that, supposedly anti-national, quality; as an imperialist, though he did not advocate the expansion of empire; and as the champion of a strong line in international affairs, though he had grasped at least as early and as firmly as Palmerston that it was becoming increasingly difficult for the country to support either the risks or the costs.

There were no, or very few, Disraelian policies, legislative or administrative, by which national unity could be promoted or national purpose effectively implemented. Yet there was a sense of the direction in which the nation and the party ought to be travelling, and a rhetoric that assumed an underlying consensus for the journey. Disraeli's art and legacy lay not in the manufacture of measures but in the management of impressions. He was perhaps the first Conservative practitioner to tear at the heart of the prevalent liberal ideologies of his day by denying that politics and government were a primarily ratiocinative activity. The appeal to the imagination which Sidonia advocates, the injunction to give people something to adore and to obey, may look like a summons to cynical manipulation of an immature public mind, but they were simply the reflection of Disraeli's sincere beliefs about the nature of politics, the recognition of what moved himself as well as others in the sphere of political thought and action. Image-making, for Disraeli, was not charlatanism, but the necessary technique whereby the force of idea, in the power of which to shape external reality he never lost his romantic faith, could be brought to bear on the common understanding. He more or less single-handedly hewed out the central plank of his party's platform for a century by creating the image of the Conservatives as the national party, a title to which the much broader church of Gladstonian Liberalism had arguably a superior claim, especially if the nation were to be defined as British rather than (as usually by Disraeli) English. The values of Toryism were presented as the natural emanation of the national character, the social structure it defended and the institutions it upheld as the guarantees of national liberty and order. National identity was appropriated as the possession of a party and the national credentials of half the political nation were impugned. The emphasis on national unity, reinforced by the pressure of growing economic, imperial and military competition between states after 1870, became a partisan tool against the movers and shakers in British society. The platform parties at Conservative election meetings who, until well after the Second World War, rose behind a table draped with the Union Jack to lead the audience in 'Land of Hope and Glory', were paying tribute to the device of appropriating the symbols and imagery of the nation which Disraeli had done as much as anyone to develop.

As Disraeli seemed to subsequent generations of Conservatives to have pre-empted the future by seizing, in an age of nationalism, the national cause, so he appeared, in the era of class conflict and electoral democracy, to have devised the formulas with which a party of property and hierarchy could treat for the survival of their privileges with a predominantly working-class constituency. Disraeli's rhetoric of national identity and the mutual interest and interdependence of classes effectively dissolved the problem of social cleavage which he had dramatised in *Sybil*, by treating it as an aberration from the norm of social relations. He saw it as caused mainly by the excesses of Liberal individualism, and by an inattentiveness on the part of property to its social duties which could be compensated if its representatives showed, by the passing of social legislation such as that which distinguished Disraeli's second ministry, that the national institutions were responsive to the people's needs. The 1867 Reform act enabled the Conservative party to claim that it had been willing to trust the people with political power. The watchwords of empire and social reform proclaimed in Disraeli's 1872 speeches supplied, under party auspices, a national mission and a symbol of national power in which rich and poor alike could be summoned to take pride, and a concrete expression of the bonds of interest and sympathy between them in the generation of the social efficiency by which alone the tasks of empire could be sustained. Disraeli cultivated no personal rapport with the emergent mass electorate, but he produced the imagery and the phraseology with which it could be cajoled in Tory terms. He led Conservatives to see that it might be exploited as a resource as well as feared as an enemy, because he grasped that, as a shrewd Liberal politician, R. B. Haldane would put it shortly after his death, 'a democracy has not got, as is assumed in practice, a body of definite opinions for the expression of which in Parliament it is seeking for delegates, but ... is an assembly of human beings earnestly seeking guidance from those of whose sympathies it is sure'.[9]

'The mind of a seer in the body of a mountebank', wrote Austen Chamberlain, unconsciously avenging his father. Disraeli's apparent prescience in grasping the conditions of Conservative survival in an era of nationalism, imperialism and democracy which he himself hardly entered endowed him with the reputation of preternatural political vision even amongst those Conservatives who doubted his genuineness and denied his right to belong to their club ('A Jew', Chamberlain thought, 'may be a loyal Englishman & passionately patriotic, but he is intellectually apart from us & will never be purely & simply English'). The sense of tectonic forces grinding just beneath the surface of day-to-day events imparted to his writings and speeches a resonance far beyond their immediate occasion; his darting at the latest events, in philosophy or science as in politics, gave his works not only topicality but a modernity that seemed to reach from the present into the future. If *Endymion* read like the product of a mind gently slipping back into its past, the chapters of *Falconet* which Disraeli completed shortly before his death were quite different. Once again, to use Israel Zangwill's words, 'his books palpitate with world-problems'. While the Buddhist missionary, Kusinara, who has come to see what may be done about the decay of faith in England, suggests another of Disraeli's oriental prescriptions for European ills, the intellectual German, Hartmann, and his mysterious associate look forward to a coming catastrophe of the human species: 'these immense armies, these new-fangled armaments – what do they mean? Destruction in every form must be welcomed.' A distinguished stranger appears, in classic Disraelian vein, to announce, by way of small talk at a fashionable party: 'Society is resolving itself into its original elements. Its superficial order is the result of habit, not of conviction ... Creeds disappear in a night. As for political institutions, they are all challenged, and statesmen, conscious of what is at hand, are changing nations into armies.'[10] Where Disraeli meant to go from this apocalyptic opening, no one knows, but once more he was sensing the vibrations in the air, seeking to make out the distant murmur of what was to come, catching, it almost seems, some faint, anticipatory sound of the guns of August 1914.

In the last analysis, however, Disraeli lives on as a source of political inspiration less because of his contributions to Conservative strategy and discourse, or his sense of profound forces shaping the flow of events, or his attributes of the seer, than because of the brilliance and excitement that he found in, and imparted to, political life. He not only said, but made others feel, that politics was 'the great game'. Above all, he enthralled the young. An opponent, W. V. Harcourt, told him, on his leaving the Commons for the Lords: 'To the imagination of the younger generation, your life will always have a special fascination. For them you have enlarged the horizon of the possibilities of the future.' Disraeli's ascent to the first place, had, as he wished it to have, the aura of a romantic epic. 'What is a great life', asked the hero of de Vigny's *Cinq-Mars*, a work contemporary with *Vivian Grey*, 'but a thought of youth carried out by maturity? ... all that our whole existence can do, is to come close to that first sketch.'[11] Disraeli's life has glittered in the gaze of aspiring youth as an example of how wit, audacity and unshakeable purpose (or, for some, cynicism, effrontery and unblushing opportunism) may triumph over dullness, prejudice and convention. The root of Disraeli's appeal is the adventure he made of his life, by consciously living it as an adventure.

The determination to shape himself and his career along the lines of force supplied by destiny imparted to Disraeli's life an earnestness easily missed by those who could see only the dexterity of the actor-manager, producing himself in whatever part suited the evening's audience. Lady Dorothy Nevill, one of the few people to know him well, believed that 'at heart he had a profound contempt for frivolity'. The task in hand was too serious. Life, he told the mechanics' institutes at Manchester in 1859, was not a lottery but a science: 'certain qualities and certain talents, properly handled and properly managed, must lead to certain results'. The realisation of the self required a constant application of physical and moral energy. 'The great majority of men', the princess of Tivoli tells Lothair, 'exist but do not live, like Italy in the last century. The power of the passions, the force of the will, the creative energy of the imagination, these make life.' To pursue life in this sense was Disraeli's ethical creed. Consciousness, not conscience, was his game. Morality lay in the present realisation of genius, not the future salvation of the soul. As Waldershare puts it, in *Endymion*: 'One should never think of death. One should think of life. That is real piety.'[12]

That the prizes of mature achievement could not convey the keenness of enjoyment that had beckoned to eager youth was a disadvantage that Disraeli had to put up with, grumbling the while to the long-suffering Lady Bradford that life as prime minister was 'not a complete existence. It gives me neither the highest development of the intellect or the heart; neither Poetry nor Love.' His final triumphs were not without their flavour, not only in politics but in society. Perhaps it was the conquest of society that was the more satisfying. Though *Endymion* is about a young man's rise to be prime minister, by benefit, as usual, of will and women, it is not so much a political novel as a paean to the metropolitan society of Disraeli's beginnings, where the real centre of power had often seemed to the impetuous newcomer to lie. That the elite ruled as much through the drawing-room as the debating chamber Disraeli never doubted. 'I can move in society, without which a public man, whatever his talents or acquirements, is in life playing at blind-man's-buff', Endymion tells Lady Montfort. High politics and high society stood, and might fall, together. In the aftermath of the defeat of 1880, no prospect of the 'revolutionary age' which he announced to Lady Chesterfield seems to have depressed Disraeli more than that 'the chances are that even you and I may live to see the final extinction of the great London season, wh. was the wonder and admiration of our youth'.[13] Eminence in both the social and the political worlds was the summit of Disraeli's aspiration and the seal of his settlement in England.

It was never a complete settlement, rather a sojourn of the migrant spirit before it took wing again. Disraeli's inspiration came from outside England's atmosphere, his leaps of mind occurred in travel beyond its shores. Among 'you English' (a phrase Charles Dilke heard him use shortly before his death), he left no heir, only the record of his striving and the glitter of his words. The engine of will and appetite and endurance and effort that accomplished his marvellous career drew its power from sources we cannot fully know. Endymion's worldly triumph is the result more of his devoted sister's impulsion than of his own. Disraeli's last completed novel ends with her words, as she rejoices with her brother in their old nursery, which she has insisted on revisiting. '"Here it is; here we are. All I have desired, all I have dreamed, have come to pass. Darling, beloved of my soul, by all our sorrows, by all our joys, in this scene of our childhood and bygone days, let me give you my last embrace".' Sarah never saw her brother prime minister; this last scene it had not been possible to stage. What hint, if any, of the inner springs of his journey Disraeli meant to give in painting it, we cannot tell. '"That is matter of history", said Lothair, "and that, you know, is always doubtful."'[14]

NOTES

References are in most cases consolidated to cover a whole paragraph. In any given note, references to the same source are grouped together, following the order of the source. Where that might make it difficult to connect a particular reference with the relevant passage in the text, the former is immediately followed by a key word or key words from the latter, placed in brackets.

INTRODUCTION

1 M. Freeden (ed.), *Minutes of the Rainbow Circle, 1894–1924*, Camden Fourth Series, vol. XXXVIII (London, Royal Historical Society, 1989), pp. 160–1.

2 Stanley, p. 179; W. S. Blunt, *My Diaries: Being a Personal Narrative of Events 1888–1914*, 2 vols. (London, 1921), vol. II, pp. 71–2; Roy Jenkins, reviewing vol. IV of the *Letters*, in *The Observer*, 9 July 1989.

3 B. R. Jerman, *The Young Disraeli* (Princeton: London, 1960).

4 P. Smith, 'Disraeli's Politics', *Transactions of the Royal Historical Society*, 5th series, 37 (1987), 65–85.

5 Blake, pp. 761–3; P. R. Ghosh, 'Disraelian Conservatism: a Financial Approach', *English Historical Review*, 99 (1984), especially pp. 268, 293–5.

6 J. Vincent, *Disraeli* (Oxford, 1990). For a recent effort to incorporate serious consideration of Disraeli's political ideas into a general biographical study, see J. Ridley, *The Young Disraeli* (London, 1995).

7 Blake, pp. 49–50, 204; R. Blake, *Disraeli's Grand Tour: Benjamin Disraeli and the Holy Land 1830–31* (London, 1982).

8 I. Zangwill, *Dreamers of the Ghetto* (London, 1898), chapter 10, 'The Primrose Sphinx'; P. Rieff, 'Disraeli: the Chosen of History', *Commentary*, 13 (1952), 22–33; Sir I. Berlin, 'Benjamin Disraeli, Karl Marx and the Search for Identity', *Transactions of the Jewish Historical Society of England*, 22 (1970), 1–20; T. M. Endelman, 'Disraeli's Jewishness Reconsidered', *Modern Judaism*, 5 (1985), 109–23; S. Weintraub, *Disraeli* (London, 1993). See also T. M. Endelman and A. R. J. Kushner (eds.), *Disraeli's Jewishness* (forthcoming).

9 R. Maitre, *Disraeli: Homme de Lettres* (Paris, 1963); D. R. Schwarz, *Disraeli's Fiction*

(London, 1979); C. B. Richmond, 'Benjamin Disraeli: a Psychological Biography 1804–1832', unpublished M.Litt. thesis, University of Oxford, 1982. See also W. Stafford, 'Romantic Elitism in the Thought of Benjamin Disraeli', *Literature and History*, 6 (1980), 43–58, and C. B. Richmond and P. Smith (eds.), *The Self-Fashioning of Benjamin Disraeli* (Cambridge, 1998/9).

10 R. Faber, *Beaconsfield and Bolingbroke* (London, 1961), p. 82; Blake, p. 766.

11 Carnarvon to Cairns, 20 April 1881, in Sir A. Hardinge, *The Life of Henry Howard Molyneux Herbert Fourth Earl of Carnarvon 1831–1890*, ed. Elisabeth Countess of Carnarvon, 3 vols. (Oxford, 1925), vol. III, pp. 62–3; D. W. R. Bahlman (ed.), *The Diary of Sir Edward Walter Hamilton 1885–1906* (Hull, 1993), p. 291 (24 March 1895); Disraeli to Metternich, 12 Oct. 1848, in *Letters*, vol. V, 1725.

I THE THEATRE OF LIFE

On Disraeli's background and early formation, in addition to M & B and Blake: Richmond and Smith (eds.), *Self-Fashioning*, cited in n. 9 to the Introduction; J. Ogden, *Isaac D'Israeli* (Oxford, 1969); C. C. Nickerson, 'Disraeli and the Rev. Eli Cogan'; T. Braun, 'Cogan and Disraeli', *Disraeli Newsletter*, 2 (1977), 14–17, 18–27; B. R. Jerman, *The Young Disraeli* (Princeton: London, 1960); R. Maitre, *Disraeli: Homme de Lettres* (Paris, 1963); D. R. Schwarz, *Disraeli's Fiction* (London, 1979); C. B. Richmond, 'Benjamin Disraeli: a Psychological Biography 1804–1832', unpublished M. Litt. thesis, University of Oxford, 1982; T. Braun, *Disraeli the Novelist* (London, 1981).

Influence of continental romanticism: S. Prawer (ed.), *The Romantic Period in Germany* (London, 1970), and R. Ashton, *The German Idea: Four English Writers and the Reception of German Thought 1800–1860* (Cambridge, 1980), for the Germanic strains by which Disraeli was touched.

Bildung and character: S. Collini, 'The Idea of "Character" in Victorian Political Thought', *Transactions of the Royal Historical Society*, 5th series, 35 (1985), 37–8.

1 *CF*, pt I, ch. 7.

2 Blake, p. 7.

3 *CF*, pt I, ch. 8; pt II, ch. 9.

4 M & B, vol. I, p. 33; *VG*, bk I, ch. 8.

5 *VG*, bk I, ch. 7.

6 'Mutilated Diary', *Letters*, vol. I, p. 447.

7 E. J. Morley (ed.), *Henry Crabb Robinson on Books and Their Writers*, 3 vols. (London, 1938), vol. II, p. 511.

8 'Mutilated Diary', *Letters*, vol. I, p. 447.

9 *VG*, vol. III of first edition (excised from later editions).

10 *YD*, first edition (excised from later editions).

11 *CF*, pt III, ch. 17 ('education', 'physiological ignorance'); pt V, ch. 18 ('Destiny'); pt VI, ch. 1 ('demonstration').

12 'Mutilated Diary', *Letters*, vol. 1, p. 447.

13 G. Steiner, *In Bluebeard's Castle: Some Notes Towards the Re-definition of Culture* (London, 1971), pp. 18–22; *YD*, bk 11, ch. 7.

14 Richmond, 'Benjamin Disraeli', p. 39.

15 *CF*, pt 11, ch. 15.

16 *Alroy*, pt 1, ch. 1; *CF*, pt 1v, chs. 5 and 6.

17 *Letters*, vol. 1, 73 ('Philistines'); *YD*, first edition (excised from later editions).

18 *Letters*, vol. 1, 76 (to Colburn), 111 (to Sarah); *YD*, bk 11, ch. 5 (Squib), bk 111, ch. 7 (society). The passage on the conduct of life from thirteen to twenty-two appears in the first edition of *YD*, and was excised from later editions.

19 *YD*, bk 11, ch. 7 ('truth of the creed'). The other passages appear in the first edition and were later excised.

20 *Letters*, vol. 1, 56; *YD*, first edition, later excised.

21 *Letters*, vol. 1, 92, 96, 98 (Cadiz), 101 (Albania, costume), 103 (to Austen).

22 *Ibid*., vol. 1, 101, 103; *CF*, pt v, ch. 15; *Venetia*, bk v1, ch. 8.

23 *Letters*, vol. 1, 94 (Granada), 104 (Athens), 118 (Austen); Blake, p. 62 (Clay).

24 *The Bradenham Edition of the Novels and Tales of Benjamin Disraeli, 1st Earl of Beaconsfield*, 12 vols. (London, 1926–7), vol. 1v, p. ix (1845 preface); J. S. Hamilton, 'Disraeli and Heine', *Disraeli Newsletter*, 2 (1977), p. 8. Cf. M & B, vol. 1, pp. 192–3.

25 *Letters*, vol. 1, p. 447 (diary), 194 (critics); *Bradenham Edition*, vol. 1v, p. xi (1845 preface).

26 *Letters*, vol. 1, p. 447 ('Mutilated Diary' on 'ideal ambition'), 296 (Austen), 297 (to Sara Austen, 'all great works'), 350 (Blessington); 'Preface' to *The Revolutionary Epick* (London, 1834).

2 THE THEATRE OF POLITICS, 1832–1837

1 *A Year at Hartlebury or The Election*, vol. 1, ch. 2, and cf. vol. 11, ch. 8 (for attribution of passages to Sarah or Benjamin, see J. Matthews, 'Cherry and Fair Star', Appendix 1 to the re-issue by John Murray, London, 1983).

2 'Mutilated Diary', *Letters*, vol. 1, p. 446; M & B, vol. 1, p. 124 (Meredith); Blake, p. 80.

3 *VG*, bk 1, ch. 8; Blake, pp. 99–104; *YD*, bk v, ch. 11; *Letters*, vol. 11, 542.

4 *Letters*, vol. 11, 630.

5 M & B, vol. 1, p. 361; *The Tragedy of Count Alarcos* (London, 1839), preface.

6 *HT*, bk 111, ch. 4 ('a female friend'), bk v1, ch. 13 ('money'); *Letters*, vol. 111, 882 (bachelorhood); *Sybil or: the Two Nations* (London, 1845), bk 1v, ch. 10 ('melancholy'); *YD*, first edition, later excised.

7 *Letters*, vol. 1, 169; vol. 111, 882.

8 *Ibid*., vol. 111, 954 (to Mary Anne, 8 July 1839), 996 (to Pyne), 1194 ('great business'); vol. 1v, 1435 (sixth wedding-anniversary ode, Aug. 1845), 1257 (to Isaac, Aug. 1842), 1370 (Shrewsbury).

9 *Ibid.*, vol. III, 1197.

10 C. B. Richmond, 'Benjamin Disraeli: a Psychological Biography 1804–1832', unpublished M.Litt. thesis, University of Oxford, 1982, pp. 23–32, on Disraeli's early readings in politics; *VG*, bk II, ch. 2; R. O'Kell, 'Ixion in Heaven: the Representative Hero', *Disraeli Newsletter*, I (1976), 14–25; 'Mutilated Diary', *Letters*, vol. I, p. 447; *CF*, pt VII, ch. 2. Three years after Contarini, in 1835, in an essay for his school-leaving examination, Karl Marx, who had contemplated a literary life, concluded that a young man should choose a career 'based on ideas of whose truth we are wholly convinced' and offering scope in working for humanity; he who worked only for himself might be a great scholar or writer but never a truly great man (S. S. Prawer, *Karl Marx and World Literature* (Oxford, 1976), p. 2).

11 *Hartlebury*, vol. I, ch. 14; *Letters*, vol. I, 120.

12 *Letters*, vol. I, 117.

13 *Ibid.*, vol. I, 179 (to Sarah), 198 (to Austen).

14 *Ibid.*, vol. I, 193; W. H. Greenleaf, *The British Political Tradition*, vol. II, *The Ideological Heritage* (London, 1983), pp. 264–5; Byron to Hobhouse, 26 June 1819, in L. A. Marchand (ed.), *Byron's Letters and Journals*, vol. VI (London, 1976), p. 166; *Reminiscences*, p. 37.

15 *Letters*, vol. I, 215; M & B, vol. I, p. 218; *CF*, pt I, ch. 5; *Hartlebury*, vol. II, chs. 2 and 7.

16 *Letters*, vol. I, 221, 239.

17 *Ibid.*, vol. I, 356, 363; R. W. Davis, *Disraeli* (London, 1976), p. 40.

18 B. Mallet, *Thomas George Earl of Northbrook GCSI: a Memoir* (London, 1908), p. 33.

19 'Mutilated Diary', in *Letters*, vol. I, p. 447; 'On the Life and Writings of Mr. Disraeli, By His Son', preface to I. Disraeli, *Curiosities of Literature*, 14th edn, 3 vols. (London, 1849), vol. I, p. liii; M & B, vol. II, p. 371.

20 *England and France: a Cure for the Ministerial Gallomania* (London, 1832), p. 13; *Letters*, vol. I, 95 (Bradenham), 141 ('John Bull').

21 Blake, pp. 10, 49–50.

22 *England and France*, pp. 13, 50.

23 *Hartlebury*, vol. II, ch. 1; *What is He?* (London, 1833), p. 16.

24 *The Works of Lord Bolingbroke*, 4 vols. (London, 1844), vol. II, p. 352; *Vindication*, pp. 186–7.

25 *Vindication*, pp. 187–8; *Letters*, vol. II, 409.

26 *Vindication*, pp. 192–3.

27 *Ibid.*, pp. 180–3.

28 L. Colley, *In Defiance of Oligarchy: the Tory Party 1714–60* (Cambridge, 1982), p. 173, and see also her 'Eighteenth-Century English Radicalism Before Wilkes', *Transactions of the Royal Historical Society*, 5th series, 31 (1981), 1–19.

29 Gladstone quoted in D. Southgate, *The Passing of the Whigs 1832–1886* (London, 1962), p. 201.

30 Richmond, 'Benjamin Disraeli', p. 25 (Bacon); J. Lee, 'Political Antiquarianism Unmasked: the Conservative Attack on the Myth of the Ancient Constitution', *Bulletin of the Institute of Historical Research*, 55 (1982), 166–79.

31 *Letters*, vol. II, 406 (address to the electors and inhabitants of Taunton, 13 June 1835), 409 (to Edwards Beadon, 2 July 1835), 458 (to *The Times*, 28 Dec. 1835).

32 *Vindication*, p. 193; *The Crisis Examined* (London, 1834), pp. 15–16.

33 *Letters*, vol. II, 380, 406 (primitive Toryism), 458 ('obsolete associations', 'unconnected with its parties'), 459 (Peel's opinion), 629 (Maidstone address).

3 THE THEATRE OF PARLIAMENT, 1837–1846

For Young England, see R. Faber, *Young England* (London, 1987), *Letters*, vol. IV, Introduction.

On the novels, in addition to T. Braun, *Disraeli the Novelist* (London, 1981); R. Maitre, *Disraeli: Homme de Lettres* (Paris, 1963); and D. R. Schwarz, *Disraeli's Fiction* (London, 1979); see R. O'Kell, 'Disraeli's "Coningsby": Political Manifesto or Psychological Romance?', *Victorian Studies*, 23 (1979), 57–78, and 'Two Nations or One? Disraeli's Allegorical Romance', *Victorian Studies*, 30 (1986–7), 211–34.

For the Conservative party, and the protectionist controversy: R. Stewart, *The Foundation of the Conservative Party 1830–1867* (London, 1978), and *The Politics of Protection. Lord Derby and the Protectionist Party, 1845–1852* (Cambridge, 1971).

1 *Coningsby or: The New Generation* (London, 1844), bk VI, ch. 2; *Letters*, vol. IV, Appendix III (draft of memorandum for Louis Philippe).

2 *Letters*, vol. IV, 1217, 1222, 1224–6.

3 *Ibid.*, vol. III, 732, 734.

4 *Ibid.*, vol. II, 672–3, 686 (maiden speech); vol. III, 738.

5 *Crisis Examined*, p. 31; *Letters*, vol. II, 557, vol. III, 908.

6 *Letters*, vol. IV, 1229.

7 *Ibid.*, vol. IV, 1370.

8 *Coningsby*, bk III, ch. 2.

9 *Sybil*, bk I, ch. 3 (English history), bk VI, ch. 13.

10 *Ibid.*, bk II, ch. 5, bk III, ch. 5 (statistics).

11 *Ibid.*, bk I, ch. 5 ('Mammon'), bk II, ch. 5 (Morley), bk III, ch. 5 (Norman yoke); *The Voyage of Captain Popanilla* (London, 1828), ch. 4; *Vindication*, ch. 2.

12 M & B, vol. II, p. 231; S. G. Checkland, *The Gladstones: a Family Biography 1764–1851* (Cambridge, 1971), pp. 244–5; Ferrand quoted in D. Southgate, 'From Disraeli to Law', in Lord Butler (ed.), *The Conservatives. A History From Their Origins to 1965* (London, 1977), p. 121.

13 B. Disraeli, 'The Midland Ocean', in *Book of Beauty* (London, 1843), reprinted in *Letters*, vol. IV, pp. 394–5.

14 July 1845 preface to *CF*, in *Bradenham Edition*, vol. IV, p. ix; *Vindication*, ch. 3; J. S. Mill, *A System of Logic Ratiocinative and Inductive* (1843), in J. M. Robson (ed.), *The Collected Works of John Stuart Mill*, vol. VIII (Toronto and London, 1974) p. 905.

15 *Coningsby*, bk III, ch. 1 (famous men), bk IV, ch. 10 (Sidonia); *Sybil*, bk VI, ch. 13.

16 *Sybil*, bk I, ch. 3 (Burke); bk I, ch. 1 (de Vere); and *passim* (for Marney and Mowbray).

17 *Ibid.*, bk I, ch. 3 (Marney, Whigs); *Coningsby*, bk VIII, ch. 3.

18 *Sybil*, bk IV, ch. 3; *Letters*, vol. IV, 1428.

19 *Letters*, vol. IV, 1433 (to *The Morning Post*, 16 Aug. 1845, for Blumenbach); *Coningsby*, bk IV, chs. 10, 15.

20 *Coningsby*, bk IV, ch. 15 ('sufficiently pure'), bk IX, ch. 4 (brains); *Sybil*, bk II, ch. 11.

21 *Coningsby*, bk IV, ch. 4; *Letters*, vol. IV, Appendix V, p. 378 (marriage); B. Disraeli, *Whigs and Whiggism. Political Writings*, ed. W. Hutcheon (London, 1913), p. 50 (Hume, 1838); M & B, vol. II, pp. 88 (1840 speech), 142 (1843 speech), 233 (Shrewsbury, 1844); *Letters*, vol. IV, 1370 (Shrewsbury); *Sybil*, bk III, ch. 4.

22 *Sybil*, bk III, ch. 8; *Coningsby*, bk IV, chs. 1–2.

23 *Sybil*, bk I, ch. 3 (Shelburne), bk II, ch. 7 (manufacturers).

24 *Sybil*, bk II, ch. 10 (poor children, 'Temple'); P. J. Keating, *The Working Classes in Victorian Fiction* (London, 1971), p. 8.

25 *Sybil*, bk II, chs. 3 (Marney), 9 (Shoddy-Court); bk IV, ch. 4 (unions, Chartism); bk V, ch. 10 (unions); bk VI, chs. 7 ('Hell-cats', strikers), 8 (women), 9 (factory population); B. R. Jerman, 'Disraeli's Fan Mail: a Curiosity Item', *Nineteenth-Century Fiction*, 9 (1954–5), 67 (Leeds Mechanics' Institution).

26 *Sybil*, bk IV, ch. 15 (the people), bk V, ch. 2 ('future principle'); *Coningsby*, bk VIII, ch. 3.

27 *Letters*, vol. IV, 1407; *Coningsby*, bk V, ch. 8 (Sidonia), bk VII, ch. 2 ('national opinion', representation); *Vindication*, pp. 65–102 (and cf. *Whigs and Whiggism*, p. 59).

28 'Mutilated Diary', in *Letters*, vol. I, p. 447; *Coningsby*, bk IV, ch. 13.

29 H. C. G. Matthew, 'Rhetoric and Politics in Great Britain, 1860–1950', in P. J. Waller (ed.), *Politics and Social Change in Modern Britain. Essays Presented to A. F. Thompson* (Brighton, 1987), p. 50; *Coningsby*, bk III, ch. 1 (spirit of the age), bk IX, ch. 4 ('new ideas'); *Letters*, vol. IV, p. 378 (Commonplace book); K. Marx and F. Engels, *Manifesto of the Communist Party* (1848), in L. S. Feuer (ed.), *Karl Marx and Friedrich Engels: Basic Writings in Politics and Philosophy* (Fontana edn, London, 1969), pp. 71–2.

30 *Letters*, vol. IV, 1402.

31 *Sybil*, bk IV, ch. 14; *Coningsby*, bk II, chs. 5–6 (Tamworth, 'Tory men'); bk V, ch. 2 (crown a cipher).

32 *Letters*, vol. II, 606 (Disraeli on Oastler, 1837), vol. III, 1065 (Attwood), vol. IV, 1379, note 2 (writing of *Sybil*), 1407, note 5 (Cooper), 1410 (Hodgskin); M & B, vol. I, p. 374 (poverty a crime, 1837), vol. II, p. 83 (monarchy of the middle classes, 1839); F. C.

Mather (ed.), *Chartism and Society: an Anthology of Documents* (London, 1980), p. 225 (O'Connor, 1844).

33 C. S. Parker, *Sir Robert Peel From His Private Papers*, 3 vols. (London, 1891–9), vol. III, p. 425.

34 M & B, vol. II, pp. 133–4 (tariff), 176 (Ireland); *Coningsby*, bk II, ch. 1; *Sybil*, bk I, ch. 3.

35 M & B, vol. II, pp. 139, 141.

36 P. J. Jupp, 'The Landed Elite and Political Authority in Britain, *c.* 1760–1850', *Journal of British Studies*, 29 (1990), 53–79.

37 *Letters*, vol. III, 747; *Coningsby*, bk IX, ch. 6.

38 M & B, vol. II, pp. 356–7.

4 A LEADING PART, 1846–1865

Disraeli's Jewishness: in addition to the references given in note 8 to the Introduction: H. Fisch, 'Disraeli's Hebraic Compulsions', in H. J. Zimmels, J. Rabbinowitz and I. Finestein (eds.), *Essays Presented to Chief Rabbi Israel Brodie on the Occasion of His Seventieth Birthday* (London, 1967), pp. 81–94; A. Gilam, 'Anglo-Jewish Attitudes Toward Benjamin Disraeli During the Era of Emancipation', *Jewish Social Studies*, 42 (1980), 313–22; B. Jaffe, 'A Reassessment of Benjamin Disraeli's Jewish Aspects', *Transactions of the Jewish Historical Society of England*, 27 (1978–80), 115–23; C. Roth, *Benjamin Disraeli, Earl of Beaconsfield* (New York, 1952), ch. 6; M. C. N. Salbstein, *The Emancipation of the Jews in Britain: the Question of the Admission of the Jews to Parliament, 1828–1860* (London, 1982), ch. 5.

Politics of mid-Victorian Budgets: P. R. Ghosh, 'Disraelian Conservatism: a Financial Approach, *English Historical Review*, 99 (1984); H. C. G. Matthew, 'Disraeli, Gladstone and the Politics of Mid-Victorian Budgets', *Historical Journal*, 22 (1979), 615–43.

1 *Letters*, vol. IV, 1513 (28 Aug. 1846).

2 *Ibid.*, vol. IV, 1474 (to Richard Bentley, 13 March 1846), 1551 (address to Buckinghamshire electors, 22 May 1847).

3 *Ibid.*, vol. IV, 1519 (to Manners, 19 Sept. 1846), 1575, note 1 (£900 a year), vol. V, 1730 (to Mary Anne, 18 Oct. 1848); *Reminiscences*, p. 148 (to Francis Espinasse, 27 March 1860); Salisbury Papers, Lady Janetta Manners to Salisbury [10 June 1880].

4 *Lord George Bentinck: a Political Biography* (London, 1851), chs. 24–5.

5 *Tancred or: The New Crusade* (London, 1847), bk I, ch. 6.

6 *Ibid.*, bk II, ch. 1.

7 *Ibid.*, bk III, ch. 7.

8 *Ibid.*, bk II, chs. 1 ('What ought I to DO'), 11.

9 *Ibid.*, bk II, ch. 11 (comforter), bk III, ch. 5 (youth and debt), bk IV, ch. 7 (Mount

Sinai), bk v, ch. 3 (new social system), bk vi, ch. 3 (divine dominion).

10 *Letters*, vol. iv, 1530; *Tancred*, bk iv, ch. 3.

11 *Tancred*, bk ii, ch. 14 (race), bk iii, ch. 4; *Sybil*, bk ii, ch. 12.

12 *Coningsby*, bk iv, ch. 15 (Sidonia); *Tancred*, bk iv, ch. 4; *Lord George Bentinck*, ch. 24 (Saxon and Celt).

13 *Tancred*, bk ii, ch. 14 (Saxon race); *Coningsby*, bk iv, ch. 10 (Saxons in first class); *Lord George Bentinck*, chs. 27 ('traditionary influences'), 28 ('great contention').

14 *Letters*, vol. ii, 636, note 3, citing C. Oman (ed.), *The Gascoyne Heiress* (London, 1968), p. 248 (Lady Salisbury); vol. iv, pp. lxxxix, xciii (*Punch* cartoons, 7 June 1845 and 26 June 1847), 1340; *Letters*, vol. vi, 2493 (Disraeli to Mrs Brydges Willyams, 28 Feb. 1853); P. Rieff, 'Disraeli: the Chosen of History', *Commentary*, 13 (1952).

15 *Letters*, vol. ii, 683 (to Sarah, 5 Dec. 1837); *Tancred*, bk v, ch. 5.

16 'On the Life and Writings of Mr. Disraeli. By His Son', preface to I. Disraeli, *Curiosities of Literature*, 14th edn, 3 vols. (London, 1849), vol. i, pp. xx–xxii (ancestry), xxiii (grandmother).

17 *Letters*, vol. iv, 1388 (to Monckton Milnes, 29 Dec, 1844); *Lord George Bentinck*, ch. 24; *Coningsby*, bk iv, ch. 10; *Tancred*, bk v, ch. 6.

18 'Mutilated Diary', *Letters*, vol. i, p. 447 ('ideal ambition'); Stanley, pp. 32–3 (cf. Stanley's original notes in *Letters*, vol. vi, Appendix 1A, pp. 535–6); R. Patai (ed.), *The complete Diaries of Theodor Herzl*, 5 vols. (New York & London, 1960), vol. ii, p. 548 (15 May 1897).

19 I. D'Israeli, *The Genius of Judaism*, 2nd edn (London, 1833), pp. 10, 99, 211, 263, 265; *Alroy*, pt vi, ch. 3.

20 *Lord George Bentinck*, ch. 24; *Reminiscences*, p. 103.

21 *Reminiscences*, pp. 103–4; M & B, vol. iii, pp. 68–70, 73 (1847 and 1850 speeches); *Jewish Chronicle*, 9 Aug. 1850; *Letters*, vol. v, 1790 (to Newcastle).

22 T. M. Endelman, 'Communal Solidarity Among the Jewish Elite of Victorian London', *Victorian Studies*, 28 (1985), 491–526; *Lord George Bentinck*, ch. 23.

23 I. D'Israeli to Francis Douce, 1794, quoted in Ogden, *Isaac D'Israeli* (Oxford, 1969), p. 195.

24 *Letters*, vol. iii, 1038 (to Sarah, ?28 Jan. 1840), vol. iv, 1451 (to Lionel de Rothschild, 3 Dec. 1845); Roth, *Beaconsfield*, p. 70.

25 *Letters*, vol. iv, 1458 (to Avigdor, 28 Dec. 1845); *Tancred*, bk iii, ch. 1 ('oriental intellect' and French Revolution), bk iv, ch. 4; M & B, vol. iv, p. 350.

26 J. Michelet, *Le Peuple* (1846), ed. L. Refort (Paris, 1946), p. 123, note 1; E. Drumont, *La France juive devant l'opinion* (Paris, 1886), p. 52; H. S. Chamberlain, *Foundations of the Nineteenth Century* (1899), trans. J. Lees, 2 vols. (New York, 1977), vol. i, p. 271.

27 *Vindication*, p. 205; *The Table Talk and Omniana of Samuel Taylor Coleridge* (Oxford, 1917), p. 191 (25 July 1832); M. Vereté, 'The Restoration of the Jews in English Protestant Thought 1790–1840', *Middle Eastern Studies*, 8 (1972), 3–50.

28 *Tancred*, bk iii, ch. 7 ('little nations'), bk iv, ch. 3 (Arabs); B. Cheyette, *Constructions*

of 'The Jew' in English Literature and Society: Racial Representations, 1875–1945 (Cambridge, 1993), pp. 43ff (George Eliot); *Reminiscences*, p. 89 (Great Rebellion).

29 *Letters*, vol. VI, 2352 (cf. 2236), Appendix 1A, pp. 535–6; Stanley, pp. 31 (1851), 179 (1861).

30 *Coningsby*, bk IV, ch. 15.

31 R. S. Surtees, *Mr Sponge's Sporting Tour* (London, 1852; originally appeared in instalments, 1849–51), ch. 15; J. Morley, *The Life of William Ewart Gladstone*, 3 vols. (London, 1903), vol. III, p. 476.

32 *Letters*, vol. IV, 1617; W. Bagehot, *The English Constitution* (1867), Fontana edn (London, 1993), p. 176.

33 M & B, vol. III, pp. 122 (Stanley to Disraeli, 21 Dec. 1848), 135 (Beresford); *Letters*, vol. V, 1755 (Disraeli to Stanley, 26 Dec. 1848); Stanley, pp. 1–2.

34 Blake, p. 369 (Lennox on Derby, Jan. 1857).

35 C. C. F. Greville, *A Journal of the Reign of Queen Victoria from 1837 to 1852*, 3 vols. (London, 1885), vol. III, p. 403 (10 April 1851); Stanley, p. 72 (Derby on Disraeli, 1852); J. Vincent (ed.), *A Selection From the Diaries of Edward Henry Stanley, 15th Earl of Derby (1826–93), Between September 1869 and March 1878*, Camden Fifth Series, vol. IV (London, Royal Historical Society, 1994 [1995]), p. 37 ('bored'); *Letters*, vol. VI, 2596 (to Mary Anne, 12 Dec. 1853), 2669 (to Lady Londonderry, 7 Aug. 1854).

36 *Letters*, vol. V, 1943 (to Stanley [Derby], 28 Dec. 1849), p. 535 (Disraeli's subsequent reminiscence of the attempt to form a government in Feb. 1851); *Lord George Bentinck*, ch. 27.

37 *Letters*, vol. V, 1947 (Londonderry), 1992, 2000 (Sarah); M & B, vol. III, p. 219 (Beresford); Stanley, pp. 17, 96.

38 M & B, vol. III, pp. 382–5; letters to Lennox in *Letters*, vol. VI.

39 Stanley, pp. 31 ('rural pursuits'), 33 ('gratitude'); *Reminiscences*, pp. 117–18, 130 (library and trees); M & B, vol. IV, pp. 173–4 (Tyrwhitt Drakes).

40 M & B, vol. IV, p. 330 (to Mrs Brydges Willyams); *Reminiscences*, p. 94 (fruit and flowers).

41 *Reminiscences*, p. 108 (Guizot); Stanley, p. 29 (July 1850); A. Macintyre, 'Lord George Bentinck and the Protectionists: a Lost Cause?', *Transactions of the Royal Historical Society*, 5th series, 39 (1989), 141–65.

42 *Lord George Bentinck*, ch. 1; Stanley, pp. 50, 107.

43 Cartoon, 'The Ministerial Crisis', *Punch*, 8 March 1851, reproduced in M & B, vol. III, facing p. 290; Charles Dickens, *Bleak House* (London, 1853), ch. 40.

44 Stanley, pp. xv (Vincent), 121 (Disraeli on Palmerston, Feb. 1854).

45 A. C. Howe, *The Cotton Masters 1830–1860* (Oxford, 1984), p. 132 & n. 176.

46 R. Stewart, *The Foundation of the Conservative Party 1830–1867* (London, 1978), appendix 8, p. 384.

47 Stewart, *Conservative Party*, p. 311 (Derby, Malmesbury); Stanley, p. 48 ('public

curiosity'); M & B, vol. III, p. 492 (Disraeli's circular); A. Hawkins, *Parliament, Party and the Art of Politics in Britain, 1855–59* (London, 1987), p. 46.

48 Stanley, pp. 167, 173.

49 *Reminiscences*, pp. 108–9 (Bright and Cobden); Stanley, pp. 40–1; Blake, pp. 231–2 ('school of Manchester'); *Letters*, vol. VI, 2480 (to Malmesbury, 26 Jan. 1853).

50 A. Offer, *Property and Politics 1870–1914. Landownership, Law, Ideology and Urban Development in England* (Cambridge, 1981), pp. 167–9; *Letters*, vol. V, 1989 (Disraeli to Granby, 8 April 1850).

51 M & B, vol. III, pp. 346 ('first ball'), 353 ('his books'); address to the electors of Bucks, 2 June 1852, *Letters*, vol. VI, 2304.

52 Stanley, p. 89.

53 Stewart, *Conservative Party*, p. 314 (Jolliffe to Derby, 23 Oct. 1855); Blake, p. 355; *Letters*, vol. VI, 2804 (Disraeli to Stanley, 18 Dec. 1855), and Appendix IV.

54 M & B, vol. IV, pp. 74 (1857 address), 254 (Disraeli to Derby, 9 Oct. 1858); Ghosh, 'Disraelian Conservatism', p. 284 ('expenditure depends on policy').

55 M & B, vol. III, p. 396 (commercial treaty); E. D. Steele, *Palmerston and Liberalism 1855–1865* (Cambridge, 1991), p. 56.

56 Hawkins, *Parliament and Party*, p. 276.

57 M & B, vol. IV, pp. 176 (to Stanley, 24 Oct. 1858), 183 (to Derby, 13 Aug. 1858).

58 Ghosh, 'Disraelian Conservatism', p. 282; M & B, vol. IV, pp. 99 ('atrocities'), 127 (to Pakington, 3 April 1858).

59 B. Disraeli, *Whigs and Whiggism. Political Writings*, ed. W. Hutcheon (London, 1913), pp. 102–3, 106 (Disraeli on the constitution in *The Morning Post*, 4 Sept. 1835), and see also *Vindication*, pp. 22–3; *Lord George Bentinck*, ch. 27.

60 M & B, vol. III, pp. 99–102, 285 (1848 and 1851 speeches); *Letters*, vol. IV, 1551 (1847 address); P. J. Chilcott, 'British Politics and the Elementary Education Question, 1850–70', unpublished D.Phil. thesis, University of Oxford, 1990, p. 80.

61 *Letters*, vol. V, 2191 & n. 1 (Disraeli to Derby, 30 Oct. 1851, with latter's letter of 26 Oct.); vol. IV, p. 79 (to Derby, 21 April 1857); Stewart, pp. 353–4.

62 M & B, vol. IV, pp. 193 ('our colleagues'), 208–9 ('democracy').

63 Stewart, *Conservative Party*, p. 319 ('everyone knows'); M & B, vol. IV, p. 266 ('monopoly'); Stanley, p. 168; Chilcott, 'British Politics' p. 151 (Derby to Whiteside, 8 June 1862).

64 Stanley, p. 182.

65 Stewart, *Conservative Party*, p. 312 (Jolliffe); Stanley, pp. 33 (Disraeli's character), 156 (1858), 187 (Walpole).

66 *The Crisis Examined* (London, 1834), p. 16; Stanley, pp. 33 ('ruling passion'), 182–3 (Disraeli on Albert, Jan.–Feb. 1862 – 'court-influence', 'Venetian constitution'), 218 (Schleswig-Holstein); M & B, vol. IV, p. 394 ('the Ideal').

67 M & B, vol. IV, pp. 283 (to King of the Belgians), 359 (to Malmesbury); *Letters*, vol.

VI, 2335 (to Lennox, 18 July 1852).

68 *Ibid.*, vol. IV, pp. 361-2 (Aylesbury), 371-4 (Oxford).

69 Stewart, *Conservative Party,* p. 352 (Derby to Disraeli, 24 July 1865); M & B, vol. IV, pp. 416-17 (to Derby); Stanley, pp. 208, 227.

70 *Reminiscences*, p. 95; M & B, vol. IV, p. 331 (to Mrs Brydges Willyams).

5 TOP OF THE BILL, 1865-1881

The Reform crisis of 1866-7: M. Cowling, *1867: Disraeli, Gladstone and Revolution. The Passing of the Second Reform Bill* (Cambridge, 1967); G. Himmelfarb, 'Politics and Ideology: the Reform Act of 1867', in *Victorian Minds* (London, 1968), pp. 333-92; F. B. Smith, *The Making of the Second Reform Bill* (Cambridge, 1966).

The Conservative party in the post-Reform era: E. J. Feuchtwanger, *Disraeli, Democracy and the Tory Party. Conservative Leadership and Organization After the Second Reform Bill* (Oxford, 1968); R. Shannon, *The Age of Disraeli, 1868-1881: the Rise of Tory Democracy* (London, 1992).

Disraeli and social reform: P. R. Ghosh, 'Style and Substance in Disraelian Social Reform, *c.* 1860-80', in P. J. Waller (ed.), *Politics and Social Change in Modern Britain. Essays Presented to A. F. Thompson* (Brighton, 1987), pp. 59-90; P. Smith, *Disraelian Conservatism and Social Reform* (London, 1967).

Imperialism: C. C. Eldridge, *England's Mission: the Imperial Idea in the Age of Gladstone and Disraeli, 1868-80* (London, 1973); F. Harcourt, 'Disraeli's Imperialism, 1866-1868: a Question of Timing', *Historical Journal*, 23 (1980), 87-109, and 'Gladstone, Monarchism and the "New" Imperialism, 1868-74', *Journal of Imperial and Commonwealth History*, 14 (1985), 20-51; N. Rodgers, 'The Abyssinian Expedition of 1867-8: Disraeli's Imperialism or James Murray's War', *Historical Journal*, 27 (1984), 129-49; S. R. Stembridge, 'Disraeli and the Millstones', *Journal of British Studies*, 5 (1965), 122-39.

Eastern question: R. Millman, *Britain and the Eastern Question 1875-1878* (Oxford, 1979); A. P. Saab, 'Disraeli, Judaism and the Eastern Question', *International History Review*, 10 (1988), 559-78; M. Swartz, *The Politics of British Foreign Policy in the Era of Disraeli and Gladstone* (London, 1985).

1 M & B, vol. IV, p. 424; Stanley, p. 237.

2 Stanley, pp. 237-8 (moderate measure); M & B, vol. IV, p. 426 (to Derby).

3 British Library, Additional MSS. 50063A, f. 93, Northcote's diary, 29 June 1866 (typescript copy).

4 F. B. Smith, *Second Reform Bill*, pp. 132-3 (dating to 21 July 1866 Disraeli's letter to Derby printed in M & B, vol. IV, pp. 452-3, under the date of 29 July); A. E. Gathorne-Hardy, *Gathorne Hardy First Earl of Cranbrook: a Memoir*, 2 vols. (London, 1910), vol. I, p. 209 (Disraeli to Hardy, 18 May 1867); M & B, vol. IV, p. 453

(Derby, Sept. 1866); B. Mallet, *Thomas George Earl of Northbrook GCSI: a Memoir* (London, 1908), p. 33.

5 M & B, vol. IV, p. 474.

6 *Ibid.*, vol. IV, pp. 484, 489.

7 Stanley, p. 294.

8 Disraeli to Hardy, 18 May 1867, cited in note 4, above.

9 Disraeli to Derby, ?21 July 1866, cited in note 4, above; M & B, vol. IV, pp. 524 ('furniture'), 534 (Corry); Stanley, p. 341 (July 1869).

10 Stanley, p. 296; M & B, vol. IV, p. 533 (Carlton Club).

11 M & B, vol. IV, pp. 528 (to Beauchamp), 552–3 (Mansion House); *Hansard's Parliamentary Debates*, 3rd series, vol. CLXXXVI, cols. 6–7; *Sybil*, bk v, ch. 2.

12 Himmelfarb, 'Politics and Ideology', pp. 382–3; J. Vincent, *Disraeli* (Oxford, 1990), p. 16.

13 Blake, pp. 460 (to Derby), 476; F. B. Smith, *Second Reform Bill*, p. 41.

14 Stanley, pp. 197, 222.

15 W. D. Jones, *Lord Derby and Victorian Conservatism* (Oxford, 1956), p. 193 (Malmesbury); Carnarvon Papers, Public Record Office, 30/6/169, fos. 89–90 (Bagehot); N. E. Johnson (ed.), *The Diary of Gathorne Hardy, Later Lord Cranbrook, 1866–1892: Political Selections* (Oxford, 1981), p. 43 (28 June 1867); Sir W. Gregory, *An Autobiography*, ed. Lady Gregory (London, 1894), p. 100; M & B, vol. v, p. 484.

16 *The Times*, 12 June 1867; M & B, vol. IV, p. 563 ('popular institutions').

17 *The Chancellor of the Exchequer in Scotland, Being Two Speeches Delivered by Him in the City of Edinburgh on 29th and 30th October 1867* (Edinburgh and London, 1867), pp. 35, 36–7, 44.

18 *Ibid.*, pp. 33–4, 35ff.; Hughenden Papers (Bodleian Library, Oxford), B/XX/M/138, Manners to Disraeli, 24 Oct. 1866.

19 M & B, vol. v, p. 88 ('without deviation').

20 *Ibid.*, vol. v, p. 24.

21 *Ibid.*, vol. v, p. 51.

22 E. D. Steele, *Palmerston and Liberalism 1855–1865* (Cambridge, 1991), p. 238 (Gladstone).

23 Shannon, *Age of Disraeli*, p. 75 ('victory'); Gathorne-Hardy, *Cranbrook*, vol. I, p. 282 (Hardy to Disraeli, 24 Sept. 1868).

24 P. Smith, *Disraelian Conservatism*, pp. 126–7 (electoral statistics); M & B, vol. v, p. 98 (Disraeli to Queen Victoria, 23 Nov. 1868).

25 Stanley, p. 347.

26 M & B, vol. v, p. 103 ('utmost reserve'); J. Vincent (ed.), *A Selection From the Diaries of Edward Henry Stanley, 15th Earl of Derby (1826–93), Between September 1869 and March 1878*, Camden Fifth Series, vol. IV, (London, Royal Historical Society, 1994 [1995]), p. 61 (abdicated).

27 Stanley, p. 347 ('literature, philosophy'); *Lothair* (London, 1870), ch. 21 ('town').

28 Johnson (ed.), *Diary of Gathorne Hardy*, p. 150 (9 Feb. 1872; Hardy's quotation of Cairns); A. Maurois, *Disraeli. A Picture of the Victorian Age* (Penguin edn, Harmondsworth, 1937), p. 164.

29 J. Winter, *Robert Lowe* (Toronto, 1976), p. 279.

30 Vincent, *Diaries of … 15th Earl of Derby*, pp. 102–3; T. E. Kebbel (ed.), *Selected Speeches of the Late Right Honourable the Earl of Beaconsfield*, 2 vols. (London, 1882), vol. II, p. 491.

31 'General Preface', in *Bradenham Edition*, vol. I, p. xv.

32 *Lord George Bentinck*, ch. 27.

33 *Lothair*, chs. 11 ('Standing Committee'), 54 ('Madre Natura'); M & B, vol. v, p. 268 (Glasgow).

34 Bagehot, *The English Constitution*, pp. 248, 251; *Sybil*, bk v, ch. 10.

35 'General Preface', in *Bradenham Edition*, vol. I, pp. xv–xvi; *Lothair*, ch. 76; Stanley, p. 340.

36 Harrowby Papers, vol. LII, fos. 246–9: Cross to Sandon, 28 Aug. 1871.

37 *Lothair*, ch. 30; Salisbury Papers, G. M. W. Sandford to Salisbury, 15 July [1871] (Disraeli on likely Liberal dissensions); Vincent, *Diaries of … 15th Earl of Derby*, pp. 83–4 (8 July 1871; Disraeli thinks Liberals fear legislation 'in the Socialist or Trades Union sense'); *The Standard*, 14 Oct. 1871; Kebbel, *Selected Speeches*, vol. II, p. 531 (Crystal Palace).

38 Kebbel, *Selected Speeches*, vol. II, pp. 512 ('health of the people'), 527 ('great body of the people'); Ghosh, 'Style and Substance', pp. 61 ('the race'), 65 (Aylesbury speech, 1868; 'national efficiency'); *Chancellor of the Exchequer in Scotland*, pp. 25–7, 39–43 (Edinburgh speeches, 1867).

39 M & B, vol. III, pp. 24, 253, 333–6, vol. IV, p. 476 ('deadweights'); *Letters*, vol. v, 1943, 2205, 2209, vol. VI, 2358 ('millstone'); *Vindication*, p. 208; Kebbel, *Selected Speeches*, vol. II, pp. 529–31 (Crystal Palace).

40 Kebbel, *Selected Speeches*, vol. II, p. 530 ('unappropriated lands').

41 Shannon, *Age of Disraeli*, p. 142 (Disraeli's response to Grey); Harcourt, 'Disraeli's Imperialism'; Rogers, 'The Abyssinian Expedition'.

42 M & B, vol. IV, pp. 372 (Oxford, 1864), 407 ('duty'), 410 (Commons, 1865), 559 (Skelton).

43 Kebbel, *Selected Speeches*, vol. II, p. 527 (second Reform act; cf. pp. 501–2); M & B, vol. v, p. 130 ('my hope').

44 Vincent, *Diaries of … 15th Earl of Derby*, p. 103.

45 Kebbel, *Selected Speeches*, vol. II, pp. 532–3.

46 Johnson (ed.), *Diary of Gathorne Hardy*, p. 154 (5 April 1872); Kebbel, *Selected Speeches*, vol. II, p. 516 ('exhausted volcanoes').

47 Kebbel, *Selected Speeches*, vol. II, pp. 492 ('party man'), 524; *Lord George Bentinck*,

chs. 27–8.

48 Harrowby Papers, 4th series, box '1868–76': Harrowby to Lord Henry Ryder, 10 Jan. 1873; M & B, vol. v, p. 235 ('hotel life'); Vincent, *Diaries of ... 15th Earl of Derby*, p. 126 (retirement).

49 P. Smith, *Disraelian Conservatism*, pp. 183–5.

50 *The Times*, 26 Jan. 1874 (address); P. Smith, *Disraelian Conservatism*, pp. 191–4 (electoral statistics).

51 *Sybil*, bk iv, ch. 2.

52 M & B, vol. v, p. 246 (shoe, July 1874); Vincent, *Diaries of ... 15th Earl of Derby*, p. 220.

53 M & B, vol. v, pp. 238 ('everything to woman'), 249 ('to *love* a person').

54 *Lothair*, ch. 35; M & B, vol. v, pp. 244 ('heart'), 308 ('Power and the Affections'), 349 (mittens).

55 M & B, vol. v, pp. 47 (Lady A. Stanley, 1868), 286.

56 *Ibid.*, vol. v, pp. 334 (Victoria's advice, 1874), 344 ('rose immensely'), 375–6 (Gladstone); Vincent, *Diaries of ... 15th Earl of Derby*, p. 202 (21 March 1875; 'spoilt child'); Kebbel, *Selected Speeches*, vol. ii, pp. 493–4 (Manchester speech).

57 M & B, vol. v, p. 414.

58 For this issue, J. Bentley, *Ritualism and Politics in Victorian Britain: the Attempt to Legislate for Belief* (Oxford, 1978).

59 P. Smith, *Disraelian Conservatism*, p. 198, note 4 ('not harassing the country'); M & B, vol. v, p. 308 (Cross).

60 Viscount Cross, *A Political History* (privately printed, 1903), p. 25; M & B, vol. v, pp. 294 (Disraeli to Queen Victoria, 23 Feb. 1874), 347 ('my dream').

61 M & B, vol. i, p. 222.

62 *Hansard*, 3rd series, vol. ccxix, col. 259.

63 M & B, vol. v, pp. 306–7 (Disraeli to Northcote, 4 April 1874); Offer, pp. 252, 404.

64 Diary, 11 Jan. 1875, in E. Hodder, *The Life and Work of the Seventh Earl of Shaftesbury, KG*, 3 vols. (London, 1888), vol. iii, p. 355.

65 M & B, vol. v, p. 377 (to Lady Bradford, 7 May 1875).

66 *Hansard*, 3rd series, vol. ccxx, col. 1190 (Salisbury); D. J. Mitchell, *Cross and Tory Democracy: a Political Biography of Richard Assheton Cross* (New York and London, 1991), p. 75; R. McKibbin, 'Why Was There No Marxism in Great Britain', *English Historical Review*, 99 (1984), 320.

67 Ghosh, 'Style and Substance', pp. 75–6. (Mansion House); P. Smith, *Disraelian Conservatism*, p. 199 (Cross, Carnarvon, Bagehot); Vincent, *Diaries of ... 15th Earl of Derby*, p. 250 (and cf. p. 448, October 1877); *Hansard*, 3rd series, vol. ccxxv, col. 525 (permissive legislation, June 1875).

68 Marquis of Zetland (ed.), *The Letters of Disraeli to Lady Bradford and Lady Chesterfield*, 2 vols. (London, 1929), vol. i, pp. 124 (to Lady Bradford, 19 July 1874),

260 (to Lady Chesterfield, 29 June 1875); M & B, vol. v, pp. 371–2 (to Lady Bradford and to Queen Victoria, 29 June 1875 – labour laws), 374 (to Lady Bradford, 26 Feb. 1875 – 'country can rally').

69 Zetland (ed.), *Letters to Lady Bradford and Lady Chesterfield*, vol. 1, p. 260 (to Lady Chesterfield, 29 June 1875 – 'lasting affection'); *Derby Reporter*, 16 Nov. 1877 (Plimsoll); pamphlet, *How to Meet the Radicals* (London, n.d. [1885]).

70 M & B, vol. v, pp. 474 (to Lady Bradford, 7 April 1876), 483 (Disraeli to Victoria, 2 July 1876); P. Smith, *Disraelian Conservatism* pp. 255–6 (Northcote).

71 M & B, vol. v, p. 475, vol. vi, p. 449 (to Lady Bradford, 26 April 1876, 6 Aug. 1879).

72 M & B, vol. vi, p. 14 (to Lady Bradford, 3 Nov. 1875).

73 Blake, p. 570.

74 M & B, vol. iii, pp. 182–3 (Disraeli in 1848), 258 (1850), vol. iv, p. 231 (1859); Ghosh, 'Disraelian Conservatism: a Financial Approach', *English Historical Review*, 99 (1984), pp. 284 ff.

75 M & B, vol. iv, pp. 468 (Earle), 469 ('Reaction'), 474 (to Victoria, 16 Aug. 1867).

76 Kebbel, *Selected Speeches*, vol. ii, pp. 521–2 (Manchester).

77 Millman, *Eastern Question*, p. 106.

78 M & B, vol. vi, p. 13 (to Lady Bradford, 6 Sept. 1875).

79 *Ibid.*, vol. iv, p. 467.

80 Millman, *Eastern Question* pp. 3–4 (Disraeli and Germany), 108 ('a secondary part').

81 J. Morley, *The Life of William Ewart Gladstone*, 3 vols. (London, 1903), vol. ii, pp. 552–3; E. A. Freeman, *The Ottoman Power in Europe, Its Nature, Its Growth and Its Decline* (London, 1877), pp. xviii–xix.

82 B. Jaffe, A Reassessment of Benjamin Disraeli's Jewish Aspects', *Transactions of the Jewish Historical Society of England*, 27 (1978 80), pp. 116 117, 120 (Kalisch, Oliphant); *Letters*, vol. iv, 1287 (Crockford's), 1294 (frigate); *Hansard's Parliamentary Debates*, 4th series, vol. xlv, col. 29 (Salisbury, 19 Jan. 1897).

83 Millman, *Eastern Question*, p. 454; Jaffe, 'Disraeli's Jewish Aspects', p. 120 (Balkan Jews).

84 Shannon, *Age of Disraeli*, pp. 268–9.

85 M & B, vol. iii, p. 183 ('nationality'), vol. iv, p. 339 (Poles), vol. vi, p. 13 (to Lady Bradford, 1 Oct. 1875); *Letters*, vol. i, 103 (Navarino); D. W. R. Bahlman (ed.), *The Diary of Sir Edward Walter Hamilton 1880–1885*, 2 vols. (Oxford, 1972), vol. i, p. 187 (Gladstone); *England and France*, p. 45.

86 Mitchell, *Cross*, p. 125 (Cairns, Sept. 1876); Millman, *Eastern Question*, pp. 258 ('sacerdotal crew'), 274 ('St Sophia'); A. J. Balfour, *Chapters of Autobiography*, ed. Mrs Edgar Dugdale (London, 1930), p. 113 ('the party').

87 Millman, *Eastern Question*, p. 347 ('prestige'); Vincent, *Diaries of … 15th Earl of Derby*, pp. 337 ('bold strokes'), 475 ('great acuteness'); Shannon, *Age of Disraeli*, pp. 270 (Salisbury's view), 276 (Disraeli to Corry).

88 Millman, *Eastern Question*, p. 93 (Britain treated like Bosnia); cf. Vincent, *Diaries of ... 15th Earl of Derby*, p. 296, 15 May 1876, for a similar complaint by Disraeli; N. A. M. Rodger, 'The Dark Ages of the Admiralty, 1869–85', pt II, 'Change and Decay, 1874–80', *Mariner's Mirror*, 62 (1976), 35 (Hornby); M & B, vol. IV, p. 579 ('Admirals'), vol. V, p. 461 (principles of foreign policy).

89 Millman, *Eastern Question,* pp. 192 (Crimean War), 306 (Gladstone), 326 ('peace-at-all-price'), 555, note 32 ('fear of responsibility'); M & B, vol. VI, pp. 130 ('mawkish sentimentality', 'Only say'), 133 (Queen's letter for cabinet).

90 M & B, vol. VI, pp. 84 ('key of India'), 92 (Guildhall speech); Shannon, *Age of Disraeli* p. 300 (Hart Dyke).

91 M & B, vol. VI, pp. 324 ('last blow'), 328 (to Lady Bradford, 26 June 1878); Lady G. Cecil, *Life of Robert Marquis of Salisbury*, 4 vols. (London, 1921–32), vol. II, p. 287 ('dimmest idea'); Bahlman (ed.), *Diary of Sir Edward Walter Hamilton 1880–1885*, vol. I, p. 70 (4 Nov. 1880).

92 M & B, vol. VI, p. 379 (Lytton).

93 *Tancred*, bk IV, ch. 3; M & B, vol. IV, p. 166 ('imagination', 1858); Shannon, *Age of Disraeli*, p. 278 (Salisbury); B. S. Cohn, 'Representing Authority in Victorian India', in E. Hobsbawm and T. Ranger (eds.), *The Invention of Tradition* (Cambridge, 1983), 185–207, on the Imperial Assemblage.

94 M & B, vol. VI, pp. 125 ('how great is the power'), 194–5 (enforcing Queen's policy), 207 ('Sovereign and Minister'), 226 ('All his own thoughts'), 233–6 (correspondence in first person).

95 E. A. Freeman quoted in Blake, p. 607; for Disraeli and nationalism see especially, D. Feldman, *Englishmen and Jews: Social Relations and Political Culture 1840–1914* (New Haven and London, 1994), ch. 4, 'Disraeli, Jews and the Eastern Question' (Crosbie quoted p. 113), and A. S. Wohl, '"Dizzy-Ben-Dizzy": Disraeli as Alien', *Journal of British Studies*, 34 (1995), 375–411.

96 P. Smith, *Disraelian Conservatism*, p. 312, note 1.

97 J. Vincent, *Pollbooks: How Victorians Voted* (Cambridge, 1967), p. 47.

98 M & B, vol. VI, pp. 403–4 (to Lady Bradford, 27 Dec.: 1878), 475 ('stars', Aug. 1879).

99 *Ibid.*, vol. VI, p. 500.

100 *Ibid.*, vol. V, p. 482.

101 Shannon, *Age of Disraeli*, pp. 370 (sources of funds), 376 (election losses).

102 P. Smith, *Disraelian Conservatism*, pp. 316 (Disraeli's explanation of defeat), 318 (to Manners); Zetland (ed.), *Letters to Lady Bradford and Lady Chesterfield*, vol. II, p. 266 (to Lady Bradford, 2 April 1880 – 'enlightened masses').

103 M & B, vol. VI, pp. 576–7 (meeting of 19 May), 582 ('great attack'), 590 ('landed interest'); Shannon, *Age of Disraeli*, p. 410.

104 M & B, vol. VI, p. 596 (Disraeli to Salisbury, 27 Dec. 1880); Vincent, *Diaries of ... 15th Earl of Derby*, p. 416 (and see also p. 198 for an earlier reference to Disraeli's

dislike of the middle classes).

105 Shannon, *Age of Disraeli*, p. 416 ('late colleagues', 'like gentlemen').

106 M & B, vol. vi, pp. 524 ('woods of Hughenden'), 583 ('in his library'), 608 (to Lady Bradford, 16 March 1881 – 'famous women').

ENVOI: THE PRIMROSE SPHINX

1 *New Statesman and Society*, 7 Oct. 1994, pp. 18–19; J. Vincent, 'Was Disraeli a Failure?', *History Today*, 31/10 (Oct. 1981), 5–8, and *Disraeli* (Oxford, 1990), especially pp. 50–6.

2 Blake, p. 407.

3 J. Parry, *The Rise and Fall of Liberal Government in Victorian Britain* (New Haven and London, 1993), p. 110, note.

4 Blake, p. 758.

5 Bahlman (ed.), *Diary of Sir Edward Walter Hamilton 1880–1885*, vol. ii, p. 425; *Hansard's Parliamentary Debates*, 3rd series, vol. cclxxiv, col. 613 (Churchill, 1 Nov. 1882).

6 Margaret Thatcher interviewed by Brian Connell, *The Times*, 9 May 1977; Richard Nixon, interviewed by G. D. Horner, *The Times*, 10 Nov. 1972; Norman Tebbitt, reported in *The Guardian*, 14 Nov. 1985; Vincent, *Disraeli*, especially pp. 87–90; *Endymion*, bk 1, ch. 40; M & B, vol. vi, p. 588 (Disraeli on Chamberlain, Aug. 1880).

7 M & B, vol. iv, p. 373 (speech at Oxford, Nov. 1864).

8 *Ibid.*, vol. v, p. 133.

9 D. A. Hamer, *Liberal Politics in the Age of Gladstone and Rosebery: a Study in Leadership and Policy* (Oxford, 1972), p. 233 (Haldane, Nov. 1889).

10 R. C. Self (ed.), *The Austen Chamberlain Diary Letters. The Correspondence of Sir Austen Chamberlain with His Sisters Hilda and Ida, 1916–1937*, Camden Fifth Series, vol. v (Cambridge, 1995), pp. 136, 138 (27 June, 11 July 1920); *Falconet*, chs. 8–9. For the likely influence on Disraeli of the topicality of Russian nihilism (which he mentioned on his death-bed), see D. Painting, 'Disraeli's "Revolutionary Mind": From Proudhon to Bakunin', *Disraeli Newsletter*, 4(1) (1979), 27–38.

11 *Endymion*, ch. 27 ('great game'); M & B, vol. v, p. 498 (Harcourt to Disraeli, 14 Aug. 1876); A. de Vigny, *Cinq-Mars* (Paris, 1826), ch. 20.

12 R. Nevill (ed.), *The Reminiscences of Lady Dorothy Nevill* (London, 1906), p. 200; M & B, vol. iv, p. 267 (life a science); *Lothair*, ch. 56; *Endymion*, ch. 27.

13 M & B, vol. v, p. 247 (to Lady Bradford, 3 Aug. 1874), vol. vi, p. 581 (to Lady Chesterfield, 27 June 1880); *Endymion*, ch. 66.

14 M & B, vol. vi, p. 603 ('You English'); *Endymion*, ch. 101; *Lothair*, ch. 73.

INDEX